CAPITALISM, SLAVERY, AND REPUBLICAN VALUES

CAPITALISM, SLAVERY, AND REPUBLICAN VALUES

Antebellum Political Economists, 1819–1848

by Allen Kaufman

Foreword by Elizabeth Fox-Genovese and Eugene D. Genovese

 UNIVERSITY OF TEXAS PRESS, AUSTIN

Library of Congress Cataloging in Publication Data
Kaufman, Allen, 1947–
    Capitalism, slavery, and republican values.
    Includes bibliographical references and index.   1. Economics—United
States—History—19th century.   2. Political science—United States—
History—19th century.   I. Title.
HB119.A2K38   1982   330'.0973   82-11188
ISBN 0-292-76019-1

To my mother and to the memory of my father

CONTENTS

FOREWORD

by Elizabeth Fox-Genovese and Eugene D. Genovese

Modern political economy took root in the same merchant capital as the mercantilism—or at least the mercantilist policies—that it so sharply repudiated. Adam Smith, like the physiocrats, assumed a special responsibility to explain the natural workings of capitalist production in a period in which the industrial system had not yet provided capital with the technology that would secure its triumph as the dominant mode of production. From its inception, modern political economy combined, and frequently conflated, revolutionary economic analysis with a wide variety of social and political norms. Never a simple description of the mechanisms of production and exchange, nor even of prevailing social relations, political economy always inextricably included the fundamental precepts of bourgeois ideology. The charges leveled by Smith and the physiocrats against the mercantilists juxtaposed natural growth and optimal development against the artificial distortions of mercantilism. Smith and the physiocrats linked their economic analyses to specific judgments of proper social order, although they differed sharply over what was indeed proper, as well as over the motive force of capitalist growth. These differences, too well known to require recapitulation, deeply influenced the development of political economy at least until the 1840s, for Smith and the physiocrats, working within adjacent if not identical intellectual traditions and observing the same data, arrived at radically different political conclusions.

Smith and the physiocrats, like Ricardo and Malthus, like Raymond, Dew, and Cardozo, prided themselves on correct observation of prevailing social and economic conditions. And scholars like C. B. MacPherson, following Marx himself, have urged us to read the political economists carefully for their insights into their own societies. But these early political economists laced their depictions of things as they are with heavy doses of things as they should be. They correctly assumed that the value of their prescriptions depended heavily on the accuracy of their analysis of existing conditions and frequently also on their historical account of how those conditions came to be. It is now accepted in some quarters, although not in all—neoclassicists are notoriously resistant—that they understood features of their own societies that more recent theories tend to obscure. Within limits, the physiocrats provided a more cogent analysis of the eighteenth-century French economy than many subsequent theorists and scholars. But it behooves us to respect the limits as fully as we respect the insights.

Industrial capitalism did not triumph decisively in any nation until the 1840s, much later in many. Once it had secured its position in Great Britain, it could serve as a model for theorists in other nations as well. But from the 1760s, when Smith and François Quesnay, the great physiocrat, began publishing their major works, until the 1840s the picture remained confused, the outcome not yet certain. At the beginning of this period, merchant capital appeared to foster the most compelling system of economic relations, whatever our retrospective judgments about the greater ultimate significance of emerging capitalism. Capitalist social relations had in fact securely established themselves in Great Britain and had provided the foundations of the North American colonies. But those relations, however firmly grounded in fundamental property relations, remained hemmed in with custom, social or antisocial interest, monopoly, privilege, and the competing claims of merchant capital itself.

In short, capitalism—the mode of production based on freedom of capital and the transformation of labor power into a commodity—could appear to contemporaries as a tendency within merchant capital, rather than the reverse. To contemporaries, as to many subsequent commentators, market relations appeared as the most dramatic and dynamic manifestation of social change. The genius of Smith and Quesnay, however great their differences, transferred the principles of exchange from relations between finished commodities or raw materials to the process of production. The goods that arrived at market had already participated in exchange relations, or—and this point is critical—could theoretically have done so. In their hands, exchange moves from the contingent mediator of the products of production to the substance of production itself. From this privileged position, exchange no longer facilitates occasional relations between established social groups; it dictates social relations. Its dictatorship derives direct from nature: the earth for the physiocrats, human nature for Smith. Accordingly, Kaufman rightly insists that Smith naturalizes society and socializes nature. The social division of labor is natural, flows from the integrity of the individual and the sanctity of private property, and brooks no artificial intervention.

Smith's political economy is permeated with his psychology. Hence, Kaufman reviews the intellectual ties that bind *The Theory of Moral Sentiments* to *The Wealth of Nations*. The passion for approbation of the one and the interest of economic aggrandizement of the other can be shown to be compatible and structurally similar in the ways in which they bind the individual to society. But the core of the psychology remains individualistic. This individualism conflates, and thus obscures, two different intellectual currents. The psychological individualism reflects the subjective self-consciousness of the religious, intellectual, and increasingly social male self in whose name the great battles for individual liberty were being waged. The economic individualism reflects the independent agent in the process of production and exchange—the owner of capital, the seller of labor power. Absolute private property, especially the property in one's self and one's labor that repudiates dependency, bridges the two concepts of individualism while it obscures the extent to which they diverged.

Absolute property did characterize English and American societies and did distinguish them from other societies in which various forms of seigneurial privilege persisted. But even in England and America, absolute property coexisted with multiple forms of dependency, especially that of slaves, women, and a variety of economically unfree laborers. Nor were the political implications of absolute property extended to those whose only property was in their own labor. The rhetoric of individualism echoed older traditions that stressed the prerogatives of the head of the household as landowner, military chief, and political agent. In many respects, this rhetoric faithfully captured the economic relations of merchant capital, in which the market provided for the exchange of the products of households rather than the labor of individuals. Political economists grasped the significance of the growth of a working class composed of masterless individuals, but they did not immediately envision the extent of its potential growth or the political consequences that might flow therefrom. Their differing estimates of these matters, like the differences in their own experience, help to account for their various expositions of political economy.

Kaufman presents Smith as setting the stage for subsequent developments in political economy. We may be permitted to chide him for having somewhat slighted the potential contribution of physiocracy to his treatment, but we should hardly question the importance of Smith. Smith principally sought to defend one analysis and practice of political economy against another. He understood that different classes benefit from mercantilist policies than from economic freedom; he underscored the economic contributions of some as against the parasitism of others. Yet, ultimately, Smith remained rooted in a world more influenced by merchant capital than by industrial capitalism. He retained reasonable confidence that labor would benefit from the freedom of capital and the extension of the social division of labor. His successors, notably Malthus and Ricardo, lacking this confidence, writhed over the relations among classes.

Kaufman carefully locates the debate that pitted Malthus against Ricardo in the political and social context of early nineteenth-century Britain, specifically the protracted struggle over the repeal of the Corn Laws. That debate still bore traces of Smith's view of a war between two competing economic systems, but both participants assimilated the industrial and agrarian elements into a single society depicted as divided among three classes: landlords, capitalists, and workers. This analysis reflected, in Kaufman's judgment, the realities of British development in which the landlord class had been integrated into industrialization.

Kaufman's reconstruction of the familiar tenets of Malthusian and Ricardian political economy not merely supports his contention that normative judgments and class allegiances inform economic analysis, but also sets the stage for his main subject—antebellum American political economy. To argue somewhat differently than Kaufman, although not in opposition to his arresting conclusions, the debate between Malthus and Ricardo confirmed the multiple strands from which the major political economists wove their theories. Kaufman emphasizes the importance that early political economists ascribed to the categories wages, profits, and rents, and he exposes the relation between these categories of the classes associated with them.

Whatever the differences between Malthus and Ricardo, Kaufman argues, they concurred in attributing a utilitarian role to the aristocracy that represented the agrarian sector they both regarded as necessary to the preservation of property. The landlords emerge in their work as modern versions of classical heads of the *oikos*. Malthus and Ricardo differed over the protection the landlords merited and on the role of the landlords in an emerging industrial capitalism. But both accepted the inevitability of a large working class that would depend upon wages for survival. In this respect, both, albeit Malthus regretfully, broke with the legacy of merchant capital; both accepted industrial capitalism as the dominant tendency, if not the full reality. But this acceptance could not obliterate the legacy of older concepts and values.

Smith, Malthus, and Ricardo provided the principal questions and analytic tools for American political economists. Hence, we have no quarrel with Kaufman's decision to focus on them, but we do suggest that his slighting of other members of the Scottish historical school, the physiocrats, and even Jean-Baptiste Say leads to an unnecessary sacrifice of valuable nuance. His discussion of the British predecessors nonetheless illustrates the combination and recombination of elements that constitute the development of political economy in different places and periods.

Early nineteenth-century American political economists confronted a very different set of problems than their British counterparts did. Relative to the British, Americans enjoyed an abundance of land and suffered a scarcity of labor. It has frequently been argued that these two facts promoted the development both of single-family farms in the North and plantation slavery in the South, and that the development of industrial capitalism in Britain became a major condition of its development in the United States. The debates over an appropriate tariff policy for the new republic, which exploded in the Nullification Crisis, reflected both the discrete pattern of American development and its relation to British development. The tariff question contributed decisively to the development of divergent American schools of political economy by prompting the clarification of issues and by sharpening the points of disagreement between North and South; and the development of both the Northern and Southern schools illustrates the extent to which any political economy constitutes an interweaving of much more than technical elements.

American political economists accepted the analytic categories of their British predecessors but informed them with different intellectual and political commitments. Wages, profits, and rents did not even have the same social and economic referents in the United States as they did in Britain. The British increasingly came to identify capitalism with industrialization, although after 200 years or so of agrarian and largely preindustrial capitalist development, they had more reason than others to know better. In their internal debates, they easily transferred the attributes of one to the other. Understandably, enclosure, the dispossession of the peasantry, and the growth of free labor all predisposed the British to view industrialization as a natural outgrowth of capitalism.

Americans, in contrast, from their earliest settlements benefited from the advantages of capitalism without industrialization. For them, absolute private property did not necessarily result in landless wage labor, manufacture, or economies of scale. For many, capitalist relations in agriculture developed on the basis of exchange of the surplus rather than economies of scale in production. Where economies of scale in agricultural production seemed to emerge, they were based on slave labor rather than free labor. And even in the South, participation in the capitalist market rested upon the solid foundations of subsistence agriculture for the producing unit. Many Americans, North and South, viewed the possible consequences of industrialization with alarm. They remained committed to an individualist and agrarian republicanism. But Northerners and Southerners differed radically on the best means to preserve their own cherished social relations.

Kaufman selects Daniel Raymond as the best exemplar of Northern political economy. He argues convincingly that Raymond has been unjustifiably neglected and makes a good case for Raymond's theoretical sophistication. But, as he shows, Raymond's very sophistication underscores his ideological conservatism within the capitalist tradition. Raymond wants the economic benefits of industrialization without its social cost, especially without the emergence of a propertyless working class. Rhetorically, he clouds industrialization in a language of anticapitalism. He especially rejects the class divisions taken as natural by his British counterparts. Raymond refuses to classify property or other economic relations as natural.

Rent, he insists, derives from a legal rather than a natural relation, and, to anchor the point, he collapses rent and profit and restricts capital. In the manner of Rousseau, he denies that the individual's right to property can be absolute. He charges Smith with having confused capital with labor. Raymond does not accept the thesis that capital employs labor; to the contrary, he holds that labor manages capital. Capital for Raymond means simply property—not money or commodities produced for profit. He thus ends with a double economic conception that imperfectly joins a commitment to independent producers and to the exchange value of commodities. In Kaufman's judgment, "Raymond helps to systematize a political discourse that attempts to reconcile precapitalist relationships with capitalist growth, and particular interests with the general welfare." For Raymond, in short, the tariff would provide protection for the development of indigenous American manufactures that would include none of the disruptive social relations suffered by the British.

Raymond's political economy may be idiosyncratic, but it does not effect a radical break with the tradition from which it derives. In some respects, Raymond reaches back beyond Smith to the democratic side of the Lockean tradition. His vision of independent producers belongs to a venerable tendency in early capitalist thought. His insistence on the social, as opposed to the natural, character of property is surely indebted to Rousseau, Godwin, and Paine. Understanding the relation between economies of scale and a dispossessed working class, he rejects the apparent consequences of the concentration of capital, but he does not reject production for market. He favors domestic control of the labor force, rather than the sale of labor power. In short, he remains wedded to patterns characteristic of merchant capital, which he believes capable of generating the economic growth characteristic of industrial capitalism without the social dislocation. His combination of economic progressivism and social conservatism much resembles that of the physiocrats, for all the differences in specifics. Like the physiocrats, he takes Britain as a case study from which other nations might select and reject elements at will. His choices contrast sharply with those made by his Southern counterparts and are all the more interesting for the ways in which they reveal how little he understood about how much they had in common.

Northerners like Raymond found Southern slavery unacceptable. Yet, with the single difference between slave labor and family labor, the economic organization favored by Raymond strongly resembles that which prevailed in the South. Raymond no more favored the intrusion of wage labor or market relations into the sanctity of the paternalistic domestic unit than proslavery Southerners did. To the extent that Raymond countenances the industrial employment of labor, he countenances the gainful employment of surplus labor—labor unnecessary to the basic social unit of farm or shop. In this respect, his view of free labor could be likened to the Southern practice of hiring slaves. To be sure, property in man contravenes the most fundamental bourgeois commitment to each man's property in himself, but Raymond—a racist like most of his compatriots—insists upon the social character of all property relations. The conflict over the tariff highlights the complexity of his opposition. We can accept his ideological opposition to slavery, even while calling attention to its inconsistencies. But the crux of his quarrel with slavery may well have been a quarrel over free trade versus protection and over economies of scale versus small autonomous units. Slavery emerges, in Raymond's critique, as a potential road to massive and disruptive industrialization—to the emergence .of class conflict as the foundation of American society.

Southerners themselves diverged in their estimates of the role of slavery in economic development. But the Southern school of political economy, whatever its internal differences, steadfastly defended the slavery itself against the meddling of Northerners. For Southerners, as for Northerners, the question of the tariff long appeared to be central. In this respect, the debates over the tariff should, as Kaufman argues, be understood as analogous to the debates over the Corn Laws in Britain. For, like the debates over the Corn Laws, those over the tariff polarized Americans on fundamental issues of economic development. In Britain, this polarization set landlords and their clients against industrialists and theirs in such a way as to make the conflict between competing classes visible to all. In the United States, the class issue remained confused by marked regional divisions that nonetheless rested upon competing systems of class relations. Industrialization and economic development, as distinct from simple economic growth, forced both Northerners and Southerners to confront the implications of the transfer of labor from the domestic to the public sectors. So long as competing labor systems could be subsumed under the direction of virtuous, paternalistic republicans, conflict between the various labor systems could be contained. There were and are those who have maintained that the individual freedom promoted by American republicanism itself depended upon the existence of slavery. Ideological opposition to slavery took shape in tandem with growing conflict over the correct national economic policy. Conflict over economic policy did not determine opposition to slavery in any crude sense, but it contributed much to making slavery a national issue. And once it had become a national issue, the ideological differences frequently obscured the importance of economic conflicts.

Just as Raymond's work reveals the uneasiness of Northerners when confronted with the social implications of industrial capitalism, so the work of Southern political economists reveals their uneasiness about the relation of slavery to social stability and economic development. Like the

Northerners, the Southerners worked with the discrete elements of political economy, rather than with an integrated system of political economy. Their consideration of the specific categories of wages, profits, and capital offers a fresh perspective on contemporaneous perception of economic development under conditions in which the outcome could not be taken as preordained. If Northerners like Raymond sought to preserve autonomous, propertied individualism as the foundation of a prosperous economy free from the strains of class conflict, Southerners sought to protect slavery as a guarantee of social stability. By accepting the legitimacy of chattel slavery, Southerners practiced what Raymond had merely asserted, namely the social as against the natural constitution of property. For slavery manifested the most severe limitations on the natural right of property in oneself, namely the social right of property in another.

Southerners did not necessarily rest the defense of slavery on the social nature of property. To have done so, they might have had to accept the implications of Raymond's theory that property rights derived from direct participation in the social compact. Many Southerners returned to a defense of man's property in man as natural, but by a novel route—racism. This tactic implicitly permitted them to accept the bourgeois commitment to the individual's right to property in himself regardless of class, even as they defended the white man's right to property in those of another race. Other Southerners placed less emphasis on race, for which they substituted a direct attack on the bourgeois doctrines of individualism and innate rights. An important group of proslavery theorists defended slavery because of its contribution to social order and social responsibility.

If the defense of slavery united Southerners of different views, it did not produce a monolithic justification for slavery. Just as Northerners, groping for a hegemonic justification for capitalism, differed in their assessments of the path toward and even the desirability of economic development, so did Southerners differ in their assessments of the proper relation between slavery and the development of the nation. Not merely did they differ, as has frequently been demonstrated, over slavery as a positive good or a necessary evil; they also differed over the desirability of slavery and its compatibility with economic development.

Kaufman juxtaposes Thomas Dew, against Raymond, as the exponent of Southern political economy. Dew staunchly defends slavery on the grounds of the racial inferiority of the black population. But Dew also accepts the economic superiority of free labor. He never perfectly reconciles these two views. Rather, he reworks Smith's concept of historical stages of development in such a way that social development passes through only two stages, a pastoral and an advanced. In fact, Dew collapses all economic organization, up to and including merchant capital, into the pastoral stage. Referring only to the recent past, he argues that masters can own and command labor, the products of which they market in a commercial system. His analysis conforms to the recent history of merchant capital. He bypasses the variety of precapitalist labor systems to concentrate on chattel slavery, which he justifies on the grounds of the manifest inferiority of blacks to whites. The ownership of labor is warranted in the pastoral system not merely because of its economic viability, but more important because of the civilizing responsibilities of the masters towards their slaves.

Dew recognizes that an advanced and dynamic economy requires free labor. He never satisfactorily explains how the racially inferior slaves can be expected to mount high enough on the rungs of civilization to perform effectively as free laborers. The starkness of his racist justification for slavery in the pastoral stage leaves scant place for the environmentalist and historical attitudes that would allow for the gradual socialization of blacks to the ways of whites. But Dew, perhaps at least partially because of his Virginia background, does believe that slavery will eventually die out. With respect to economic development he holds that pastoralism will naturally yield to the emergence of manufacture and intensive garden farming, both of which support economic development and require autonomous labor. At the same time he recognizes the contradiction between chattel slavery and the pursuit of profits and even allows that slavery may deter masters from aggressive market attitudes. Politically, however, slavery ensures optimal relations among whites of different economic standing. In short, Dew remains mired in the contradictions that historically characterized Southern slavery.

Other Southern political economists responded differently to the challenge of reconciling slavery and economic development. Dew's dilemma resulted from his commitment to slavery and his recognition of its incompatibility with economic development. In this sense, he combined the positive good and necessary evil arguments on the grounds of the racial inferiority of blacks. He proved unable to transcend the conflict between the genetic racial arguments and the social arguments that insisted upon the necessary relation between the labor system and the economic productivity. Others, most flamboyantly George Fitzhugh, are able to brush aside these problems and to reject the lure of economic development. They, too, accept the inevitable relation between economic development and free labor, but find the attendant claims, like those of psychological individualism, incompatible with social stability and the material well-being of the labor force. Slaves are better off than free workers. Society as a whole is better off free from the disruptive effects of competitive economic individualism. The price of economic development is soaring much too high.

Jacob Cardozo differs with both Dew and Fitzhugh. In his judgment, economic development and diversification are desirable and perfectly compatible with slavery. Cardozo displays far more confidence than Dew in the ability of slaves to adapt to manufacture. Basing his convictions on his appreciation of the hiring-out system, he confidently predicts that slave character and moral capacity will develop in conformity with the tasks to which slaves are set. He does not entirely clarify how slavery will adapt to a transition from basic manufacture to full industrialization, but the problem does not trouble him. Cardozo reserves his doubts for the behavior of those masters who may fail to recognize the advantages of economic development and diversification.

The differences among Dew, Fitzhugh, and Cardozo reveal the variety of political economies that could emerge even within a single class committed to the defense of slavery. Their defense of slavery differentiates all of them from Raymond. And all of the Americans differed sharply from their British predecessors. Kaufman's compelling argument reveals Southern Americans, by and large, as more comfortable with economies of scale, the emergence of a dependent labor force, and the place of capitalists—including landlords—in society than Northerners such as Raymond are.

By a striking reversal, Southerners, with the single exception of their commitment to slavery, appear more receptive to the central features of industrial capitalism than many Northerners do. To be sure, some Southern theorists reject industrial capitalism in its entirety, but even they firmly grasp its essential principles, whereas Raymond, with his commitment to free labor, has to repudiate the implications of economic development.

Kaufman demonstrates the ties that bind the thought of Raymond to that of Dew, fundamental opposition over labor notwithstanding. In his judgment, both Dew and Raymond elevate "a precapitalist relationship to the level of theoretical necessity in guaranteeing the preservation of the 'natural'—that is, the capitalist—order." This excellent insight leads to a consideration of the most important larger problems of antebellum Southern thought.

Kaufman shows how important a contribution the Southern political economists made to the slaveholders' ideology, and he properly lays heavy emphasis on the extent to which they shaped the increasingly militant proslavery argument. Yet, they—or at least their specifically economic writings—did not achieve the popularity accorded to the political, religious, and social theorists and propagandists. The explanation does not lie primarily in the nature of economic discourse, which then as now might pass as an infallible cure for insomnia. Significantly, when the militants bring out their ideological big guns in 1860, in the form of E. N. Elliott's massive 908-page anthology, *Cotton Is King and Pro-Slavery Arguments*, they do include a long essay on economics—"Cotton Is King, Or Slavery in the Light of Political Economy," by David Christy of Cincinnati. Whatever its merits as propaganda, it hardly compares in economic sophistication with the best efforts of Dew or Cooper, Tucker or Cardozo, or even of John Taylor of Caroline, for that matter.

Kaufman, in one of his finest contributions, leads us to a deeper explanation that lays bare the central dilemma of antebellum Southern thought: no Southern political economist can reconcile a commitment to slavery with anything that can pass for a scientific economics without ending in a funeral dirge over his preferred social system. The more able and honest the writer, the more thoroughly his efforts unwittingly expose the impossibility of defending slavery and science at the same time. George Fitzhugh, a lazy ignoramus in these matters, probes deeper and sees more clearly than his intellectual betters: he repudiates political economy and all its works, for he knows exactly, if intuitively, where it is leading.

In this and other respects, Kaufman joins a swelling group of younger Marxist historians who are illuminating Southern intellectual history and the ideological development of the slaveholding class. It should be enough to mention Mark Tushnet on the law, Jack Maddex on religion, and, if somewhat tangentially, Steven Hahn on the yeomanry. Mark Tushnet, for example, in his brilliant book *The American Law of Slavery*, demonstrates with unprecedented specificity and depth the dilemma that arose from having a social system based on property in man embedded in a worldwide capitalist mode of production, the ideological premise of which was the right of every man to property in himself. Kaufman exposes that very dilemma in the sphere of political economy and, by extension, in scientific thought in general. While building on Melvin Leiman's pioneering essay in Marxist scholarship, *Jacob N. Cardozo: Economic Thought in the Antebellum South*, he carries the argument to wider terrain and thereby offers rich insights into the complexity of merchant capital's contradictory impact upon the evolution of the modern world.

Kaufman makes his case for the ideological aspect of economic thought and, in so doing, makes his case for the advantages of Marxist method. He would, however, doubtless agree that his version of Marxism is not the only legitimate one in the world today. Understood as a process of intellectual—and political—labor, Marxism cannot be reduced to a single interpretation, much less a formula, nor can it be treated as a revealed truth to be justified or, worse, "applied." If, therefore, bourgeois critics find much to contest in Kaufman's bold book, so will Marxists, albeit on another level of discourse.

For ourselves, we suspect that he will have to retreat from his surprisingly uncritical reliance on the work of J. G. A. Pocock, whose talents are by no means in dispute but whose method and ideological commitment will likely prove much less assimilable to a Marxist interpretation than Kaufman seems to think possible. And for that matter, we confess to being puzzled by his attraction to the superficial and often misleading work of

Keith Tribe, although we happily concede that not much damage ensues from this indiscretion. More important, we do not share Kaufman's Frankfurt school orientation and, more specifically, his attachment to Marx's utopian humanism. These quarrels are for another time and place. Indeed, we have only admiration for Kaufman's determination to make his own standpoint as clear as possible. He could have, with little difficulty, avoided criticism by a heavy dose of fudging. Instead, he has convincingly elaborated his primary theses on the specific problems at hand while providing valuable if controversial reflections on some important larger implications.

With this book Allen Kaufman launches what promises to be an outstanding career.

ACKNOWLEDGMENTS

I am indebted to at least two groups of people for helping me see this book through to publication. One is the student body of the Rutgers University Graduate Program in History for its unflinching support when my unorthodox views threatened to end a very short career in history. Among my fellow students were Howard Green, Allan Wheatcroft, Philip Rosen, Terry Poe, Susan Tracy, Jack Reynolds, Dan Schaeffer, Mary Wright, David Szatzmary, and Larry Henry. The other group, more immediately concerned with the project at hand, is made up of the scholars who advised me during its writing. Ross Thomson has earned my special thanks for his extraordinary comprehension of the role of economics in history and for his tireless generosity in minutely commenting on the manuscript. Rudolph Bell, for reminding me that narrative history is not necessarily inimical to exegesis, and Lloyd Gardner, for his general support, are also thankfully acknowledged. And Norman Markowitz, the one friend and scholar who both supported me personally in the Rutgers University History Department and advised me professionally with this book, deserves and gets my double thanks.

The foreword to this book makes obvious my reasons for acknowledging the support and understanding of Eugene Genovese and Elizabeth Fox-Genovese; that support extended throughout most of the period of my writing and gave me much appreciated encouragement.

Less immediate, but of significant importance to my general intellectual development, was the interaction I enjoyed with students of economics: Anwar Shaikh, David Levey, Ron Blackwell, Patrick Clawson, Farrokh Khalili.

A.K.

INTRODUCTION

This work is an interpretive essay on antebellum political economy. Both the subject matter and the exegetical method employed may seem far removed from social and labor history. Yet these disciplines were my original area of study, and they directed me to political economy. Like so many students of American history in the past decade, I was drawn to a social history of America's working people as a way to challenge consensus history and to revise class analysis in American historiography. The strategy seemed certain enough. Marx's *Capital* offered the theory required for examining conflicts in the work place, while anthropological and sociological studies provided cultural concepts for discussing workers' resistance to capital's appropriation of the labor process.

Others then pursued this combined course of study, while I became more intrigued with Marx's text. At first I pondered the economic questions: was the labor theory of value a "metaphysical" concept? under what conditions did the falling rate of profit hold? Marxist discourse had by that time become critical of Marx's political economy. Certainly, Marx believed that he had discovered the fatal internal contradictions of capitalist accumulation. Yet in the presentation a moral voice could be heard urging the reader actively to resist "capital" as a social evil in itself. The broadened Marxist discourse offered space for discussing that voice.[1]

I turned first to the economists who preceded Marx, then to political philosophy, and finally to moral philosophy. That preliminary investigation gave me an ear for the political meaning of Marx's vocabulary. He may have countered Bentham's defense of the market as guarantor of equality and freedom, but Marx recast those concepts and used them to project a legitimate political and economic order. By laying bare the laws and motion of capitalist accumulation, Marx showed that the conditions of capitalist production violated the premises of equality and freedom on which the bourgeois order was founded. He further identified the working class as that social force which could take those premises most seriously and which could create a truly equal and free society.

Marx saw the working class as the agent of social change because its economic situation gave it strength enough to vie for political power and because its battles over wages and working conditions would shatter the illusion of equality and freedom in a capitalist order. But in naming the working class the gravedigger of capitalism, Marx had to assume that its members believed themselves to be ethical and sovereign individuals who assessed rationally their social and political relationships in terms of equality and freedom.[2]

Once *Capital* is interpreted in this fashion, it takes on political meaning in two ways. First, the work reveals a certain moral conception. That is to say, *Capital* rests on particular assumptions regarding human nature and derives from them a notion of the good society. Second, the positive results of the economic analysis, namely the theory of accumulation and the tendency for the falling rate of profit, describe the circumstances and the possibilities by which the good might come into full existence. Consequently, by explicating the concepts of equality and freedom in economic life and by showing the possibilities for their realization, *Capital* offers itself, even if in an underdeveloped way, as a "legitimating" or "hegemonic" ideology which could serve as the rational core for a political movement comprised of sovereign and ethical individuals.[3]

From this reading, it became clear that just as the labor process is a contested area between workers and capitalists (even if it isn't a contest of equals), so too is the ideological/political arena. Only here the struggle is not between workers and capitalists per se but between organized political coalitions. That these coalitions may consist of divergent interests, whether defined in economic or noneconomic terms, follows from society's own multiplicity of interests. What cements this coalition is a shared conception of a good or just society, or conceptions of the good which significantly agree. Such a formulation does not deny the initial premise of interest, since it is only through a shared conception of the good that the legitimacy of interest can be affirmed and that competing legitimate interests can be ranked.[4] Of course, for political allegiance to persist there must be some correspondence between the satisfaction of legitimate ends and the shared standard (or compatible standards) of justice. For example, market inequities may be accepted if they are believed to be either materially beneficial (a rising standard of living) when compared to some other position (the state of nature, feudalism, self-sufficiency) or necessary for the preservation of other more important values and institutions (personal liberty, ethnic communities, trade unions, electoral democracy).[5] Furthermore, this political consensus can occur even under conditions of intense economic class struggle.

It now seemed theoretically possible to accept some of the consensus school's formulations and still view American history in terms of class analysis. If Louis Hartz is right to consider America a "liberal" polity, then it seemed that unanimity had to be continually re-created and won.[6] The battle involved conflicting economic class interests as well as opposing concepts of social justice and of America's historic mission. So instead of studying the class struggle as it involved control of the labor process, I decided to investigate the class struggle pertaining to the definition of the good society. In particular, this study would involve the development of American political discourse, its relationship to party politics, and in turn the relationship of party politics to state power and economic development.

Antebellum America became my starting point because it presents an anomaly in consensus theory. If there is any agreement among those writing on antebellum history, it is that the Civil War was not the result of inexorable economic forces. The tariff, a national bank, a national transportation system, and other matters were all negotiable if the party system had been capable of managing the conflicting interests and achieving a workable national unity.[7]

Here the agreement among historians ends. An abundant, complex, and conflicting literature exists on the reasons for the collapse of the second party system and the political crisis of the 1850s. Some blame "blundering" politicians, uncompromising moralists, or the "excesses" of democracy, while others argue that differences in the distribution of racial populations or differences in the labor systems created what might be considered two civilizations with competing moral, political, and economic concerns.[8] These explanations are much debated and need not be explored in this work. However, I find with some qualification that the thesis of a contending labor system is the most persuasive.

Given this and the earlier proposition regarding the moral or ideological premise of politics, a study of antebellum politics should investigate the way in which contemporary political discourse normatively evaluated (legitimated or "de-legitimated") the various labor systems. For the antebellum period the dominant mode of discourse was republican theory. But as studies by Rush Welter, Major Wilson, and others have shown, important conceptual differences existed among the discourse's practitioners.[9] These studies have not directly examined the connections between republican political theory and antebellum political economy. Consequently, the literature does not provide an integrated analysis of contemporary debates on political principle and organization and rival views on the "natural" laws regulating production.

Where such a body of literature does exist—say, in the case of Eric Foner, Eugene Genovese, or even Barrington Moore, Jr.—greater detail is needed not only to clarify but to help resolve some persistent problems. Both Foner and Moore would agree that industrialists and yeoman farmers could cement an economic alliance from their interests in developing a Northern home market; both historians would agree that the notion of free labor provided a political standard for defining the general welfare, and both would consider this alliance as consistent with the needs of industrial capitalist development. Yet these conclusions ignore the proposition in economic theory that capitalist production expands with wage labor and is limited by family farming.[10] Economic historians, particularly Gavin Wright, seem to have resolved this paradox by showing how the family farm within the context of American development was conducive to capitalist accumulation. This approach may describe the economic integration of precapitalist forms into an emerging industrial capitalist economy, but it does not necessarily explain how farmers could strike a political bargain with industrialists. After all, farmers would hardly consider themselves free if they found themselves forced to sell their labor power to capitalists.

One explanation for this unity of precapitalist and capitalist classes is that the consequences of capitalist development were not yet known. But this does not seem likely since the case of England, with its dispossessed peasantry and its moneyed aristocracy, haunted the American imagination.[11] A second explanation, one consistent with Foner's work, argues that a theory of class harmony could emerge by making use of America's special circumstances. Its seemingly limitless supply of land and its republican institutions could harmonize the interests of capitalist and independent laborer. This may be so, but the idea needs greater specification.

A comparable problem arises when one considers labor in manufacturing. As Alan Dawley and Anthony Wallace have shown, artisans and proletarians alike found capitalist relationships far from satisfying but joined a political alliance with capitalists against slave power.[12] Certainly it would be useful to understand why and how this political unity of opposites (workers and bosses) was accomplished.

If the reconciliation of precapitalist and capitalist relationships poses problems in appreciating Northern development, these are magnified when considering the South. How did the South accommodate a system of labor which denied freedom and retarded economic growth to a political theory which affirmed individual freedom and celebrated limitless economic growth as the ends of society? Eugene Genovese has offered one solution: the South finally did not make the accommodation. In his study of George Fitzhugh, Genovese persuasively argues that Southerners wanted to establish a republic based on static conceptions of the good compatible with a nonacquisitive economy.[13] No one can deny that Fitzhugh articulated one particular solution, but before 1848 there was general agreement that the principles of free trade in its narrow sense best served Southern interests and that free trade in its broader meaning provided the most compelling arguments for political association. Even in the 1850s, fire-eaters no less prominent than J. B. DeBow still upheld free trade values and looked to Thomas R. Dew for inspiration and legitimation. This evidence suggests that important Southern thinkers continued the effort to reconcile slavery with modern republican discourse, and that effort needs further study.

In addressing these questions, my study of antebellum writings on political economy has thus coincided with the work of two other American historians: Drew McCoy and Paul Conkin.[14] While Conkin's focus is apparently the result of his recognition that political economy before the Civil War is an important and virtually unknown topic, I think that McCoy's motives for writing are rather close to my own. The connection between economic analysis and normative judgments about capitalist and precapitalist relationships in a republic directs the researcher to political economy. As I indicated earlier, political economy does not make a radical distinction between normative standards and positive results, as does neoclassical economics. Unlike Marx, who radically historicized the discipline, classical political economists as well as American practitioners believed their findings to be deduced from nature. They also believed that policy had to follow from those dictates if the conditions of the natural order were to be established and perpetuated. Instead, by uncovering the causes of wealth, political economy sought to deduce from human nature "natural" social relationships and to formulate distributive policies that would reproduce and expand those conditions. In other words, these economists did not define their object of study as scarcity, and so differ from neoclassical economists who consider problems of efficiency to be scientific but matters of distribution normative.

Perhaps one explanation for this unity of normative and positive statements is that economics had only recently separated itself from political theory. As Cropsey, Pocock, and Hirschman have demonstrated, the shift in republican discourse from virtue to interest defined and legitimated economics as a separate sphere of study.[15] Eighteenth-century theorists no longer considered human nature, the first principle of political theory, to be essentially static or principally political; rather they conceived human nature to be as fluid and as creative as commerce itself, so that economic activity became the sphere for moral improvement. As a result, class, defined in terms of relations of production, assumed the central role in understanding the natural conditions of society. At the same time, class defined the subject and object of politics (that is, who constitutes a nation's citizenry and how they should organize their government). Human nature remained the first principle of political discourse, but the definition of human nature had shifted from a political to an economic one.

There are also certain formal aspects of political economy which make it attractive for historical study. As a systematic exposition it demands clearly defined categories and rigorously argued connections among those categories. In this respect, political economy, unlike political party debate, defines itself as a scientific discipline, even if practice falls short of that standard. Thus, as a dimension of political discourse, political economy offers the historian a systematic body of carefully defined concepts that are available for formal criticism.

By limiting my subject to an intellectual discipline, I was able to use methods developed by intellectual historians to recover the discourse of American political economy which sought to reconcile economic growth with republican "virtue." Furthermore, a historical analysis of the "science" of political economy reveals its practitioners' historically bound assumptions, ambiguities, and strategies as well as the fact that their particular challenges were embedded in America's transformation from a preindustrial to an industrial capitalist order.

These historical concerns are for the most part absent from those studies in the history of economic thought which aim to evaluate texts in terms of their shortcomings or contributions by the standard of current economic doctrine. While such studies dehistoricize texts by treating them as mere antecedents of current thinking, they do provide relevant material for the historian; alleged ambiguities, ill-formed concepts, or logical contradictions may point to historical assumptions and/or other circumstantial factors that distinguish previous scientific endeavors from present dogma. In this way, the continuing pursuit of a "true" conception of the economy may be combined with the more "relativist" practices of the historian.[16]

In combining these approaches I first select those treatises which are usually considered or which appear to me to be the most rigorous formulations of a particular position. Then I discuss their ambiguities or logical inconsistencies. In the case of English political economy, I employ Marx's critique.[17] In comparing the classical and antebellum economists, I use the theory of capitalist development which distinguishes between a preindustrial and an industrial phase of development.[18]

This procedure permits me to establish the normative/political character of political economy and to specify its central "moral" dilemma. It also allows me to compare the structural similarities and differences between the Corn Law debates and the tariff debates, since each addressed the problem of distribution between industrial and agrarian interests during the process of industrialization. And then I describe how Northern and Southern economists defended their regions' precapitalist relationships as a solution to the moral/political dilemma of capitalist accumulation. Within that description I discuss the existence of those precapitalist relationships in terms of American economic development, and in turn use that discussion to explain the contradictory structure of antebellum political economy.

Thus, while this method shows the links between nineteenth-century economic development (the relations and forces of production) and economic thought, it does not reduce the principal concerns of political economy to matters of profitability, efficiency, and the like. For contained in those categories are questions regarding the proper social constitution of the natural order and the policies required for its perpetuation. And found therein is a conception of the social good that can provide the political basis for the reconciliation (or lack of reconciliation) of class interests and hence the foundations of republican rule.

I do not presume to write a general history of antebellum political economy. Rather I intend to present systematically the legitimating concepts within the discourse and, where possible, to show their connection to the structure of production on which the political economists reflected. By retrieving political economy in this manner, I hope to use it as an interpretive tool for reevaluating the political equilibrium and disequilibrium of the antebellum period. Although this requires a separate study of the political and constitutional debates preceding the Civil War, my analysis of the second party system and my concluding remarks suggest the direction that such a study might take.[19]

The antebellum writings examined in this study come from the period between 1819, when Daniel Raymond published the first American treatise on political economy, and 1848, when Henry Carey published *The Past, the Present and the Future*. Carey's work ended the uncritical acceptance of the Ricardian/Malthusian notion of diminishing returns. Both of these works are protectionist tracts, yet Carey's introduced a theoretical shift in the protariff argument. It permitted the protectionist forces to reconcile the manufacturer's demand for protection and the farmer's and laborer's concern for cheap western lands. This undercut the Southern free-trade argument that these interests were irreconcilable. Politically, Carey's theoretical breakthrough allowed the inclusion of a strong protective tariff and a homestead policy on the same platform, and it frustrated the South's hope for an alliance with the West. It also coincided significantly with the ideas of radical labor or agrarian theorists such as John Pickering and George Evans. Since these theorists did not immediately address the tariff on which my book is structured, I will treat them, along with post-1848 writings in political economy, elsewhere.

The period from 1819 to 1848 is politically important as the time when national party politics prevailed. In 1848, when the Mexican War was ended and the debate began concerning slavery's expansion into the western territories, the second party system collapsed, and with that collapse the Civil War became more of a possibility.

England offers both the classic model for capitalist development and the classic tradition of political economy, and it is there that my discussion must begin. Chapter 1 starts with a presentation of Adam Smith's *The*

Theory of Moral Sentiments to suggest that his understanding of human nature allows him to displace politics for economics as the arena for moral development. In *The Wealth of Nations* Smith establishes the vocabulary of political economy and formulates the moral dilemma that accompanies "natural" economic growth at the expense of the laboring population. Chapter 2 examines Ricardo's and Malthus's efforts to resolve the dilemma in the context of England's industrial revolution.

The remaining five chapters discuss works of American antebellum political economists who attempt to reconcile the early stage of economic growth to the long-term outcome that brings degradation to labor and the potential threat of a radicalized working class. For the Northern protectionist Daniel Raymond, the solution lay in a utopian schema of state intervention that would allow limitless growth and the perpetuation of independent labor. Unlike Raymond, the Southern free-trader Thomas R. Dew accepted the formation of a working class as natural and inevitable. Yet he dissented from the English free-trade theorists by defending slavery based on race as consistent with the natural order. Consequently, he could reason that slavery and racism were the means to politically restrain the laboring population in the United States. While the South Carolinian Jacob Cardozo agreed that slavery was politically prudent, he recognized that slavery limited to the plantation was inconsistent with natural economic growth. He suggested reforms that would make slavery economically as well as politically sound.

It should be noted that the writing of this book was essentially completed by September 1980, and therefore I have not been able to incorporate discussion of other studies published since that time.

CAPITALISM, SLAVERY, AND REPUBLICAN VALUES

1. ADAM SMITH *on the Wealth of Nations and the Poverty of Labor*

It hence becomes apparent that despite an excess of wealth, civil society is not rich enough, i.e., its resources are insufficient to check excessive poverty and the creation of a penurious rabble.
—Friedrich Hegel, *The Philosophy of Right*

Adam Smith's Project

Antebellum debates among American political economists began with Adam Smith, whether they agreed with him, as the Southerners generally did, or disagreed, as the Northern protectionists did. By systematizing economic thought and directing it against the mercantilist policy of his day, Adam Smith founded the science of wealth that the Americans attempted to perfect.

Smith contributed to the political and economic controversies that arose after England subordinated traditional restrictions on economic freedom.[1] The major breakthrough of the new order was signaled by the Civil War and the Glorious Revolution. The Settlement of 1688 resolved serious practical and economic questions that had been raised during the Civil War and the interregnum. When James II abdicated, Tories and Whigs put aside their bitter doctrinal divisions to draw up a declaration of rights that William would be obliged to honor if he was to become England's sovereign. The bill of rights effectively transferred sovereignty from the king to Parliament and shifted the balance of political power accordingly. A political revolution had thus finally been accomplished with only the slightest modification of existing political institutions. Despite the years of war, the struggle did not culminate in the social dislocations that would characterize Europe's next epochal uprising—the French Revolution.

The newly empowered Parliament was itself principally composed of landed property owners, whether aristocrats or gentry.[2] Yet the revolution triumphed over the monarch's feudal conservatism because significant factions of the dominant landed class had been making a gradual economic transformation to capitalist practices.[3] Titles and gentlemanly manners often masked a commitment to enterprise and a dependency of annual rents on commerce.[4]

Private property won victories during the Civil War not only at the expense of the king and his feudal allies but also at the expense of labor. During the interregnum, the radicals who had challenged private property were defeated, although the danger of radicalism remained. The memory of the forces unleashed by the disputes among the propertied classes at the outset of the Civil War softened the differences between Tories and Whigs. Both accepted William and Mary as their conditional sovereigns and protectors against the poor and propertyless, whose very presence was construed as a threat of political chaos that could erupt with the slightest weakening of the established order.[5]

With order preserved and the king's rights curtailed, Parliament passed legislation according to its prerogative. It established the colonial system, the Bank of London, a national debt, a modern system of taxation, and a protectionist system, laying the legal foundations on which the economic edifice of the eighteenth century was built. Of all the acts passed by Parliament just preceding and during the years modern historians call the Industrial Revolution, the enclosure acts are the most revealing.

Although the precise effect of the enclosure acts on the growth of a propertyless class in the eighteenth century has become a contested area in English historiography, the intent of the acts remains above dispute.[6] In issuing these orders of expropriation Parliament dismantled the ancient rights of Englishmen and replaced them with the natural rights of *homo oeconomicus*. By the time England entered the nineteenth century it had become the classic model of capitalist development. Unlike the rest of Europe, England had uprooted and "pauperized" its peasantry and created a new three-tiered society of capitalists, landlords, and workers that claimed to be grounded in nature's moral *principia*.

The new order did not succeed without critiques from among the landed gentry.[7] Country opposition rested in large part on James Harrington's *The Commonwealth of Oceana*. Through his interpretation of Machiavelli, Harrington had devised a political theory that combined the religious concerns of the Puritan saints with a secular conception of polity, transforming a saint into a citizen. Harrington's citizens were persons of property, for it was property—in particular, landed property—that bestowed economic independence and the freedom to bear arms at one's own discretion. Like Machiavelli, therefore, Harrington stressed that the command of arms and citizenship were synonymous, but unlike Machiavelli he made arms depend on property relationships and consequently blamed the decline of the republic on a maldistribution of property rather than on corruption. Despite his emphasis on land as a condition of freedom and citizenship, Harrington allowed commerce to enter his system and thus found that membership in the gentry could be compatible with commercial enterprise so long as that enterprise was land-based.[8]

In the Country's reformulation of Harringtonian republicanism, decline was still associated with a lack of independence, but not with a faulty distribution of land. Instead, the growth of the king's power through parliamentary patronage and the existence of a standing army to protect English commerce came to be associated with corruption. Furthermore, the national debt, which gave the king new financial powers, undermined the economic security which commerce based on property and specie had allegedly secured. The congealed labor (value) that gold embodied for Locke had represented the actual state of propertied relationships. However, credit and paper money replaced labor with caprice. The natural conditions of social life established with the Settlement of 1688 were being slowly eroded.

The economic conditions of the new order consequently shifted political questions about polity's ends and means into the realm of economic theory. The growth of economics (political arithmetic) was related not only to the increasing need for economic expertise in affairs of state but also to questions of republicanism.[9]

Both mercantile and landed interests agreed that trade was the main condition of freedom and that it necessitated the triad of classes. The bitter polemics among propertied interests focused on the particular means that could be consciously applied to preserve the political and social values of the settlement within a general economic process that, as Hume defined it in his *History of England*, proceeded independent of conscious design.

Adam Smith's rigorous economic theory analyzes the common ground on which the Court and Country fought their battles. Although his ideas are decidedly Court or Whig, he cannot be accused of sacrificing science for polemics. In his impartiality and thoroughness, Smith succeeds in systematizing the tradition of bourgeois thought as it had developed through the debates of the Civil War and the Augustan period. Self-interest becomes the basis rather than the nemesis of moral ends and hence of legitimate political rule; embodied labor no longer distinguishes natural from unnatural economic pursuits but characterizes all economic life; far from indicating an unstable government, credit and national debt are shown to presuppose political stability; the standing army is proven to ensure the liberty of all propertied owners. Finally, the lack of constraint that conservatives feared as a sign of political decline becomes, in Smith's system, the opportunity for economic growth and the means of actively informing history rather than contemplating the erosion of an apparently fixed order based on universal principles. For Smith, the true impetus of social life is the human being's propensity to "truck, barter, and exchange"; sociopolitical activity is both economic and historical.

Human Nature, Ethical Life, and the Good Society

While essentially correct, the above statement regarding Smith's conception of human nature is too concise to account for the complexities developed in *The Theory of Moral Sentiments*. In this work Smith, like the classical and scholastic social philosophers, premises his theory on a conception of the good.[10] But as a son of the eighteenth century and an iconoclast, he defines the political good as nothing more than the preservation of life, so that the end of society is given by the only empirically verifiable drive in nature.[11] In this way Smith converts the human passions from obstacles to the social good into vehicles toward it, especially since Smith counts sympathy and the need for approbation among the biological drives. He reasons that both these moral sentiments follow necessarily from the passion for preservation as soon as we interpret it to include the reproduction of the species. The family and the group thrive on extended love and approbation, which permit us to be virtuous; our inherent sympathy coupled with imagination enable and drive us toward morality and sociability.[12]

By making the passions moral, Smith prepares for an argument that will shift the focus of social theory from politics to economics. We will see, however, that Smith's success depends on the reader's readiness to accept an ambiguous outcome, namely that nature's social order is unjust by human moral standards.[13]

Once morality is rooted in biological necessity, the legitimate end of government, according to *The Theory of Moral Sentiments*, is to guarantee the free exercise of the passions. From this Smith argues that the basis of political obligation is a concept of the just society, a society that ensures the natural right of individuals to preserve themselves, provided that they do not interfere with the self-preservation of others.[14]

Several important consequences follow. Political association, now merely protecting the free exercise of the passions, no longer provides the arena in which moral capacities develop. The separation between political life and civil society creates the ethical space for the separation between the state and the economy. The parallel structure between Smith's moral and economic writings is all the more apparent if one agrees with Hirschman, who concedes that Smith treats a multiplicity of passions in his moral philosophy but reduces that multiplicity to a single passion, approbation, and finally to a single interest, economic aggrandizement.[15] Although Smith starts from the passion of approbation, he assumes that economic aggrandizement is the best way to satisfy vanity. Economics is consequently the best indicator of the "natural order."

Unfortunately for Smith, a residuum of human morality survives to plague his otherwise rigorous exorcism of traditional moral philosophy. While the state could achieve perfectability by simply ensuring individual rights, for Smith individual perfection is synonymous with benevolence, the very sentiment that makes him lament the natural society with its propertyless and morally degraded laboring population.[16] Smith's repeated pangs of conscience in *The Wealth of Nations* reveal both the ambiguity in his theory and the sincerity of his moral sentiments.[17] Classical political economy after him would inherit but not resolve the ethical and political challenges presented by the existence of a working class.

Homo Oeconomicus: The Division of Labor and History

The crux of Smith's ambiguity in *The Wealth of Nations* is his concept of human nature, now entirely reduced to *homo oeconomicus*. The natural drive for self-preservation and the social capacity become identical with the drive for accumulation and the capacity for trade. Consequently, Smith describes both the barbaric and the advanced stages of history as natural, since they are united by the propensities of human nature, latent in the first and manifest in the second.

By grounding his thought on the mercurial notion of human nature, Smith in fact confuses the poles of his exposition: he socializes nature by attributing social phenomena to inherent human drives, and he naturalizes society by explaining social formations as manifestations of natural instincts.[18] Despite the logical limitations of this conflation of the social and the natural, it establishes a "scientific" conception of nature as the authority to which Smith and later English political economists would appeal in their advocacy of capitalist relationships.

In the first paragraph of *The Wealth of Nations* Smith distinguishes between the necessaries and conveniences of life and implies that the latter is the subject of economics, because conveniences mark the generous civilized state, where a division of labor creates a social surplus as opposed to the pitiful "savage nations" that merely subsist.

Smith first posits the division of labor to be social rather than technical and then empties its social determination by making the division of labor a result of an instinctual drive. He can describe the natural, barbarous state of hunters and gatherers as a "society" of individual producers who enter into exchange relationships:

> In a tribe of hunters or shepherds a particular person makes bows and arrows, for example, with more readiness and dexterity than any other. He frequently exchanges them for cattle or for venison and with his companions; and he finds at last that he can in this manner get more cattle and venison than if he himself went to the field to catch them.[19]

The existence of the individual commodity producer in the barbarous state collapses the distinction that Smith makes between the early and rude stage of development and the advanced or commercial one (or more generally between barbarism and civilization). Commodity production unifies these stages conceptually; what differentiates them is the relationship the direct laborer has to the implements of production. In the early and rude stage labor is in possession of stock (both the materials required for production and the goods needed to sustain the laborer during the process of production and circulation), whereas in the advanced stage the laborer is devoid of stock. Thus, Smith introduces the assumptions of commercial society into the primordial condition of humanity and thereby socializes nature.

Conversely, he naturalizes society: first, by collapsing the determination of social life into an instinctual drive and, second, by making the substance of social relationships the physical requirements of production.[20] In Smith's theory value regulates the social act of exchange, but value itself does not derive from the determination of the exchange relationships. Instead, he conceives of value merely as a physical condition of production whether the products of labor are exchanged or not. His reasoning follows Locke's doctrines of natural law and makes value congealed labor—that is, the toil and trouble expanded in production:

> If among a nation of hunters, for example, it usually costs twice the labor to kill a beaver which it does to kill a deer, one beaver should naturally exchange for or be worth two deer. It is natural that what is usually the produce of two days or two hours labor, should be worth double of what is usually the produce of one day's or one hour's labor.[21]

Smith's concept of human nature allows him, on the one hand, to establish commodity production as the constant of human life and, on the other hand, to account for the change from barbarism to civilization as the result of the propensity to trade. His discussion of economic growth thus provides a framework for social change, and economics rather than politics becomes the appropriate subject for historical research.

The results of Smith's own research suggest a fourfold stage of history based on economic organization.[22] The first is the early and rude stage, characterized by the hunting and gathering mode of subsistence. Here, human life remains closely linked to its biological origin, notwithstanding some division of labor and exchange. The universal poverty that prevails establishes the egalitarian society that does not require any formal political organization, since social interests do not conflict one with another.[23]

Smith describes the second stage as a pastoral one, in which private property begins to be concentrated and, as a result, a state becomes necessary. For the agricultural stage, the next period, Smith distinguishes two substages, one having an allodial form of property ownership and the other a feudal form. With time, land becomes concentrated in the hands of a few families who maintain their control through the institutions of primogeniture and entail, perpetuating a monopoly on land and subordinating the laboring population. While productivity increases during this stage, society remains in a condition of poverty since the division of labor is "underdeveloped," particularly between agriculture and manufacturing. Political instability resulting from the concentration of power in rival families further exacerbates the economic malaise of the agricultural period.

The final and most advanced stage in Smith's schema is the commercial stage. Here the division of labor is fully matured; manufacture has broken from agriculture and created a home market in a two-sector economy. Both stock and land have been completely appropriated by capitalists and landlords respectively, creating a three-class society in which the propertyless class supplies the labor. The cash nexus replaces the servile relationship of the feudal order as the socially cohesive element, and political stability is ensured since property is divided among a greater number of people than in the previous feudal stage.

Although Smith views each of these stages as necessary in the development of a nation, he does not suggest that each nation will inevitably develop from one stage to the next. A desire to improve one's economic condition provides the motor force, but movement will occur only where historical circumstance permits favorable conditions. The importance of contingency in Smith's theory of history is best illustrated in his detailed discussion of the transition from the feudal to the commercial stage. Positive factors include the accessibility of navigable rivers or the ocean and the alliance of the feudal kings with the cities against the lords, but they do not include the conscious intervention of the state.[24] Rather, the interaction of individual self-interests facilitates the advance of history.[25] In the transition commerce plays the salutary role of undermining the oppressive hold of the lords over the laborers; commerce advances individual freedom.[26]

Civilized Barbarism and Barbaric Civilization

Although Smith describes a fourfold division in his discussion of human history, his economics employs a simpler twofold separation between barbarism and civilization; this distinction is based on commerce and manifests the human being's latent natural propensities for freedom.[27]

Smith's equivocal distinction between barbarism and civilization is that a division of labor exists in the advanced stage. Although that distinction is never absolute in his theory, a corollary determinant of the two stages proves more useful; it is the relationship of labor to the process of production. The rudimentary division of labor in primitive life never takes away labor's stock or its control over the labor process and its products.

Smith conceives of all primitive laborers as independent producers enjoying an impoverished equality that breeds no resentment. The resulting freedom exists within a kind of primitive republicanism that can prevail in the absence of a state and a legal system.

By contrast, resentments are inevitable in the advanced stage. The deepened division of labor divorces the laborer from both stock and land, concentrating them in the hands of capitalists and landlords. The only possession of propertyless laborers is their own ability to work, so that they are forced periodically to exchange labor for wages.

While Smith believes that self-love is natural to all people, he nonetheless credits certain individuals with virtues that greatly enhance their ability to acquire wealth. Of those virtues, Smith particularly praises parsimony, which more than anything else explains for him the emergence of propertied and propertyless classes in the commercial stage.[28] For those fortunately endowed with this superior trait, the market offers a means to save and to invest, thereby facilitating the appropriation of the wealth of the indolent and the spendthrift. Through the market, then, society experiences a deepening of the division of labor as property is divided among those equipped to manage it and taken from those fit only to labor. The less capable people are subordinated as propertyless laborers and are further degraded intellectually into a "drowzy stupidity" by repeatedly performing the simplified tasks that result from the decomposition of crafts into detailed labor.[29] In Smith's words:

> He [the propertyless laborer] naturally loses, therefore, the habit of such [intellectual] exertion, and generally becomes as stupid and ignorant as it is possible for a human creature to become. The torpor of his mind renders him, not only incapable of relishing or bearing a part in any rational conversation, but of conceiving any generous, noble, or tender sentiment, and consequently of forming any just judgment concerning many even of the ordinary duties of private life . . .[30]

This morally degraded condition of labor presents something of a problem in Smith's theory, for labor remains the source of wealth for the nation. In consequence he formulates two contradictory theories of value. In the first theory, which explains the conditions of the early and rude stage, the value of a commodity produced equals the value that labor receives for it.[31] In the second theory, which applies to the advanced stage, the labor embodied in the commodities exceeds the wages, which only partially recompense labor's toil and trouble. In the advanced stage, the capitalist and the landlord benefit from the surplus of labor's work.[32] The value of the commodity is now composed of the respective shares of the wealth produced by labor: wages, profits, and rents. As the source of value, labor represents for Smith the standard by which prosperity could be measured: personal wealth becomes synonymous with the ability to command labor.[33]

For Smith, labor's ability to produce a value greater than its own wages characterizes the production of wealth in the advanced stage. Wealth is associated not only with the increment of goods produced but also with the profits employed in activities which generate income and those which do not—as, respectively, productive and unproductive labor. For example, the work of a laborer engaged by a capitalist to produce furniture for the market may be considered productive labor since the sale of the furniture generates income for the worker and the capitalist; labor employed by the capitalist to produce furniture for personal consumption cannot be considered productive labor, because the wages the laborer receives are deductions from the capitalist's revenue.[34]

When Smith recognizes the inevitability of class resentments in the advanced stage, he simultaneously admits the necessity of controlling those resentments by political means. As the source of wealth, labor has to be continuously employed in productive activity, and therefore it must be exploited by capitalists and landlords. At the same time, in order to reduce resentments and to ensure its cooperation, labor has to be accommodated by a body politic that grants formal equality without upsetting the economic hierarchy that increases productivity for all. If, however, the resentments of a degraded, irrational, immoral class of laborers cannot be contained by reasonable political mechanisms, Smith recommends that less friendly coercion be used. In the most dire circumstances he is not opposed to the military enforcement of order, for which purpose a standing army should be established.[35]

Preindustrial Economics

In Smith's treatment of the advanced stage two technical peculiarities stand out: his insufficient treatment of fixed capital, especially regarding its substitutability for circulating capital, and his notion that rent is a surplus (surplus value) given by nature rather than by labor.

Smith demonstrates his understanding of capitalist accumulation in carefully reasoned passages on the division of labor in which he reveals the logic of introducing machinery through an extension of the division of labor. By splintering the labor process into detailed tasks, a growing division of labor permits machinery to be invented to perform work formerly done by skilled labor. Furthermore, in his introduction to Book II, "Of the Nature, Accumulation, and Employment of Stock," Smith argues that the substitution of fixed capital—machinery or embodied labor—for circulating capital—living labor—depends on the accumulation process itself.[36]

Smith nonetheless cannot logically connect profits, the motor mechanism of capitalist accumulation, to the labor process in which value is created. More significant, he principally conceives of economic growth—that is, the extension of the division of labor—either as the continuing subdivision of crafts or the addition of external markets. He does not see the deepening of the division of labor through the introduction of machinery and the subsequent restructuring of the labor process as an independent force of growth—as the internal self-sustaining dynamic of capitalist accumulation. His exclusive focus on the extension of the market, as opposed to the deepening of it, explains Marx's assessment of Smith as the theorist of manufacturing par excellence.[37]

Smith's final failure to connect value with his concepts of the division of labor, profits, and accumulation mars his theory by omission. But his treatment of rents is even less satisfactory because of its contradictory reasoning. Smith asserts that the economic basis for rents derives from land's capacity to produce a surplus above the subsistence requirements for capitalists and laborers.[38]

He maintains that land has special productive powers when he considers the natural course of economic development and the relative powers of capital employed in the various sectors of the economy.[39] Since land and labor are joined to produce a nation's wealth, Smith makes agriculture the most productive form of investment and the initial sphere in which investment should occur if an economy is to progress naturally.

The cause of Smith's use of physiocratic language is his confusion between the production of wealth (use value) and the production of value (exchange value). The former can occur spontaneously in nature since wealth is nothing more than an aggregate of things; however, the latter can be produced only where a social division of labor exists since value is dependent on exchange.

This confusion repeats Smith's principal contradiction between nature and society. But there is more. During the period in which he writes, capital has captured production and the state, but incompletely, although the peasantry has been separated from the land. Agriculture still predominates over manufacturing, and traditional crafts generally persist in both spheres of production. Labor has been only formally subsumed by capital; the worker still controls the production process, even in the most developed trades, such as pin production. Only with the introduction of machinery will capital come into control of the production process and in so doing deepen the division of labor and create an internal dynamic for growth.[40]

Notwithstanding the remarkable economic advances of the period, most of the improvements were confined to a few industries, notably cotton and iron, and in large part postdated the publication of *The Wealth of Nations*.[41] England remained a rural nation tied to ancient ways although it was organized along capitalist lines and although its initial political break into the modern era had occurred nearly a century before. The railroad boom of the 1840s marked the close of England's preindustrial past.[42]

The State's Ordering of Nature

Formal equality before the law provides the necessary development of the just natural order, as government fulfills the duty of protecting every member of society from the "injustice of oppression" of every other member of it. The proper exercise of government will end the arbitrary and despotic rule that characterizes the "unnatural" stages of history that intervene between the primitive republicanism of the first and natural stage and the developed, true freedom of the commercial stage. Although labor is propertyless and degraded in comparison with the capitalists and landlords of civilized society, at least it is not the property of lords and masters.[43]

Throughout Smith's analysis he insists that economic advance is a necessary but not sufficient condition for ridding society of unnatural relationships. Although spontaneous economic advance in feudal Europe establishes the possibility of social progress, the potential is realized only through the functioning of the state. The very foundation of socioeconomic life, private property, demands the existence of a state:

> The origin of natural rights is quite evident. That a person has a right to have his body free from injury and his liberty free from infringement unless there be proper cause, nobody doubts. But acquired rights such as property require more explanation. Property and civil government very much depend on one another.[44]

It can be suggested, therefore, that Smith looks to the system of jurisprudence in the commercial stage of history as a means of realigning social development and fulfilling nature's end. Although a natural system of law will eliminate privilege in the form of either guilds or mercantile and aristocratic monopolies, the most significant alteration will occur in the creation of a free-labor market, since wage labor itself is the foundation, according to Smith, of the wealth in the advanced stage.

Smith equates all wealth (value) with the physical act of laboring, so slave labor itself is compatible in Smith's system with commercial enterprise; both in *Lectures on Justice* and *The Wealth of Nations* Smith discusses examples of slavery's commercial usage. However, he always condemns this institution—which includes both chattel slavery and serfdom—because he believes that it violates the laborer's natural right of self-preservation and consequently inhibits economic growth by misallocating labor and eliminating incentive.[45] Through the legislated perpetuation of free-market conditions, the state unifies the contending classes and affords a stability that allows continuous growth.[46] As a consequence of economic growth the laborer is elevated from his previously pitiful material existence.[47]

Thus, where government ensures freedom, workers can be expected to internalize the principles of the natural order from which they benefit, even if labor's gains are not as great as those of the other classes. To guarantee their adherence, Smith recommends that the state educate the working class to appreciate the natural society in which productivity is the key to freedom.[48] This education is to be restricted to what is known now as vocational training and to instruction in the moral precepts given by nature and developed by society.[49]

The Mercantilist Menace

Smith's concern with individual freedom and therefore with economic advance results paradoxically in a preoccupation with policy recommendations, though he denies that politics is the primary realm in which humanity should seek moral improvement. Economic theory can determine the correctness of certain policies, but politics has to impose them. Not to do so would allow practice to fly in the face of sound theory by permitting misallocation of resources.

In the introduction to Book IV of *The Wealth of Nations*, in which he evaluates the opposing systems of political economy, Smith defines the two objects of his inquiry when political economy "is considered as a branch of the science of the statesman": "first, to provide a plentiful revenue or subsistence for the people . . . ; and secondly, to supply the state or commonwealth with a revenue sufficient for public services."[50] Smith's theoretical antagonism to what he considers reactionary economic practice is most consistently directed against mercantilist policy, which he feels has influence not only on men of learning, but on the public conduct of statesmen and sovereigns.[51]

First, by systematizing the basic concepts of political economy Smith establishes a theoretical basis on which to criticize mercantilist thought, which lacks scientific rigor.[52] Second, Smith analyzes the historic effect of monopolies during Europe's transition from feudalism to commercial society.[53] Monopolies, more like vestiges of feudalism than harbingers of progress, interfere with the natural functioning of the market by misallocating resources. In rural areas primogeniture and entail inhibit the commercial use of land, whereas monopolies in trade favor the cities over the country. In Smith's opinion, the mercantile monopolies result from the exceptional abilities of those merchants whose profession has sharpened their calculating skills and political acumen, providing them with the knowhow to influence policy decisions in "unnatural" ways—that is, where self-interest conflicts with the general interest.

In contrast to his criticism of mercantilism, Smith praises the natural transition of the American economy, which has made rapid progress from the agrarian to the manufacturing stage because it is unencumbered by monopolies. For Smith natural development means that a nation proceeds from agriculture to manufacturing as the agrarian sector improves its technical apparatus; as a result, the population grows, cities arise, and a home market is formed. The cities, in turn, affect rural areas by stimulating demand for agricultural goods. With the increased demand, agricultural techniques continue to develop and to stimulate production at prices low enough to engage in long-distance trade. Similarly, manufacturing develops as the division of labor deepens, reducing the cost of production and leading inevitably to manufacture for international trade. Smith notes that the American colonies have followed this natural path of development and consequently have advanced much more rapidly than the European nations, where monopolies on land and industry have retarded growth.[54]

Nature's Ordering of the State

Without the state there can be no freedom; that is clear to Smith. But he doubts that even with the state freedom can be ensured, for the state is not natural but artificial. Natural rights and duties establish only the legitimacy and the end of government, not the means. All classes and all interests within each class should enjoy the natural freedom that the state has the duty to provide. *The Wealth of Nations* begins its examination of the institutions that might ensure that end by asking which class in the advanced stage is most fit to rule. Smith's criteria for selecting that class are (1) the relationship between the income of the class and the economic growth of society as a whole and (2) the general conditions of life of the particular class. Smith easily dispenses with the working class. The laborers' conditions of life are so degenerate that Smith excludes them entirely from direct participation in the body politic.

Even though he welcomes the political participation of the capitalists, he ultimately finds their class unsuitable for rule. First, their income falls with economic prosperity because competition drives down profits.[55] Second, the severe competition among capitalists forces them to use the state to promote their narrow interests while claiming that they represent the interests of the nation.[56]

The landlord class wins almost by default. Though Smith argues that the landlords are entitled to a share of the national product because of their monopoly on land, he does not confuse the landlords, who have acquired land through commercial enterprise, with the landed aristocracy, which merely inherits land through the "unnatural" laws of primogeniture and entail. Smith illustrates the distinction between natural and unnatural monopolies on land by referring to the American colonies, where rapid economic development has made the initially abundant land progressively more scarce and prepared the way for the inevitable monopolization of land.[57] As population has continued to increase, the owners of land have been able to lease it in return for rent because of the greater demand for the use of the land's productive powers. Rent has emerged as a natural consequence of economic growth and may even be considered an index of that growth. The same line of argument would recur among later American economists. The landlords' income increases with society's advance; the demand for agricultural goods increases with population growth.

Smith qualifies his confidence in the landlord's abilities. First, the very leisure which might allow landlords to study subjects like economics and politics means that they do not labor for their rents but receive them as an apparent gift from nature. They do not develop the mental skills of the capitalists, who sharpen their wits through the economic necessity of competing on the market.[58] Landlords are consequently often ill-prepared to recommend policies that further even their own interests, let alone those of society in general.

Smith cites the ill-advised Corn Laws as a flagrant mismanagement of resources. Hoping to raise the real value of corn and thereby rents, the landlords have succumbed to the arguments of the manufacturers and the merchants, who have persuaded them to demand a bounty on corn.[59] But they have neglected to consider that the price of corn functions differently from that of other commodities; a bounty raises its money price, since less corn is produced, but not its real value. Workers require the same amount of corn for survival and reproduction regardless of the money price. The higher price necessitates either higher wages or a reduction in the laboring population through starvation. High wages will discourage capitalists from fully employing productive labor; a diminished labor force signals the general contraction of the economy. In either case, the economic growth upon which rents depend is not allowed to proceed.

Smith understands that no one class is capable of rule; he therefore favors the incorporation of countervailing forces in the body politic, especially since he recognizes that historical circumstances dictate that the old estates—the monarchy, the aristocracy, and the clergy—be represented. Through this process he hopes that a natural aristocracy of talent will rise to positions of political power.[60] For Smith political freedom is a limited concept, a means to ensure economic freedom so that the business of accumulation can proceed.

Rule by one class would be tantamount to the oppression of the ruled. Smith therefore seeks the principle of good government in the elements of its construction.[61] In its most basic form, good government prescribes the separation of the sovereign or executive branch from the judicial. This eliminates the arbitrariness from law.[62] Unlike many other Whigs, Smith does not despair of monarchy as a viable guarantor of commercial freedom.[63] He prefers the monarch to an elected official because he believes that only inherited authority can inspire sufficient respect in the populace to safeguard the nation from lawlessness. Smith further fears that the competition for an elective executive position will engender demagoguery and mislead a gullible electorate.[64]

In the best case, the powers of the monarchy are circumscribed through a deepening of the division in government by taking the legislative powers away from the executive branch and investing them in a legislative branch. The legislature is composed of an upper house of nobility and a lower house elected by the propertied classes. Apparently Smith regards the English nobility as part of the advanced economic order. The only privilege it has—and this is limited to the individual head of the noble family—is political. Thus, the English aristocracy can provide the stability and order associated with its caste while being incorporated into civil society.

2. RICARDO *and* MALTHUS *on Who* *Uses Labor Best, Capitalists or Landlords*

> Corn Law Repeal is a question of morals and general legislation, not
> limited to that object food . . . laws are an expression of the will of
> the whole society, they are carried into effect by the general power,
> and they have . . . a permanent influence over the morality and
> well-being of all. Of society, the labourers form the largest portion;
> the protection of peaceful industry is the great object of all laws, and
> if any man can show that the Corn Laws add to the rewards of the
> labourers and elevate their character, he shall have me for his fol-
> lower.—Thomas Hodgskin, "A Lecture on Free Trade"

As the Settlement of 1688 had substituted natural law for the ancient
rights of free-born Englishmen as the set of principles on which the constitution was to rest, the Industrial Revolution supplanted the last economic
remnants of a discarded past with the technological consequences of nature's revealed order.[1] By offering a scientific language by which policy decisions could be made in conformity with nature, Smith replaced political
theory with political economy as the discourse of statesmanship. However,
the peculiarities in Smith's theory produced varying interpretations of the
technical relationships among the elements of the economy and permitted
contending policy recommendations about the viability of an industrial
order.

The Industrial Revolution had only begun to crack the foundations of
England's agrarian-based economy when Adam Smith wrote *The Wealth of
Nations*. His perspicacity enabled him to observe generalized relationships
that appeared chaotic to his contemporaries and to speculate about further
developments. But Smith could not accurately describe the conflicts that
would manifest themselves during the full-blown transformation to industrial society. That work was in part left to his disciples Malthus and Ricardo, the friendly adversaries of the Corn Law debates. These debates,
like the tariff controversy in the United States, developed from the economic crisis in the wake of the Napoleonic Wars. Since the English debates focused on preserving freedom in a deepening capitalist economy,
the American political economists often sided explicitly with either Malthus or Ricardo.

Landlords' Accommodation to History

The viability of an industrial order was raised in the Corn Law debates, initiated by the Corn Law of 1815 and sustained by its modifications in 1822, 1828, and 1842.[2] Unlike the earlier corn laws, the 1815 law was designed to bolster the landlords' rent by prohibiting the importation of corn at a certain price.[3] Without foreign competition the price of corn was to be artificially maintained at the high levels reached during the Napoleonic Wars. Although Smith's theory condemned interference in the market, his vestiges of physiocratic thought offered grounds for later economists, such as Spence, Chalmers, and Malthus, to devise intricate theories to defend the policy of corn restrictions.[4] Part of the defense rested on an issue that Smith had not addressed in any significant manner—namely, economic crisis. The economic depression that followed the Napoleonic Wars forced economists to consider this question.[5]

The advocates of corn restriction and the agrarian order, of whom Malthus was the most theoretically rigorous, contended that capital was the culprit of economic crisis since its parsimonious character restricted demand. Only the landlord's disbursement of nature's gratuitous surplus could compensate for capital's miserliness. For Ricardo, the leading economic theorist of industrial capital, crises were brief aberrations caused by disproportions in the market, for capital generated its own demand through its continued revolutionizing of production. The only intrinsic barrier that Ricardo perceived to capital's ability to increase a nation's wealth was nature's limited fertility, although there were artificial constraints imposed by misguided legislators. The most important was the Corn Laws.

The works of Malthus and Ricardo written between 1815 and 1822 are the best of the innumerable tracts that emerged during the controversy that finally ended with the repeal of the Corn Laws in 1846. Although they disagreed on particular points and on substantive issues, Ricardo and Malthus remained close personal friends. But from 1825 on, the anti–Corn Law forces, with pamphlets and mass mobilization, fostered mistrust and animosity between the landlords and capitalists. In 1839 the reform forces coalesced in the Anti–Corn Law League, which found its main leadership in the radical party inspired by the principles of Bentham, Mill, and Ricardo. Inspiration could have led to revolt had the Tories, led by Peel, not repealed the Corn Laws in 1846.[6] By conceding on this issue, the landlords made their political peace with the new industrial order.

While the predominant landed class in America, that of the planters, was effectively isolated, ideologically as well as geographically, from the process that was transforming the United States from a preindustrial into an industrial capitalist society, the English gentry was integrated in the transformation by the ideology and the objectives it shared with industrial capitalists. The Tories' successful statesmanship combined a retreat of the landlord class before industrial capitalism with the preservation of both relative class harmony and aristocratic privilege in government.

Unlike the Southern planters, the English landlords were deeply involved in constructing the infrastructure for the Industrial Revolution. Increasing demand for raw materials such as coal encouraged the landlords to invest in transportation systems and new technology. Through investment in industry of capital accumulated in the agrarian sector, the landlords promoted industrial growth in the eighteenth century.[7]

The landlords continued to play this role in the first half of the nineteenth century, although their relative importance in the economy was declining. The railroad, which proved to be the major stimulus to British industrialization, found its earliest supporters among the landed gentry. Landlords reaped benefits from the railroad, but in the long run it limited their power by shifting the economy from an agrarian to an industrial base.[8] By the mid-nineteenth century, the English landlords had clearly become a junior partner to the English industrialists.

In England disagreements seemed to push to the limits of peaceful dialogue; yet the underlying agreement about the necessity of the working class and its problematic character prevented the heat of the arguments from erupting into violence. The radicalism of the French Revolution, the Peterloo Massacre, the Luddite rebellions, and the Chartist movement all reminded landlords and capitalists alike of the potential force in the working class if unity among the propertied interests were broken. Even the philosophic radical James Mill, who advocated universal male suffrage and a repeal of the Corn Laws, did not go so far as to attack either the landlord's right to rent or the institution of primogeniture.[9] An attack on the landlord's rent would be in fact an attack on private property and a challenge to the very basis of the social order. Aristocrats, integrated into the capitalist economy and members of the House of Lords, provided the continuity needed to restrain the capriciousness of the lower house.[10] Cobden's attempt to extend the anti–Corn Law campaign into a movement against primogeniture failed miserably.[11]

To the Northern American school, however, the dominant landed class did not necessarily add to the stability of the Union. Slavery was a peculiar institution since it made labor a form of property and denied the universal qualities of commodity exchange. Moreover, the radical wing of the American school believed that the corrupting influence of slavery disqualified the planters as a stabilizing force. Instead, the planters were viewed as a political power that threatened the very existence of independent labor by opposing legislation such as the protective tariff, which was designed to preserve labor's status. The planters' obstructionism threatened the American republic itself since, in the minds of the economists of the American school, independent labor constituted the social basis of the republic.

The landlords' integration both in the economy and in the discourse on political economy helped them concede to the political realities of the new industrial order. As a political force, they quickly adopted programs for political reform and for the extension of free trade in matters not directly related to corn. As early as 1770 members of the gentry such as Wyvill, Burdett, and Hunt,[12] Pitt, Perceval, and Lord Liverpool first introduced free trade into the political arena.[13] The concessions to the middle classes, the most important of which were the Reform Act of 1832 and the repeal of the Corn Laws in 1846, were within a tradition completely consistent with Whig and, for that matter, Tory political practice. But most striking in the political savoir faire of the English landed parties was their ability to adopt radical utilitarian notions about integrating the working class into the nation. The aristocracy, not the middle classes, yielded to the demands of the working class with, for example, the factory acts[14] and the Reform Act of 1867, which extended the franchise to large portions of the working class.[15] In this respect the contention of Dugald Stewart and James Mill that the aristocracy provided a stabilizing effect on the nation was certainly borne out in practice. Though in most respects England was the classical model of capitalist development, it ironically instituted a bourgeois order through the "utilitarian" politics of the aristrocracy.[16]

Corn Laws: An Incentive or an Obstacle to Productive Labor

The Ricardo-Malthus debate on the Corn Laws began with the publishing of pamphlets. In February of 1815 Malthus published *Grounds on an Opinion on the Policy of Restricting the Importation of Foreign Corn* and *An Inquiry into the Nature and Progress of Rent*, followed shortly by Ricardo's *An Essay on the Influence of a Low Price of Corn on the Profits of Stock*. In the same month West and Torrens published their pamphlets on the Corn Laws. As their titles indicate, Malthus's and Ricardo's pamphlets centered on the economic source of rents and their relationship to profits.[17] Ricardo extended his analysis of rents and profits in 1817 when he published his *Principles of Political Economy and Taxation*. He subordinated the policy issue of the Corn Laws to the question of creating a science of the economy. Malthus did not allow Ricardo the last word; in 1820 he published his *Principles of Political Economy Considered with a View to their Practical Application*.

Unlike Smith's work, the Ricardo-Malthus treatises did not attempt to systematize a general theory of society. In essence, they accepted his notion that nature, with its drive for self-preservation, should guide social development; they proceeded to refine his economic theory, specifying the relationship of wages, profits, and rents to the accumulation process.[18] In this way the Ricardo-Malthus debate attempted rigorously to establish the relationship of the capitalist, landlord, and working classes to economic growth. Ricardo claimed that the capitalists were the pivotal class in the accumulation process, while Malthus favored the landlords.

The Ricardo-Malthus debates mark a shift from a preindustrial to an industrial capitalist order, but the actual economic conditions remain still principally rooted in an agrarian world, as recent economic studies detailing the extent of mechanization and factory production in the early nineteenth century indicate.[19] The structure of the debate itself retains an agrarian vocabulary. For Ricardo and Malthus, rent becomes the pivotal economic category, and corn production becomes central to capitalist production. They make social life a mere biological process of reproduction. For both, nature imposes limitations on economic development by restricting the soil's productive power relative to human fecundity. Thus, capitalist society finally appears to be no more free from nature's tyranny than the agrarian world of Tudor England.

Such an agrarian bias cannot be found in the work of Adam Smith. Although he maintains a physiocratic bias toward agriculture, he does not impute to nature any limiting qualities. As a polemic against mercantilist policy, *The Wealth of Nations* attempts to break with the tradition of political economy in which the nation's wealth appears analogous to the ordering of a household; Smith's agrarian bias merely shows his inability to break fully with the tradition he opposes.[20] In the Ricardo-Malthus debate, however, the structure is necessary both for defining rent as the central concern and for warding off the radical theories, based on nature's limitless potential, that predicate the ultimate abolition of private property.

Yet Ricardo's and Malthus's work focuses on the problems of a modern industrial order, not immediately with regard to the transitional conflict between industrialists and the predominant agrarian capitalist class, but with regard to technological change, economic crisis, and the threat of working-class revolution. Thus, the theoretical discourse advanced by developing concepts contained only within the economic discourse and not immediately given by real economic life.

With all their differences, both Ricardo and Malthus fundamentally attempt to determine the mechanisms that will permit accumulation to continue smoothly. For them, as for Smith, accumulation is the object of social-ethical life and the substance of freedom. Even though they disagree on the nature of value, they agree that the Smithian distinction between productive and unproductive labor is sound; therefore, their efforts to ascertain the real, and hence natural, relationships among the classes hinge on the question of the proper employment of productive labor. The debate can be seen as a contention between paradigms of the proper means by which productive labor sustains accumulation—that is, produces the wealth of nations. In the Ricardian schema the capitalist functions as the pivotal mechanism ensuring productive labor's fullest "exploitation," while in Malthus's theory the landlords assume, somewhat paradoxically, the captain-of-industry role.[21]

In both, the working class emerges with all the contradictions found in Smith's theory. The source of wealth is the working class, whose power can be fully realized only when controlled by capital. Yet, as a propertyless class, the laboring masses are potentially dangerous, since the system of private property can appear to them as a source of enslavement. And in the Ricardo-Malthus debate the laboring population in England appears as a force inspired by the French Revolution. Malthus and Ricardo share theories of population and rents. Whereas for Smith the working class may be promised a future of rising incomes even as the division of labor condemns them to a life of drudgery, Ricardo and Malthus can only promise them perpetual poverty, for nature supposedly limits the production of wealth.

For this reason—and since the French Revolution is fresh in their minds—the dual problem of ideologically including the working class in civil society and incorporating it into the nation's political life becomes all the more perplexing and difficult for these economists.[22] They assume that employment and temporarily rising incomes can offset the radicalization of the working class, but they have to offer ideological and political means of ensuring that the working class will adhere to nature's order. A modicum of physical well-being may breed desire for more unless workers are convinced of the "correctness" of their subordination. Thus, while the conflict between the capitalist and landlord characterizes the debate between Ricardo and Malthus (and the period), their opposing views about whether landlords or capitalists should dominate are based on the relative ability of the contending classes to "exploit" the working class and politically neutralize it. The Corn Laws precipitated a debate on the character and destiny of the English nation among the propertied classes.

The Advent of Industrial Capital According to Ricardo

Ricardo's specific concerns in the Corn Laws controversy redefine the object of study for political economy in general.[23] According to Ricardo, its subject is no longer the nature and causes of wealth but the laws which regulate redistribution: how "the proportions of the whole produce of the earth will be allotted to each of the classes [landlord, capitalist, and working] under the names of rent, profit and wages."[24] In particular, do the laws of distribution, with their implications for economic legislation, such as the Corn Laws, and the problem of taxation, divide the total produce of society in a way that facilitates continued economic growth?

By defining the problem of distribution in terms of "the whole produce of the earth," Ricardo defines the economic product as an agricultural, physical entity.[25] The question of distribution appears to be how the agricultural product is divided among the classes so that all are fed and so that natural biological reproduction may continue. Wages afford, in his system, the bundle of necessaries required to reproduce the working class; rents are the amount paid for the use of the land's indestructible powers; and profits are the sum needed to preserve the stock required by labor in producing wealth. However, when Ricardo treats wages, profits, and rents as market concepts whose determination is subject to the law of value, he continues the ambiguity of Smith's theory and therefore determines the relative portions ultimately falling to the capitalist, landlord, and working classes. Ricardo finds Smith's component theory of value incapable of defining value because it assumes what it is intended to explain.[26] Instead, Ricardo adopts Smith's labor theory of value; labor can be designated the source of value because the division of labor transforms the act of work into a social activity.

Ricardo posits labor as the source of value and assumes that the reader is familiar with Smith's lengthy discussions on the division of labor. Since Ricardo is a follower of Bentham and Mill, his works are intimately connected with the reform efforts of the philosophic radicals. Mill encouraged Ricardo to write his *Principles* in order to explicate the economic foundations of their "radical" political efforts.[27]

As Halévy has argued, a value theory based on utility—like that developed by Say and criticized by Ricardo—makes that economic measurement rest on personal preference, which cannot be accurately measured, rather than on the easily calculable toil and trouble of producing individuals. It is the latter which, for Ricardo, grounds economics in a system subject to the Benthamite calculus of pleasure and pain.[28] This entire utilitarian project, as Halévy has demonstrated, is compatible, although not identical, with Smith's moral and economic doctrine.

Ricardo devises an economic model in which corn is the only commodity produced, for he believes that each class's portion of the product (value) produced by labor is determined by the production of corn. Corn, for Ricardo as for the other economists of his day, constitutes the major portion of labor's wages—an indicator in Ricardo's model of profits since they existed in inverse proportion. Because the rate of profit tends to equalize among industries, the ratio between wages and profits set in agriculture is logically generalized throughout the economy. Ricardo's model therefore alters Smith's theory by making the rate of profit depend on agricultural production, which regulates the wages spent primarily for corn, rather than on competition among capitals.

The dynamic of Ricardo's model depends on two concepts for which

Ricardo gives Malthus credit: the Malthusian theory of population and a differential theory of rent. Unlike Smith, Malthus argues that biological factors fundamentally regulate human population. He posits that humanity is so prolific that population grows faster than nature can produce food; consequently, human population constantly pushes toward the limit of food supply. Malthus reasons that human population advances geometrically while food advances arithmetically. Without certain checks on population growth, Malthus foresees a general crisis of overpopulation. Ricardo uses this theory in explaining wages, profits, and rents. As population increases, the demand for food increases. To meet this growing demand, less fertile land is brought into cultivation. This continual movement from more fertile to less fertile land makes the production of food more difficult and necessitates the expenditure of more labor time to procure the basic requirements of life. Agricultural production, therefore, moves in the opposite direction from manufacturing, which continually reduces labor time by introducing technology.

Since the amount of required labor varies, corn has a multitude of values. The actual market price of food, however, is set by the corn produced on the least fertile soil, since that measures the difficulty society has in providing for the entire population. Therefore, as the population increases, the price of food rises. This forces the wage rate to rise and the profit rate to fall.

If profits fall, rents rise. Following Malthus, Ricardo argues that the economic source of rent is to be found in the differential productivity of the land. The more fertile lands can produce food more cheaply; that is, they require less labor to produce the same amount of food in a given time period. Consequently, the more fertile land produces a surplus over the amount produced on the least fertile land.

This surplus constitutes the rent; therefore, the least fertile land does not afford a rent. Landlords acquire the rent because of their legal title to the land, limited in supply and possessed of "original and indestructible power."[29] Like Smith, Ricardo believes that rent is legally supported by private property, which is a "natural" condition of production.

The expansion of population and the growing demand for food benefit the landlord class in two ways. First, landlords acquire an increased share of the produce of their land every time less fertile land than theirs is taken into production. Second, as the price of food increases over time, a landlord's corn "will exchange for a greater quantity of all other goods which have not been raised in value."[30]

What then is the specific effect of rising rents on profits and wages? A rise in rents produces a fall in profits since increasing rents correspond to increasing costs of food and to increasing labor costs. Eventually, wages will absorb profits entirely. But it does not follow that workers' living conditions will improve. Increasing wages will allow them to purchase only the same quantity of the means of subsistence. As wages rise and cut into profits because of increased food prices, the costs of the means of subsistence will probably rise faster, so that the condition of the working class will actually deteriorate.

As the rate of profit steadily declines because of wage increments, the capitalists will be discouraged from investing and will eventually stop doing so. Accumulation will cease and society will begin to decay. Decay is inevitable in Ricardo's theory; its certainty is ensured by the limitation of nature's powers of production, which causes the food prices and wages to rise and the rate of profit to fall. Nature is the cause for the inevitable collapse of society; the landlords' increasing wealth is the first indicator of doom.

The increasing wealth of the landlord class offers Ricardo no solution to the problem of the falling rate of profit. He does not assume that the landlord class will invest its wealth in productive activities and thereby continue accumulation; instead he assumes that the landlords will spend their revenues unproductively in luxurious living. If the landlords were to invest productively, they would be functioning as capitalists; as such they would eventually suffer from the falling rate of profit and at last lose their motivation to continue acting as capitalists.

The only possible solution to the falling rate of profit is to increase nature's productive powers by means of technology. But Ricardo argues that this, too, is only temporary; improved means of cultivation and fertilizing can increase nature's productivity only within meager limits. Eventually the meanness of nature will assert itself, and as the quantity of fertile land becomes ever more scarce, the rate of profit will once again enter its inevitable decline. The working class must live more or less at a subsistence level. In Ricardo's opinion these are inevitable facts of life.

For Ricardo the capitalists most closely represent society's interests while the landlords stand opposed to them. Economic growth depends on expanded investments. The capitalists' motivation to expand production is based on increasing returns, so that the best guarantee for the continued growth of the economy is to ensure relatively high profits that may be invested. Ricardo recommends that taxes not fall on capital since they would "proportionably diminish that fund by whose extent the extent of the productive industry of the country must always be regulated."[31]

More important, he recommends that the Corn Laws be abrogated. He does not call for the expropriation of the landlords' property so that rents could be redistributed to the capitalist class.[32] Although such a policy could not resolve the problem of the falling rate of profit, it certainly could give accumulation new vitality.

So radical a recommendation does not appear in the *Principles* and most likely never entered Ricardo's mind, for to expropriate the landlords' property would be a direct assault on private property. There is still another possible way to redistribute the landlords' wealth to the capitalist class: tax the landlords' rent and redistribute it to the capitalist class. Ricardo rejects this method because it would be a class policy, unjust and uneconomical. He perceives too many technical problems that would have to be solved if the state were actually to tax the landlord and not the tenant farmer.[33]

For Ricardo free trade in corn would allow cheap food to enter the English market. Wages would consequently fall and profits rise with economic growth stimulated. As a result, the landlords' strangling grasp on the economy would temporarily be loosened, at least until corn prices once again rose as demand outstripped supply.

In demonstrating that the labor process itself determines distribution, Ricardo perceives the social character of production and thereby distinguishes himself as the theorist of industrial capital. He also contends that a short-run economic crisis is not a result of limitations in capitalist production but of disproportionality—a proposition that Malthus will seriously challenge.

Ricardo advocates capital's short- and medium-term solvency by adopting Say's law that supply creates its own demand. Ricardo's adoption of that law contains the same ambiguity found in his corn model, for at one moment the law functions as a natural imperative and at another as a derivation from the social character of capital. In accepting Say's law, Ricardo assumes that the aim of production is consumption and not the profits that propel economic development. Hence he assumes that economic life is directly created by the human being's physical needs.[34]

For Ricardo, Say's law functions in a manner consistent with production for profit. Capital itself can generate a demand sufficient to meet the requirement of profitability and thus can prevent a crisis of underconsumption. This theory can be found in his discussion of machinery's effect on the working class. In the first two editions of the *Principles* Ricardo argues that machinery benefits the working class because it facilitates production and lowers the costs of commodities. By the third edition, in which he adds a chapter on machinery, Ricardo has come under the influence of "labor" economists such as Barton, who argues that because it replaces workers and creates massive unemployment, machinery is detrimental.[35]

Ricardo finally agrees with labor economists on one point: the unemployment that results is only temporary. The decreasing price of commodities caused by machinery allows the capitalists greater savings, which are reinvested to create new and greater demand for labor. The introduction of machinery indicates a growing economy and rising labor costs. To limit technology is to prepare the way for premature economic stagnation and to prevent the deepening of the market. In Ricardo's model, capital finds no internal limits to its growth, only those imposed by nature, which condemns the working class to misery while the wealth of the nation advances. Perhaps this is the greatest paradox in Ricardo's works. At the moment when society is on the verge of liberating itself from nature's restrictions on production, the leading theorist of the new industrial order can only forecast nature's inevitable triumph, not humanity's.

Malthus's Agents of Providence

Malthus believed the application of Ricardo's erroneous theory would cause serious disruptions in the economy and foster political unrest among the lower orders of society. Significantly, in opposing Ricardo, Malthus developed concepts which question his own original formulations about population and rent.[36] In order to maintain his defense of the landlord class, Malthus expressed a vision of sustained economic growth in the language of the natural order.

First, he rejected the labor theory of value. According to Malthus, many circumstances, like monopolies, government policies, and the varying durability of capital, cause prices to deviate significantly from the labor embodied in them, making a labor theory of value useless. Consequently, Malthus pursued Smith's component theory of value in contradistinction to Ricardo. While the components of price are wages, profits, and rents, each of these in Malthus's view is determined by the law of supply and demand. If, for example, a rare skill is required to produce a commodity, labor commands a high price because there is a small supply of it compared to the demand; if unskilled labor is called for, then wages will be low because of an abundant supply. Profits, too, are determined by supply and demand. According to Malthus, capitalists are entitled to profits in return for "previous accumulation of objects which facilitates further production."[37] They can increase labor's productivity enormously, but their returns are not proportional. Instead, the improved state of production makes the supply of commodities more accessible so that prices fall—and with them, profits—until they reach the lowest level that can maintain capital's service. Rent offers no exception. Landlords like capitalists and workers receive the going return for their contribution to production; the only limitation is that the return be sufficient to induce the landlords to offer their resources for use.[38]

Because, for Malthus, supply and demand determine the cost of production, they ultimately help determine the commodity's exchange value by setting its lower limit. If the price at which a commodity sells is not sufficient to remunerate worker, capitalist, and landlord, its production will come to a halt. Malthus calls the cost of production the "necessary price," rather than the "natural price" referred to by Smith, since it is the price necessary "to bring the commodity regularly to the market."[39]

Malthus pushes his objection to Ricardo's ostensibly objective labor theory of value to the ultimate conclusion. Value, according to Malthus, depends mostly on the subjective principle of demand, even within his supply-and-demand paradigm: "the true way of considering costs is, as the necessary condition of the supply of objects wanted."[40] Nothing could be more in keeping with Malthus's definition of value as the will and power to possess commodities. With this assertion Malthus converts caprice from a force corrosive to the nation, as it is perceived by others, to the very foundation of economic regularity. Smith has countered objections to the allegedly capricious capitalist order by arguing that embodied labor offers an objective measure of value. For Malthus, that objectivity is illusory, but his equation of caprice with economic law rests on his understanding that nature imposes scarcity and orders freedom.

Malthus's conclusions regarding the relationship of rent to accumulation differ radically from Ricardo's. Following Smith, Malthus cites three causes of rent: (1) land creates a product greater than is necessary to physically sustain both the agricultural worker and the capitalist, (2) corn creates its own demand and always commands a necessary price, and (3) since fertile land is comparatively scarce, the conditions for a "natural" monopoly and a landlord class are created.

Malthus takes great pains to make the landlord's monopoly of the land last among the causes. That monopoly enhances the production of the surplus because private property is the most productive form of ownership, but Malthus insists that rent results from natural surpluses rather than from monopolies, however beneficial they may be. Because of this confusion, which Malthus attributes to Ricardo, Malthus argues that the landlords are unjustly characterized as parasitic.

Unlike Ricardo, Malthus points to nature's beneficence rather than its meanness to explain rent. For Malthus, rents are a "bountiful gift of nature," and they alleviate labor's pain and misery in obtaining food. In turn, the additional time this natural beneficence allows society may be devoted to manufacturing luxuries and to other pursuits which create a high civilization: "the surplus, which a given quantity of land yields in the shape of rent . . . is finally an exact measure of the *relief* from labour in the production of food granted to him by kind Providence."[41]

Although Malthus projects a correlation between increasing national wealth and rising rents, he cannot deny that profits fall as rents rise. If, moreover, advancing rents can be considered Providence's contribution to social opulence, Malthus has to demonstrate that the landlords' behavior serves Providence's ends. Malthus's discussion of technology and underconsumption tackles both problems.

For Malthus, the finite productivity of land will not be able to keep up with the productive powers of humanity. Consequently, in some distant future when land has been exhausted, the increasing price of corn will cause stagnation in the economy and conflict over the limited resources. Technology will be relatively powerless to alleviate the crisis. On these general points Malthus and Ricardo agree. Unlike Ricardo, however, Malthus stresses the positive short-term effects of technology in raising the living standards of capitalists, workers, and landlords.

Drawing from the impressive empirical data on the impact of technology on English agricultural productivity in the eighteenth and early nineteenth centuries, Malthus argues that applying science to production can both control the long-term trend of diminishing returns in agriculture and keep wages from eroding the rate of profit. Consequently, technology can mitigate the potential conflict between landlords and capitalists over distribution by guaranteeing a stable profit rate even as accumulation advances.[42]

Technology in manufacturing can also enhance profits by lowering the nonagricultural component of the wage. Growing labor costs will be offset further by substituting fixed for circulating capital. Malthus believes that these countervailing forces—agricultural improvements, lowered costs of manufactured goods, and substitution of fixed for circulating capital —can offset the falling rate of profit for at least a century.

By increasing the total social product, technology can alleviate the potential conflict over distribution between the working class, on the one hand, and the capitalist and landlord classes on the other. In Ricardo's universe this short-run solution offers little comfort against that inevitable clash.[43]

In discussing the potential of technology to resolve all economic contradictions in the short run, Malthus goes so far as to suggest that technology can overcome nature's limited supply of fertile land. His conception of nature's meanness has two essential effects on his defense of the agrarian order. First, to counter radical utopian visions such as Godwin's, Condorcet's, and Owen's, Malthus argues that nature imposes restrictions on production. Second, without a theory of restricted production, Malthus could not give the landlords the importance he does, but would have to allow for the possibility of a changing economic balance in favor of industrialists. The theory of population makes rents the pivotal economic category and the focus of economic inquiry for Malthus and Ricardo. Moreover, in Malthus's theory, if technology were capable of overcoming nature's meanness, then social organization could not be understood in terms of increasing land's productivity, since agriculture and manufacturing would technically be equivalents. Thus, Malthus would not have economic grounds for defending policies favoring agriculture against those favoring manufacturing.

Malthus on the Landlords' Utility

In sharp distinction to Ricardo, Malthus maintains that increased wealth of landlords leads to increased unproductive spending and to profits for the industrialists. Initially, Malthus concurred with Ricardo that the profit rate governs the accumulation process and that in the long term the rate of profit tends to fall. Ricardo, however, by assuming Say's law, sees the falling rate of profit as the only real obstacle to sustained growth, whereas Malthus identifies it as only one of two checks on accumulation; the other, more significant in the short run, is underconsumption.

Malthus rejects Say's law for three reasons: (1) it treats commodities "as if they were mathematical figures, or arithmetical characters, the relations of which were to be compared, instead of articles of consumption, which must of course be referred to the numbers and wants of consumers"; (2) it does not consider indolence and love of ease as a feature of human nature; and (3) it assumes that savings are a simple transfer of expenditures so that labor, which is "employed by those whose object is to save, will create such an effectual demand for commodities as to encourage a continued increase or produce."[44] For Malthus, underconsumption provides a check on accumulation. If demand is not sufficient to establish a price that can remunerate the capitalists for their services, then production will come to a halt.

Two conditions cause the imbalance: (1) the increasing employment of labor in productive enterprises, and (2) the capitalists' propensity to save. Malthus reasons that accumulation results in a growing employment of productive labor. The increasing number of commodities must be bought at the necessary price, which only the propertied class can afford. Labor's purchasing power does not keep pace with its productive powers.[45] The propertied classes are not equal in their creation of demand for manufactured goods, mainly, Malthus argues, because capitalists would rather save than spend and thus intensify underconsumption. Even when this parsimonious behavior leads to growing expenditures on capital goods, the problem is not resolved, for expenditures only bring more productive workers into the picture and further exacerbate the imbalance between demand and supply.

Malthus offers three mechanisms by which demand can be made effective. The first is foreign trade. The second is proper distribution of land. Highly concentrated ownership of land restricts demand by limiting the amount of food and luxuries consumed directly.[46] But if a vicious distribution reduces the production of wealth, so does one that continually subdivides property by eliminating primogeniture and distinctions of inheritance based on sex. Such a system generates an impoverished state in which all live equally in poverty and great numbers perish. The only rich members of society will be those who received salaries from the government. Malthus points to France, which was experimenting in such laws, and warns that by eliminating the wealthy landowner one ensures not only poverty but also political unrest, since the aristocracy balances the mob and the crown.

The third and most important mechanism for ensuring an effective demand is the unproductive consumption of luxuries, not only by landlords and their retainers but also by government employees. All state employees and all military units and public projects are included as government expenditure. Public projects are particularly important since they can employ large numbers of workers. Because they allow the state to expand and contract the supply of unproductive labor at will, Malthus assigns to the government the responsibility for intervening if the other mechanisms for establishing an effective demand should fail.

In general, Malthus eliminates the negative connotation that the term *unproductive* might have in relationship to the landlords' and the state's functions in the economy and rejects Ricardo's negative estimation of the landlord class's effect on economic growth.[47]

Malthus's analysis of underconsumption is structured by his dependence on physiocracy, which is hidden to some extent by his acceptance of Smith's notion that labor, rather than land, is the productive element in society; consequently, profits are viewed as a true contribution to society's surplus product.[48] But when one considers the actual dynamic of short-term economic growth and the source of profits, Malthus's physiocratic bias becomes more evident and more consistent with the physiocratic definition of rent he has derived from Smith.[49]

For Malthus, profits depend on rents. More important, since profits ultimately derive from nature rather than from labor, the notion of class exploitation found in Smith and Ricardo cannot exist. Furthermore, technology—that is, society's control over nature—can enhance that surplus in the near and immediate future so that per capita income may rise. Thus, there is no compelling reason for class conflict over the social product.

To maintain effective demand for manufactured goods, Malthus argues for a weighted balance in favor of country over town. Any danger of economic crisis from underconsumption will exacerbate class conflict because of the resulting masses of unemployed workers congregated in unwholesome towns. To prevent this, Malthus advises the state to retain the Corn Laws. According to him, the Corn Laws will force capital into agriculture by artificially sustaining high profits there.[50]

Apparently more important, the Corn Laws help preserve the political balance between town and country, between landlords and laborers.[51] In the end, not only would the propertied classes be harmed by free trade in grain, but so would the working class, since its economic and moral "advancement" made possible through accumulation would be interrupted.

The Political Dilemma of Increased Productivity

Malthus's preoccupation with political stability goes beyond the assumption that national prosperity will promote harmony among classes. To ensure economic and social prosperity Malthus and Ricardo agree on the need for a program to best use the working class in the production of national wealth and to promote an adequate moral propensity among workers to ensure their adherence to the capitalist order. The working class poses a serious dilemma for political theory. As owners of no property, they are degraded below the level of citizens; as owners of their own labor, they can claim to be commodity owners entitled to full citizenship.

Malthus and Ricardo both deny the right of the working class to enfranchisement, although they think that universal education should be the means of tempering working-class demands. Whereas Ricardo finally views political inclusion of the working class as consistent with that objective, Malthus insists that such a proposal is impolitic.[52] In Malthus's theory the workers' depravity stems more from their innate moral ineptitude than from the consequences of the social division of labor; education will not uplift these "helots" to the same moral or intellectual level as their propertied "masters."

Smith had proposed universal education for the working class in order to alleviate the dehumanizing effects of the division of labor and to replace the inhibiting superstitions of the laboring population with the "natural" tenets of political economy. Malthus no longer has superstition to contend with. Instead, he has to combat a radical, allegedly distorted, Smithian analysis from penetrating the working class. Godwin and Condorcet read Smith carefully and appropriated his principle of utility to devise a system that promised a future without poverty, private property, or a state.[53] These social transformations were to occur through the progress of modern industry, which would make wealth redundant and consequently egoism useless; benevolence would replace self-interest as the motivating force of human nature and the foundation of social life.

In his determination to deny the validity of these ideas, Malthus developed his theory of population, in which the development of industry lags far behind human fecundity. Without the redundance of wealth, economic necessity will continually assert itself, ensuring the permanence of egoism and private property. Malthus denies any logic to the radical proposition that the greatest happiness for the greatest number can possibly result from the state's abrogation of private property. He argues that accumulation and therefore wealth will halt in the absence of private property.

Malthus's own recommendations for state intervention were based on an artificial identity of interests consistent with class distinctions. To make sure that Condorcet, Godwin, and Owen (who is added in the 1817 edition of *An Essay on the Principle of Population*) would have no impact, Malthus gave the supposed innate inferiority of the working class a theoretical determination. In this way he justified the denial of political enfranchisement to the class that might want to act on the principles of the radicals.

He develops his objections to extending political rights to the working class both in his *Essay on Population* and in his *Principles*.[54] They are founded on the contradiction that he posits between natural abundance and human fecundity. The latter Malthus attributed to the drive for sexual gratification, which in his opinion was the primary motivating force for human action. But a close reading of Malthus reveals that he did not restrict the passion for sex to the mere act of coupling. The individual seeks pleasures of all kinds, and these desires must be gratified immediately. Therefore, contradicting Smith's premise that human nature is basically acquisitive, human nature for Malthus is improvident and immoral. Morality, the key to rational development beyond the stage of subsistence, develops only when necessity dictates constraints on pleasure:

> At an early period of cultivation, when only rich soils are worked, as the quantity of corn is the greatest, compared with the quantity of labour required to produce it, we might expect to find a small portion of the population engaged in agriculture, and a large portion engaged in administering to the other wants of society. . . . But in examining the state of unimproved countries, what do we really see?—almost invariably, a much larger proportion of the whole people employed on the land than in those countries where the increase of population has occasioned the necessity of resorting to poor soils; and less time instead of more time devoted to the production of conveniences and luxuries.[55]

Therefore, if humanity were placed in an environment in which the land could supply all the necessaries of life with little or no work, population would advance disproportionally and bring hunger rather than prosperity, immorality instead of civilization. Happily, according to Malthus, Providence has placed definite restrictions on the fertility of the soil to prevent this situation.[56]

Malthus may here be guilty of sloppy thinking: the human being is depraved because of natural limitations, but natural limitations militate against depravity. The only logical interpretation of Malthus's notions is that the exercise of selfishness engenders morality in the few who are "innately" capable of accumulation. The bulk of the population, therefore, finds itself between the Scylla of immorality that might result from abundance and the Charybdis of nature's stinginess, which forces constraints on the immoral populace. In either case, Malthus succeeds in blaming the working class for restricting wealth, either because of indolence derived from nature's plenty or from ill-advised fecundity despite nature's limitations. No matter what concept of nature his audience holds, Malthus's first concern is to discredit the radical ideas that would equalize classes.

Nature's meanness imposes, for Malthus, two types of checks on population: the "positive" checks on life's duration—misery dictated by nature and vice by society—and the "preventive" checks, including the moral restraint on sexual activity. Malthus claims that this restraint both lifts humanity from its original degraded state and points to a possible world in which human misery can be mitigated.[57] The peculiar feature of the moral, preventive check is its voluntary—and therefore particularly human—character. "Man" has "that distinctive superiority in his reasoning faculties which enables him to calculate distant consequences." In Malthus's opinion the unhappiness resulting from self-denial is slight compared to the suffering caused by "any of the other checks to population."[58]

Again, like Smith, Malthus considers his own society representative of the highest stage of history. Both follow systems of periodization that allow not only for diachronic comparison of civilizations but also for synchronic evaluation of the relative merits of coexisting classes within any given stage. Although he proves to be Smith's loyal disciple in such comparisons, Malthus apparently understands that Smith's theory of morality is contradictory. Smith asserts both that all human beings are equally acquisitive (that is, moral) and that some, those who have concentrated property, are more so than others. Malthus solves the contradiction by simply asserting the obvious: since most people cannot accumulate wealth, the masses are immoral. For all the religious rhetoric in Malthus's work, his treatises are remarkably free of any real spirituality. In that respect, the apparent differences between Smith's or Ricardo's theories and Malthus's are finally precisely that—apparent.

For Malthus, the state must maintain a healthy balance between town and country and educate the workers in self-restraint and the acknowledgement of their inferiority. Education, for Malthus, can make a disfranchised working class industrious, as comfortable as possible, and politically neutral.[59] If the state does not assume the paternalistic functions of educating workers to the "naturalness" of class society and of alleviating economic distress through unproductive expenditures, despotism will follow.[60]

Ricardo appropriates Malthus's theory of population and differential rent but not his view of the innate moral deficiencies of the working class, for that view denies the central tenet of political economy: that all individuals have an equal capacity for self-preservation or, in Benthamite terms, happiness. Ricardo's commitment to an extended suffrage has been clear since before his entry into the House of Commons. That commitment, however, is restricted to property owners. Prudence keeps Ricardo from endorsing Bentham's more radical program for universal suffrage:

> I believe that Bentham's book has satisfied [Sir Francis] that there would be no danger in Universal Suffrage but his main object might be [obtain]ed by stopping very far short of Universal suffrage. [With] such opinions it is a mere question of pru[dence] . . .[61]

Property, or a lack of it, in Ricardo's view, does not establish the right to include, or exclude, an individual from the political community. Property only indicates that an individual will have a definite interest in upholding the security of private property, one of the four objectives of government in Bentham's utilitarian analysis. For the propertyless class to be included in the polity, Ricardo requires some guarantee that it will not act rashly—that is, against the laws of the natural order—by attempting to secure legislation that would redistribute wealth or even abolish private property. Ricardo implicitly suggests universal education in the principles of utilitarian politics.

Ricardo favors ultimately enfranchising the people, including the working class, to check the possible tyranny of the aristocracy. The utilitarian notion that the end of government is to promote the greatest happiness for the greatest number practically mandates the enfranchisement of the masses. Yet, by allowing for majoritarian rule, Ricardo and his colleagues opened the way for majoritarian tyranny, a threat that obsessed American Southerners and dominated much of the antebellum debate.

3. DANIEL RAYMOND *on Wealth without a Working Class*

Dependence begets subservience and venality, suffocates the germ of virtue, and prepares fit tools for the designs of ambition. This, natural progress and consequence of the arts, has sometimes perhaps been retarded by accidental circumstance: but, generally speaking, the proportion which the aggregate of the other classes of citizens bears in any state to that of its husbandmen is the proportion of its unsound to its healthy parts, and is a good barometer whereby to measure its degree of corruption.—Thomas Jefferson, *Notes on Virginia*

The Economic Context

The discursive unity of English political economy contrasts sharply with the theoretical disjuncture between Northern protectionist and Southern free-trade political economists in antebellum America. The peculiar inversion of America's economic development, when compared to England's, structured this schism. Whereas the English economy developed by separating the laborer from the land, the American economy advanced by settling labor on the "frontier" and by providing white labor with a relatively high standard of living.

Adam Smith explained the unusual coexistence of high wages and profits in the North American colonies by pointing to the high land-labor ratio. His observations contained a critical note that was developed by Wakefield, the utilitarian colonial reformer and political economist, in his remarkable little work of 1833, *England and America*. Unlike Smith, Wakefield concluded that America's bountiful supply of land was initially a hindrance to economic development. England, he observed, had achieved economic growth by expropriating the peasantry from the land, so that labor became plentiful and cheap while land became scarce and dear.

This path of development was obviously impossible in the North American colonies. Virtually limitless land offered labor the possibility of withdrawing from the market and establishing self-sufficient homesteads. Wakefield believed that such a path of development would have eventually condemned North America to poverty.[1] Happily, for Wakefield, poverty was averted by the institutionalization of chattel slavery in the Southern colonies.[2] Slave labor produced the agricultural commodities that integrated America into the world market and provided the impetus for economic growth. Recent scholarship has partially confirmed Wakefield's analysis. Slavery did resolve the problem of labor scarcity in the South;[3] yet the plantation system retarded the rate of Southern industrialization by restricting the region's division of labor and the formation of a home market.

Comparable studies of the North, however, have refuted Wakefield's contention that yeoman farming was incompatible with capitalist development.[4] Commercial capital integrated the Northern farmer into an emergent home market whether directly through credit or indirectly through a regional transportation system. As a component of the market, the Northern yeoman functioned, in Smith's words, as a producer merchant always concerned with buying cheap and selling dear.

For the yeomanry land was a commodity that was to be bought and sold for a profit. It was good business for family farmers to purchase cheap frontier land, settle it, and finally sell it as prices rose.[5] To enhance the value of the land and the profitability of agriculture, family farmers advocated internal improvements that encouraged specialization and a growing division of labor between town and country.[6] By the close of the antebellum period, many farmers purchased from manufacturers labor-saving equipment such as threshing machines, mowers, and reapers, which eased the economic pressures of the region's high land-labor ratio.[7]

The symbiotic relationship between Northern manufacturers and farmers had two potential irritants. Industrialists feared that a rapid westward movement, beneficial to farmers, would drain the North of wage earners, while farmers feared that industrialization could undermine their economic position.[8] The Northern laboring class was also jealous of its independence; its artisanal traditions ran counter to the exigencies of industrialization while its political clout had increased with the extension of the franchise in the 1820s and 1830s.[9]

The precapitalist relationships of independent labor and slavery created a series of paradoxes about the structure and meaning of the natural order. The Northern American school theorists faced the dilemma of reconciling an economic process that promised limitless wealth at the expense of labor's independence. Southern economists faced an equally difficult task: the reconciliation of slavery to freedom and exponential growth.

The Ideological Context

Although the intellectual origins of the American Revolution were in large part British, the dominant ideology of the revolution developed along lines far more "radical" than those of the English Revolution. The Settlement of 1688 had secured the freedom of the propertied classes by shifting the locus of political power from the monarch to Parliament. Despite this substantive transformation, the new rulers had defined the legitimacy of their victory in the traditional constitutional language, which maintained the efficacy of hereditary monarchy and aristocratic privilege and so invalidated the leveling and chiliastic rhetoric of the interregnum.

The American Revolution did not produce so conservative an ideology. From English Whig thought the colonists inherited an ideology that responded to legislation such as the Currency Act, the Stamp Act, and the Townshend Acts with great foreboding, for these measures indicated that the English crown had succumbed to corruption and was violating the contractual rights and duties between ruler and ruled, crown and colony. Viewing these growing abuses, the colonists became convinced that revolution was the only solution. While the Whig system of thought offered a compelling logic for revolutionary action, it did not provide an adequate theory either for conducting the struggle or for forming a new just government.[10]

In determining the source of English corruption, the colonial patriots reevaluated the principles of Whiggism, particularly the notion that a hereditary monarchy and an aristocratic elite were necessary in a republican government to prevent a democratic tyranny. Instead, the rebels blamed hereditary privilege for English corruption, for hereditary rulers had interests opposed to the people, and power to impose them.

In rejecting the notion of a mixed government, the new American political science substituted the proposition that sovereignty resided in the monarchical parliament with a proclamation that sovereignty resided in the people. The formulation posed immediate problems for the American patriots. Traditional republican theory constructed a system of checks and balances from the fixed political virtues associated with the monarchy, the aristocracy, and the people. In the absence of privilege there would be no way to prevent a "democratic" tyranny. More specifically, how was it possible to prevent the majority from oppressing the minority, especially when the majority was poor or propertyless and the minority wealthy and propertied?

Two general solutions emerged during the constitutional debates. The first, associated with the federalists, implicitly assaulted court ideology;[11] the antifederalists followed more closely the Harringtonian line of reasoning as developed by the Country Whigs. The federalists, arguing that passion and interest must be recognized as fundamental to the human being's true nature, logically followed the political reasoning of Adam Smith except that they rejected the mixed constitution.[12]

According to federalist theorists, representation and a strict division among the functions or branches of government provided the appropriate infrastructure for avoiding tyranny. Here again they challenged traditional thought on the subject. Republican theory had condemned representation since it necessitated the surrendering of one's will to another; a strict division among the branches of government was suspected of weakening government by pitting interests against each other instead of mediating among them. The federalists countered these objections by asserting that representation actually expressed the will of the people and that through a system of multiple representation a plurality of interests could emerge, including the interests of a natural aristocracy of talent. Furthermore, a strict division averted the danger of consolidation. Through these mechanisms, the federalists cogently argued, a tyranny of either the few or the many could be avoided and a consensus about the national interest could form.

Although the antifederalists agreed that sovereignty resided in the people, they affirmed the traditional view that political virtue was the only real means of instituting and preserving a republican government. Virtue was practically synonymous with property, particularly agricultural property, which would provide the common interest for citizens.

Despite its influence this conception of republican politics was not as coherent as that of the federalists. By accepting commerce as a legitimate pursuit, the antifederalists introduced implicit difficulties in the ideal of a landed citizenry; even when restricted to agricultural production for a market, commerce assumed self-interest, change, and the concentration of wealth. The federalists were well equipped for such eventualities, for their theory was predicated on self-interest and change. It is not surprising that the federalists prevailed. Nor is it surprising that Thomas Jefferson, the foremost antifederalist theorist, rejected Ricardo's economics in favor of Destutt de Tracy's [13] and sought a solution to the dilemma of a propertied citizenry through territorial expansion. [14]

The new American political science did not stop at redefining sovereignty and making innovations in political structures; it also legitimated itself through a metahistory that transformed the mundane concerns of political life into a symbolic representation of God's will. Contractual concepts of republican thought could be interpreted as a new covenant between God and his chosen. This metahistory certainly contrasted with the strictly materialist vision of British political and economic theory. The Settlement of 1688 had expunged the chiliasm of the interregnum from political debate. Visionary political discourse had proven too dangerous for a nation whose dispossessed laboring population could best be controlled in the absence of hope. For the propertied classes of the early nineteenth century, only Providence—in Malthus's determinist conception—could enter the normative political and economic discourse.

The American dominant classes were not so cautious; there seemed no need. Nature had provided the colonists with an unsettled territory free from the corruption of England's privileged orders and the depravity of its degraded laborers. In that environment a truly natural order could be erected for humanity's freedom and salvation. Drawing on the Puritan "errand" and the Enlightenment's wish to imitate God's nature in human society, American politics preserved the millenarian fervor of the New Model Army. That fervor, however, was not expressed in the language of eschatology, for patriot and citizen had replaced the saint as the agent of God's will.[15]

Republican theory posited that individual freedom (salvation) could only occur through society and that the revolution itself was a test of America's virtue (morality) by its undaunted opposition to English corruption (sinfulness). The Great Awakening had prepared the way for this metahistory, which made the profane sacred and turned the nation's material advancement into a religious metaphor. If New England Puritanism added enthusiasm to the revolution, the American Enlightenment, with only minor exceptions, upheld the Christian end of political life, complementing the Calvinist sermons which beckoned the flock to resist the British antichrist, King George III.

By successfully rebelling against England, the American colonists had begun to see themselves worthy of God's trust, but other trials faced them, namely the challenge of writing a constitution and formulating a foreign policy in a world shaken by the French Revolution. However, for a large number of Americans, the real test of America's "virtue" was in its handling of slavery. In Enlightenment terms this institution blighted the nation's glory, for it denied the rational and autonomous principles of revolution; from a religious perspective antislavery forces condemned the institution as sinful. To these people, the Missouri Compromise of 1820 signified the nation's decline and the need for a new Jeremiah.

The Tariff Controversy[16]

During the Napoleonic Wars, America's defense of liberty demanded a series of embargo acts, a war with England, and a protective tariff to raise military revenues. Designed to demonstrate the nation's resolve among the warring European nations, the new American foreign policy unintentionally catalyzed economic growth. Formerly, U.S. mercantile activity had been concentrated in export and re-export to the belligerent European powers. With those markets cut off by legislation and with a home market created by the necessities of war, mercantile capital shifted into manufacturing. This shift, primarily into textiles, created the beginnings for an industrial base. However, an industrial revolution was aborted by the Treaty of Ghent, ratified in 1815, which ended hostilities between the United States and England and restored to England its lost American market. Cheap British manufactured goods soon strangled the infant American industries and created economic havoc.[17]

This economic downturn continued even after the renewal in 1816 of the war tariff, which anticipated and tried to offset the adverse economic effects of the recent peace. But the tariff was too weak a measure, and a renewed demand for protection emerged as early as 1817 and grew into a militant political movement that wrenched the nation out of the Era of Good Feeling and caused the profound political crisis over the Tariff of Abominations and South Carolina's nullification of it in 1832.[18]

The Compromise Tariff of 1833 forestalled a settlement of the constitutional issues raised during the Nullification Crisis. The events of 1832 and 1833 only strengthened the Southern antiprotectionist forces, both practically and ideologically. In the next decade the tariff remained a controversial issue closely related to the economic questions of per capita income, the conditions of labor, the price of land, expansion, and internal improvements as well as the general political problems of minority rights in a "democratic republic." Party politics sorted out these contending economic and sectional demands and through a process of expedient compromise formulated policy that allegedly promoted the general welfare.[19]

By 1846 legislative consensus had grown untenable. In that year a free-trade measure was passed called the Walker Tariff[20] in recognition of the leadership provided by Polk's secretary of treasury, Robert Walker. A year before, Walker had given an address on the Democratic Party's platform of territorial expansion, free trade, and a continuation of the subtreasury system. Through this report Walker attempted to refute the restrictive system, especially as formulated by Henry Clay, Polk's rival in the 1844 presidential election. Although the protectionists lost a battle, the war continued. Protectionist interests became tied to a policy of excluding slavery from the territories and making homesteads available to free white labor. Only the Civil War would finally decide the "correct" economic policy for the republic.

Like the Corn Law debates, the tariff controversy prompted a rash of polemical works. In the initial phase, from 1817 to 1819, protariff forces concentrated in Pennsylvania formed small societies for the promotion of manufacturing. They were greatly aided in 1819 when the publisher and journalist Mathew Carey, outraged by the economic distress of 1819, dedicated his pen and printing press to the protectionist cause.[21] Intellectual journals also took it up. The influential *Niles Register*, for example, defended protectionist ideas.[22] They were countered in Condy Raguet's popular journals *Free Trade Advocate* and *Banner of the Constitution*, published in Philadelphia, the protectionists' heartland.[23]

Political electioneering also spawned numerous pamphlets and memorials on economic issues. Here, too, protectionist forces took the lead in national politics when in 1827 they called a convention in Harrisburg to influence the 1828 presidential election. Free traders responded by assem-

bling in local meetings to issue pamphlets opposing the Harrisburg memorial. Perhaps the most famous of these free-trade pamphlets was "A Committee of Citizens of Boston and Vicinity Opposed to a Further Increase of
Duties and Importations," written by Henry Lee and challenged by Friedrich List.[24] The election year of 1832 witnessed both free-trade and protectionist conventions, as each faction vied for the influence necessary to re-
scind or sustain the Tariff of 1828.

Although many of these pamphlets, articles, and memorials were
characterized by solid economic reasoning, they remained polemical in
character, generally disorganized, and marred by a tendency to assert economic principle rather than elaborate it. Theoretical works did appear,
however, and though partisan, they attempted rigorously to explore the
abstract concept of wealth.[25] In so doing, the treatises firmly located the
tariff within the complex system of either Northern protectionism or free-
trade thought, either of which claimed to evaluate the tariff's efficacy in
promoting the natural order.

A significant peculiarity arises in the American texts. They do not
share theoretical premises, as the English Corn Law debates did. The free-
trade tracts adopted—with some modification—the Ricardian paradigm,
so their conception of the natural order is a familiar one. Those thinkers,
who can be identified either as Southern free-trade advocates or as members of the clerical school associated with the Northern universities, never
objected in principle to industrialization, since they saw it as a necessary
stage in commercial life.[26] Moreover, they recognized that industrialization
would transform America from a nation of independent producers to a
three-class society. Industrialization, therefore, was in itself not the issue
in their opposition to the tariff. Rather, it was a matter of timing; if agrarian
interests were denied in favor of manufacturers, industrialization would
ultimately be monopolized by the existing industrialist class. Furthermore, the tariff would distort the general economic growth by misallocating resources. In political terms, the tariff, by economically weakening the
agrarian minority, implied a violation of minority rights. Thus, the passage and maintenance of a protective tariff would indicate a fundamental
weakening of republican government.

For the protectionist school, however, these objections were ill-
founded, since they rested on the classical conception of the natural order.
While the protectionist camp included the New England economists such
as Alexander Everett and William Phillips, they were relatively peripheral
in the formulation of both economic theory and policy.[27] The American
school, led by Mathew Carey and later by his son Henry, dominated intellectually, while Henry Clay and Calvin Colton worked out the practical details of protection in their advocacy of an American system.

To the economists of the American school, the encouragement of manufacturing was something quite different from industrialization. Both processes conjure in our imagination the emergence of the factory system, the formation of an industrial working class, and the creation of a developed home market, along with other economic features that need not be enumerated. But the crucial distinction between the American school's concept of that process and our own (which consequently differentiates their notion of promoting manufacturing from our notion of industrialization) is that for the American school the laborer was not separated from the direct control of the production process. Certainly, these theorists accepted the accumulation of land and capital as a natural consequence of increasing wealth and in so doing underwrote the formation of the working class. However, they hoped to prevent the development of an impoverished working class by restricting and ensuring its skill composition. The American school could thus still assume that, over time, independent labor would fundamentally structure the economy. In this theory capital neither organized production for its own profit nor acquired any productive characteristics; in either role labor would no longer be an independent producer but a mere instrument in capital's expansion.

For these thinkers, then, the classical school was not simply a body of doctrine that inhibited national development; it in fact perverted the natural relationships between labor and society. England was a rich nation, but at what price? There, labor existed in a state of pauperism degraded physically and morally. Was this the course charted by the American Revolution? To the American school the answer was perfectly obvious.

To the more radical thinkers, England was not the only society that showed the disastrous consequences that awaited the United States if it allowed free-trade doctrine to inform state policy; the South, in whose soil classical theory had firmly entrenched its malignant roots, also seemed a harbinger of catastrophe. Radicals of the American school believed that black labor there was enchained to capital through the institution of slavery, and deduced that free white labor was degraded as a result.

Thus, a paradox emerges. On the one hand, the American school denounced classical theory as a body of doctrine derived from unnatural circumstances and consequently as pernicious. On the other hand, the school adopted a program designed to promote manufacturing and a home market with the inevitable working class—that class which served as an index of England's degeneration.[28]

The disagreements between protectionist and free-trade thinkers imply their differences in the tradition of the American Revolution. Despite their association with federalist and Whig politics, the protectionist economists adopted the antifederalist assumption that based republicanism on a "virtuous," or moral and prosperous, citizenry; hence their concern to preserve an equitable distribution of property and an educated, skilled labor force.[29] In this way virtue and interest could be reconciled. In contrast, the free-trade school, particularly the Southern branch, followed the federalist line of reasoning, which *constructed* republican government from the functional mechanisms of checks and balances. Certainly free-trade theorists venerated property, but like their English colleagues they believed that an impoverished and mentally stunted propertyless class was a necessary condition of the natural order, despite the danger such a class presented.

Daniel Raymond

The works of Daniel Raymond perhaps best illustrate the principles of the American protectionist school. At first sight this claim may seem inappropriate, since Raymond achieved little prominence in the Whig Party or in his legal practice. The paucity of secondary literature on Raymond suggests that American historians concur with the evaluation of his contemporaries.[30] A more likely candidate would seem to be Reverend Calvin Colton, who produced numerous pamphlets and an important treatise on political economy in 1848. Moreover, as a political confidant and biographer of Henry Clay, Colton had greater personal prestige and influence than Raymond.[31] In fact, Colton's personal relationship with Clay might help us bridge the gap between economic theory and political practice. However, Colton's success is no measure of the cogency of his theoretical arguments. When his work is compared with Raymond's the latter's rigor becomes evident.[32]

Raymond exerted great influence despite his lackluster career. His first work on political economy appeared in 1819 under the title *Thoughts on Political Economy*. Three years later the work was republished in an enlarged edition with a new title: *The Elements of Political Economy*. His pamphlet "The Missouri Question" became a polemical weapon in the hands of antislavery forces, and his writings won him praise among protectionists and abolitionists.

Mathew Carey hailed the volume on political economy as the most informed writing he knew on the subject. He was so impressed with Raymond's effort that he attempted to establish for him a chair of political economy at the University of Maryland. Both John Adams and John Quincy Adams admired Raymond's writings. John Quincy Adams, in fact, became embroiled in a political controversy when he formally presented the fourth edition of Raymond's *Elements* to the library of the House of Representatives, of which he was then a member. Raymond's writings were equally famous, or infamous, among free-trade advocates.[33] The Virginian Thomas R. Dew, undoubtedly the foremost Southern theoretician for the free-trade position, cited Raymond in his *Lectures on the Restrictive System*. He and Friedrich List were the only protectionists mentioned by Dew.[34] Another eminent free-trade figure, Governor Thomas Giles of Virginia, devoted an entire series of articles in the *Richmond Enquirer* to refuting Raymond's arguments.[35] Furthermore, Jacob Cardozo, a highly gifted economist who was then editor of the Charlestonian *Southern Patriot*, reviewed Raymond's volume and denounced it as an unscientific treatise that only a young and undisciplined mind could have conceived.[36]

But Raymond's importance went beyond notoriety. *The Elements of Political Economy*, the first systematic treatise on political economy published by an American, founded the American school of economics, which dominated the protectionist camp. Later writers like Phillips, Colton, Rae, and even Henry Carey would adopt many of Raymond's definitions and conventions,[37] even if his rigor was not duplicated until Henry Carey published his famous work *The Past, the Present and the Future* in 1848. With that publication, the American school entered a new period in which it rejected the theory of diminishing returns in agriculture. It therefore lies beyond the scope of this essay.

Raymond's *Elements* actually conceptualized the economy as a theoretical entity, unlike the "moral" economy for independent labor found in Colton's and Rae's work.[38] As the major theoretical work for the American school prior to 1848, Raymond's *Elements* most clearly reveals the internal contradictions of that school's overall project. For this reason alone, his *Elements* provides a useful text for us. Moreover, his work is an abolitionist tract, deeply influenced by his Calvinist New England background and intolerant of the kinds of compromises necessary for party politics. This may help to explain Raymond's failure in public life. The book's extremism makes it useful for examining the ideological spaces that separated Northern and Southern economists.

Limitless Wealth and Independent Labor

Raymond correctly perceived an ambiguity in Smith's characterization of labor and human need, and the effort to resolve it structured Raymond's theoretical work. Smith argued that the source of a nation's wealth is productive labor and that the purpose of economic activity is to satisfy human needs. These propositions might lead to the conclusion that labor is the central directing force in the economy. However, in the course of his analysis Smith places labor under the supervisory role of the capitalist and then substitutes capital for the capitalist as the motivating agent of production.

By capital Smith specifically means that portion of a capitalist's stock or property which "affords a revenue or profit" or, put a little differently, that portion of a capitalist's property that is capable of increasing its original exchange value. According to this definition, a capitalist's personal expenditure is not capital since it does not procure a profit. Thus, Smith provides two possible uses for profits: (1) their conversion into capitalist revenue and (2) their conversion into capital. If the controlling impetus of production is toward profits for investment in expanding capital, it is clear that human needs are no longer the primary object of the productive process: "The proportion between capital and revenue, therefore, seems everywhere to regulate the proportion between industry and idleness. Wherever capital predominates, industry prevails: wherever revenue, idleness."[39] In short, not only does labor seem to have lost its productive capacity, but production seems to be determined by something other than human need.[40]

There is a possible solution to this dilemma if we remember that among the needs that Smith discusses in *Theories of Moral Sentiments* is the need for approbation, which has no limits. Raymond would not be satisfied with this solution, for Smith's objection to monopolies and his assumption that a free market would benefit workers and capitalists alike had the paradoxical effect of converting moral sentiment into approbation for vanity and pride—which benefited capitalists at the expense of workers. For the American Calvinist, pride is the cause of humanity's fall and labor its punishment; but it is also the means for redemption through obedience to God and through the discovery of his laws in nature. When some members of society avoid work by subjugating others, then the moral economy and growth are forfeited. Hence, Raymond's adamant rejection of Smith's judgment that labor's subordination to capital promotes economic growth and well-being.

Although economic life is the principal realm for moral improvement for Raymond, it is a dependent one. Unlike Smith, Raymond discusses the state in more than instrumental terms at the service of the human passions. On the contrary, the state must intervene in the economy to preserve labor's independence from humanity's sinful nature and thus to direct society according to natural law. The English state was a model to be avoided; by means of primogeniture, the national debt, and other political contrivances, the aristocracy and bankers acquired a disproportionate share of wealth and divided English society into antagonistic classes. Besides fearing the instability of inevitable class struggles, Raymond is also sure that the natural order could not be based on one class corrupted by greed and another degraded by extreme poverty. His solution is a society of propertied citizens protected by a government that conforms to democratic republican principles.

If England affords an example of a nation guided by the passions, then the United States, in Raymond's words, offers "the fairest theatre on earth for acquisition of knowledge in the science of government and political economy."[41] America's government is free of aristocratic manipulation and its economy is natural, since labor, except in the South, is free from capital's degrading rule. For these reasons Raymond confidently proceeds to reformulate and to redeem political economy.

Raymond begins by arguing that labor in the state of nature is the standard for establishing a productive, moral economy. But he then posits that private property and accumulation are indicators of humanity's adherence to nature's laws so that wage labor and capital are legitimate categories. Raymond recognizes that the incorporation of capital threatens labor's independence and that contradiction would haunt him. In order to reconcile the antagonism between labor and capital, Raymond distinguishes between individual and national wealth. From his concept of national wealth, he prescribes a set of policies which the state must actively pursue to control any alarming expansion of capitalist production so as to prevent labor's physical and moral destitution.

In formulating his policy recommendations, Raymond makes special note of slavery and its harmful consequences to the nation's wealth and morality. In fact, Raymond equates slavery with capitalism and insists that it be abolished. His insistence, however, does not rest principally on an economic argument. In Raymond's theory, Southern planters constitute a political power capable of blocking legislation to protect independent labor. As such the defenders of slavery were the enemies of the republic.

The ambiguities that arise from Raymond's attempt to place the distinct economies of the early state and the advanced one in a single theoretical space stem from the contradictory character of his social reality. On the one hand, self-expanding value is the principal aim of economic activity in the antebellum North; on the other hand, preindustrial capitalist relationships—independent farmers and craft labor—still predominate over a small proportion of wage labor. Raymond accepts the validity of self-expanding value while equating morality and republican ideals with independent labor. He is consequently confronted with the utopian task of preserving labor's ownership of the means of production in a system in which capital, as self-expanding value, has informed economic relationships. Raymond's work, therefore, appears to be "transitional," since capital in its preindustrial form has organized production for self-expanding value but has not revolutionized the relations and forces of production as industrial capital would do.

Here, then, is the irony of Raymond's thought. Motivated by a profoundly religious sentiment, Raymond calls for a program of state intervention that became associated with industrialization in subsequent American historiography and economic literature. However, Raymond designed the program as an offensive strategy against industrialization, which he views as capital's encroachment on free and independent labor. For Raymond the demon capital assumes many forms: bankocracy, slaveocracy, and corporations. His intentions become clearer if compared to those of the flagrantly anticapitalist labor economists of his period.[42] Both fear capitalist accumulation and support labor's independence based on a wide distribution of property.

Raymond's work is startling in that his ideas, while easily labeled petty bourgeois, actually become, in slightly modified form, the economic program and rhetoric for "industrial capital" in the United States. It is through such rhetoric that the process of industrialization, of which the Civil War must be considered a part, becomes clouded in a language of anticapitalism.

Individual versus National Wealth

In Raymond's estimation, Smith and his disciples are doomed to failure because they gloss over the distinction between individual and national wealth.[43] In contrast, Raymond clearly differentiates between wealth's individual and national forms. Individual wealth is the *"possession of property, for the use of which, the owner can obtain a quantity of the necessaries and comforts of life."*[44] Property refers to the land, goods, and money possessed by an individual. But this definition is inadequate for Raymond in determining whether any individual may be considered wealthy; for that measure of wealth which he offers in a single sentence may lack economic rigor but is rich in concerns: "All will, I think, admit that it [the measurement of individual wealth] must be a quantity of property, for the use of which the necessaries of life which he consumes, may be obtained, without the manual labour of the owner."[45] Raymond's criterion for wealth implies a social structure including two agents: a wealthy individual who, being in legal possession of the means of production, or property, is willing to lend in return for a revenue, and a laborer either devoid of property or deficient in it who is willing to pay rent for the use of the means of production. Hence, private property and the results of accumulation are assumed in Raymond's definition of individual wealth and the method of measuring it. Raymond adds that accumulation, with its consequent social stratification, varies according to the differing talents and skills among individual commodity producers.

At first sight his description of society appears identical with Smith's advanced state, and Raymond's measurement seems to be nothing more than a slightly altered formulation of Smith's component theory of value. In both cases, labor creates revenue for others. Nevertheless, two important differences exist. Under the conditions described by Smith, labor is unpropertied, unskilled, and at the command of capital. Raymond dissents. He substitutes "rents," derived from the proprietor's leasing of land, tools, etc., for "profits." Thus, the proprietor is not a capitalist, and the laborer is not an unskilled worker, i.e., incapable of organizing the labor process. In this way Raymond can challenge Smith's notion that capital has the capacity to direct production.

> It seems scarcely credible, that a writer who presumes to instruct mankind in the science of political economy, should really suppose that capital, whether land, money or goods was an active agent, capable of either *supplanting* or of *performing* labour, which is beyond the reach or power of man to perform. It is not possible for any man to suppose that capital can really perform labour, and he who talks about labour performed by capital, must, therefore, use the language in a figurative or metaphorical sense.[46]

Raymond believes that labor's independence and consequently its morality will be saved by preserving at least two characteristics of the early and rude state: labor's ownership of the means of production and labor's technical know-how. For Raymond, the proprietor is ideally a small producer who actively engages in the labor process and who might employ several skilled wage laborers whose limited number allows them to maintain their artisanal character.

Here, then, are two contradictory systems forced into one theoretical space. To put it in terms of Smith's periodization, Raymond attempts to subordinate the advanced state to the early and rude state. Were he attempting the opposite, his theory would more closely approximate the actual historical trend. Although he recognizes the contradictions in his system, he does not attribute them to faulty reasoning but rather accepts them as insoluble without the intervention of the state.

Raymond's success in incorporating the state into his theory depends on his definition of public or national wealth. He defines a nation as follows:

> A nation, it is true, is an artificial being, or a legal entity, composed of millions of natural beings; still it possesses all the properties and attributes of being, which are distinct and strongly marked, as the properties and attributes of any natural being, and this must be constantly borne in mind, if we would reason correctly of the interests or rights of this being.
>
> A nation is a UNITY, and possesses all the properties of unity. It possesses a unity of rights, a unity of interests, and a unity of possessions; and he who professes to treat interests of this unity, but departs from them, and treats of the interests of some constituent part of it, will just as certainly arrive at a wrong conclusion.[47]

From this definition Raymond establishes the criterion for the wealth of a nation as the "capacity for acquiring the necessaries and comforts of life" for its citizens.[48] "Capacity" refers to those factors which can increase labor's productivity: (1) the state of cultivation and improvements, (2) the development and perfection of the arts and sciences, (3) the type of a nation's government, and (4) the soil, climate, and geographic location of a nation.

By conceiving of the nation as a corporate unity, Raymond implies that wealth belongs to the state and thereby undermines his earlier proposition that society is based on private property. This, in turn, suggests that the nation, being in possession of the means of production, is capable of organizing production and distribution directly without the assistance of the marketplace.[49] How are the two economies in Raymond's definition of individual and national wealth reconciled?

This question may be answered by examining the function of national wealth in Raymond's theory. His definition of individual wealth pertains to a commodity-producing society that combines accumulation and independent labor. Raymond recognizes that this situation is tenuous because the proprietor, driven by a desire to obtain greater revenues, will continually acquire property by dispossessing large sectors of the population.

For Raymond, this is not simply a theoretical possibility; it is the actual historical experience of England. Consequently, he requires a mechanism to safeguard the integrity of labor while "natural" accumulation proceeds. He finds that mechanism in his definition of national wealth and its mandate to the nation to guard labor's independence. The state can carry out this function, according to Raymond, by ensuring an equal distribution of property, alleviating the unemployment that results from underconsumption, and controlling corporate enterprises.

In prescribing these policies to the nation-state, Raymond avoids the full social implications of his definition of national wealth. Yet it is that definition which provides the legal basis for intervention that characterizes his nation-state. Since it is not the organizer of production, the marketplace still has primary responsibility in the economic process, but the state's hand is always required to guide that process, or unbridled individual greed will destroy the body politic. In order to fully understand the need for state intervention, let us first examine Raymond's theory of commodity production and its internal contradictions.

The Mechanics of Individual Wealth

Raymond's inquiry into the economics of individual wealth begins with a definition of value: "VALUE is the relationship which one thing bears to another in regards to price, and is appropriately used or significant only in exchanging one thing for another."[50] As such, value is not contained in objects for immediate consumption or in national wealth. Those things have a use value but no exchange value.

In determining the source of value Raymond first rejects Smith's and

Ricardo's labor theory of value. He reasons that circumstances conditioning production, such as fertility of the soil and the variety of machines employed in production, cause the exchange value of a commodity to deviate significantly from the labor required to produce it. Raymond thinks it absurd to make labor a homogeneous concept that regulates the values of commodities produced by qualitatively different forms of labor. Like Malthus, Raymond attributes the source of value to human wants and desires, with supply and demand setting the exact degree of any commodity's value.

Despite the regulatory function of human needs and desires, Raymond posits that the value of any commodity has a "saving price," a minimum level below which it cannot fall.[51] Otherwise, the price would not be sufficient to supply the contributors of production with their revenues. In this respect the saving price resembles Smith's natural price and Malthus's necessary price. However, Raymond's concept differs from the others in that it collapses profits into rents; only wages and rents constitute the saving price. The total product of labor, then, is divided for Raymond between proprietors and labor.

Raymond begins his analysis of rents by considering the owners of landed property. The landowner's rent is "that portion of the product of labour or an equivalent, which the proprietor . . . is entitled to, for the use of his land."[52] Unlike Smith and Malthus, who attribute rent principally to the land's productive powers, Raymond conceives of rent as determined solely by the landowner's legal right to control property that is necessary for the fulfillment of human needs and desires. Because rent is conceived of strictly as a function of private property and demand, Raymond can assert that any form of property may command a rent. Thus, tenants who own property are entitled to rent, whether what they own is agricultural implements or the means of subsistence by which they can hire agricultural laborers. Similarly, proprietors of workshops command a rent since their property is necessary for the manufacture of commodities.[53]

Wages are, of course, that portion of the social product belonging to labor, and wages vary according to particular skills. One of Raymond's illustrations is tenants who, as members of a "higher order" of labor, receive a wage for their physical efforts and their supervision of agricultural labor.

Raymond lists three circumstances that influence the proportions of wages and rents: (1) the land-labor ratio, (2) the distribution of property, and (3) the health of the economy. In so determining the levels of wages and rents, Raymond intentionally ignores the Malthusian theory of population and its effect on distribution because it is not immediately applicable to the American situation.

Not only is this true for the United States, with its vast regions of uncultivated fertile lands, but, in Raymond's opinion, it is also true for England. He is not willing to attribute the starvation of England's population to nature's discipline of a lustful working class. Instead, he points to Parliament's refusal to equitably distribute property. "Entail, primogeniture, and limitations of real property" have converted the English yeomanry, in Raymond's opinion, to the "useless paupers that clutter the countryside."[54] If the aristocratic laws were repealed and the unequal distribution of property rectified, Raymond hypothesizes, the yeomanry could be resuscitated and could revitalize the body politic. It is not surprising, after this explanation for the poverty of English labor, that Raymond characterizes Malthus's population theory as a piece of aristocratic logic contrived to justify the landlord's swollen wealth.[55]

The Threats to Independent Labor: Money Capital

Though Raymond can collapse profits into rents to try to maintain a simple commodity-producing paradigm, he cannot do the same with interest, because money has features that make it unlike all other forms of property. By being the measure of the exchange value of commodities, money measures profit, or rent in Raymond's terms, and thus provides the vehicle by which (exchange) value expands. It is this apparent self-expanding quality of money that commands an interest.

Even though Raymond offers no explanation for the self-expanding character of money, he recognizes the process by designating as capital that money whose value does expand. But he hesitates to assign the term "capitalistic" to the independent producer's pursuit of property when wealth is not immediately translated into marketable exchange value. For example, the acquisition of land by the farmer or machinery by the manufacturer is to be considered as merely augmentation of physical wealth rather than as fixed capital. In contrast, for Raymond, when the same agents use money to purchase raw materials to produce commodities, they act as merchants and use capital. Here the important factor is the expansion of the money invested, rather than the specific quality of the means of production. Therefore, Raymond accepts a notion of capital, but it differs from Smith's in being confined to money, or circulating capital, and remaining external to the production process. The means of production remain "mere passive instruments in the hands of man" rather than components in the process of capitalist production.

> Machinery is not stock, nor is stock either fixed or circulating capital as in Smith's system, any more than land is gold. . . .
> The word capital, or one of similar import is indispensable to

the merchant. The business of exchanging commodities requires it. But has the farmer, or the manufacturer any occasion of such a term of art? . . .

The farmer commences the business of agriculture on one thousand acres of land. What difference is it to him, whether it is estimated at ten, or at a hundred dollars an acre? It is for use, and not for sale or exchange—the value of it, is immaterial. . . .[56]

The manufacturer commences business upon a small piece of land, upon which there is a fall or water. He knows it is worth something, but he has no occasion for the word capital, in order to estimate or express its value.[57]

Despite his narrow and misleading definition of capital, Raymond's logic does in fact justify capital's self-expanding property and the interest with which capital may be borrowed. But this uneasiness about the anomaly of an exchange value devoid of use value causes him to be preoccupied with the rate of interest. That rate, he observes, is based on two variables: the risk of the lender and the risk of the borrower. Because one deals in the market, there is always the danger that the money's original exchange value will be lost as a result of economic fluctuations. To compensate the lender for the risk of losing this property or a portion of it, the borrower must pay an interest above the rent charged for the use of the money. The borrower runs a risk as well. If the loan does not yield profits, or worse, if the money is lost in an unfriendly market, the borrower is obliged to repay the lender. Therefore, the borrower compensates by adding an interest cost to the price of the product.

Given the peculiar determinants for interest, Raymond points out that its rate, comprised of a rent and risks, must always exceed the rate of rent on land.[58] In this way, Raymond maintains his distinction between the proprietor, who commands a rent, and the merchant or the capitalist, who commands an interest as well.

Those proprietors who desire to expand through loans or are forced by circumstances to mortgage their property will tend to lose it to the moneylender, whose activity is paradoxically both necessary to Raymond's system and corrosive to it. Such foreclosures will concentrate property in the hands of capitalists, merchants, or bankers. They, along with would-be aristocrats, are the "subversives" that the state must constantly watch over.

The potential danger that interest poses to labor is exacerbated by the free banking system. Raymond appreciates four functions of banks; they are offices of discount, depositories, loan offices, and manufacturers of money.[59] But the combination of the last two functions transforms them into parasites. As manufacturers of money, the banks could issue as much as they pleased, thereby causing inflation; as loan offices the banks could establish usurious interest rates on paper money. According to Raymond, speculation becomes rampant among capitalists who hope to take advantage of market fluctuations. He argues that property owners will speculate on the grounds that the rate of interest is higher than that of rent. The pressure of speculation on the price of property causes market fluctuations and leads to economic crisis and extensive failures. The only result is the acceleration of concentration. A force is required to constrain avarice's conflict with national wealth. Raymond's perennial solution is state intervention.

Accumulation

Although growth should be the core of his theory of national wealth, Raymond unfortunately does not treat the process in any great detail. He investigates it only briefly while discussing distribution as it is affected by growth, stagnation, and decay.[60] Yet, despite the brevity of his incursion into the question of expanded reproduction, Raymond nonetheless intuits the potentially dissolvent effect that growth could have on labor's ownership of property and once again relies on state policy to inhibit the process. The most salient feature of this discussion is that the catalyst of dissolution is not external to the labor process but actually inherent in it. It belongs neither to a hereditary aristocracy nor to a bankocracy separated from the real forces of growth; rather, labor's own quest after individual wealth is the factor that can transform a one-class society into a three-class society.

Growth, according to Raymond, is derived from nature, the source of wealth, and labor, the cause of wealth.[61] Using this definition, he identifies two forms of labor: productive labor, which is expended in producing the necessaries and comforts of life, and effective labor, which produces a nation's productive forces, such as machines, canals, and improvements in land.[62] This distinction differs from Smith's differentiation between productive and unproductive labor in that Raymond's categories are not dependent on exchange and revenue for their determination but on use value.

By increasing a nation's productivity, the employment of effective labor regulates growth. For Raymond, growth begins with agriculture, where a surplus makes economic growth possible in the first place. The immediate result of the landowners' employment of effective labor to augment their wealth is that rents decline as the overall demand for labor increases. However, proprietors are compensated by the increased value of their property and by their decreasing need for productive labor as productivity becomes built into their property. By paying less in wages proprietors gain a share of labor's product proportionate to the augmented power of their property.[63]

Raymond recognizes that agricultural unemployment may result, but he reasons that manufacturing will absorb those workers because the demands of agricultural proprietors keep pace with their increasing income. Raymond argues further that the shift from agriculture to manufacturing is advantageous to the worker since wages in that sector are "double, triple, quadruple or perhaps fifty times as great as that which goes to the proprietor in the shape of rent, interest or profits."[64] Although Raymond does not explain these high wages, he clearly assumed that the supply for skilled labor is not sufficient to meet demand. In this way Raymond sought to calm fears that agricultural labor might have concerning its fate as growth proceeded. As for the labor already employed in manufacturing, Raymond dismisses its fear of labor-saving machinery by insisting that the introduction of machinery in one trade merely increases the demand for labor in another.

Raymond's brief description of expanded reproduction develops the contradictions already implied in his definition of individual wealth, which posits the coexistence of accumulation and a one-class society. Although Raymond assumed a working class, it was limited and highly skilled, somehow—despite the continuation of its growth, the conversion of agricultural labor into manufacturing labor, and the introduction of labor-saving machinery. Here, then, is economic growth without the degradation of labor.

Central to Raymond's theory of growth is the motivation of proprietors to increase their individual wealth, which presents a dimension that Raymond attempts unsuccessfully to ignore. Both farmer and manufacturer logically tend to introduce labor-saving devices. Raymond denies that wages will fall by simply asserting that labor will receive high wages because machinery only increases the demand for labor, which he further asserts is necessarily skilled. One wonders how skilled labor freed by machinery from one trade can be so easily employed in another if the skill requirements in manufacturing are as significant as Raymond insists. Moreover, the means of increasing individual wealth are not limited to the improvement of property but extended to the acquisition of additional property, which encourages concentration, as has been discussed.

Because Raymond intuits the corrupting potential of growth, even though he refuses to deal with it squarely, he exhorts the state for a second time to regulate the distribution of property. In the first instance he demands that the state quash "aristocratic" bills. In this instance he finds it necessary for the state to intervene directly to regulate economic growth, which, if unmonitored, might not best serve national wealth.

Economic Crisis

In addition to growth, Raymond's theory has to account for economic crisis. By its very nature, commodity production precipitates periodic crises to adjust supply to demand. These market fluctuations pose no problems in Raymond's theory since they are considered temporary disruptions necessary to the proper allocation of resources. As part of this readjustment process Raymond includes the crises resulting from speculation that have been alluded to in the discussion on interest. However, historical experience—the economic crisis of 1819—has demonstrated for Raymond, first, that a longer, more serious kind of crisis unrelated to market deviations can manifest itself and, second, that state intervention is again necessary both to cure and to prevent major crises. As usual, Raymond isolates the source of economic malaise in capitalist behavior, i.e. parsimony. He finds it an unsatisfactory explanation for the transition from the early and rude state to the advanced state, which is characterized by aristocratic laws that cause an unequal distribution of property. Regarding growth, Raymond considers Smith's explanation not only incorrect but actually the cause of protracted crises.[65] Raymond admits that from an individual perspective, savings can increase one's wealth. From a national perspective, however, constricted expenditures can only be detrimental to wealth. How, Raymond asks, is it possible for a nation to increase its wealth when production exceeds consumption?

To substantiate his observation that underconsumption causes decline and distress, especially among propertyless laborers, Raymond first defines the terms of production and consumption. For him, production is the result of labor where it is intended to create the necessaries and comforts of life.[66] Thus, he restricts production to the means of subsistence in an attempt to avoid Smith's perverse logic about capital's ability to dictate production.

Raymond's definition of consumption is less esoteric; it does not refer to decomposition, as it does in the common vernacular, but to the process in which "an article [is] finally appropriated to the purpose for which it has been produced."[67] Raymond distinguishes between two uses of a commodity: immediate consumption and exchange. Because production and consumption can incorporate exchange—or, more precisely, exchange regulated by a saving price—overproduction is possible if some individuals refuse to consume. Their abstinence lowers the demand for goods so that prices fall below the saving price. It is then no longer economical for producers to bring commodities to the market, and there is a general reduction in production.[68] The effect of this contraction or crisis is least felt by those in possession of property, particularly of land. They can always sustain themselves. It is quite different for propertyless laborers who depend on employment for their livelihood. Even though the effect of the crisis is felt differently in different sectors, its overall impact on national wealth is detrimental, for production has been greatly curtailed.[69]

Raymond hopes that his argument against parsimony is persuasive enough to influence the proprietors to consume rather than to save. But he is realistic enough to doubt that moral suasion suffices; state force is the more practical ally. In keeping with its principal function of ensuring national prosperity, the state should, according to Raymond, act "to preserve the body politic from the disease of *accumulation*" by providing a sufficient demand through expenditures on public works, public service, and/or war.[70]

The State's Guardianship of Independent Labor: The Protective Tariff

To preserve labor's independence, Raymond proposes legislation to (1) guarantee labor's employment and (2) maintain an equal distribution of property. The first set of policies would maximize the employment of underutilized and marginal labor, ensure a proper balance between manufacturing and agriculture, and resolve crises caused by underconsumption. Raymond's recommendations about public monopolies, colonies, war, public works, national debt, and the protective tariff all fall into this first category of legislation.[71] For my discussion, the most important of these proposals is the protective tariff.

While Raymond's concept of national wealth economically justifies the state's promotion of a protective tariff, the legal justification is another matter. He does this by showing that in society the individual's private rights must be subordinated to collective rights. Through a discussion of natural and conventional rights, Raymond attempts to bridge the space between individual and national wealth, and in the process he subordinates private property to national interest.

The equal rights that the human being enjoys in the state of nature from the beginning fall into the categories of personal and collective. To the personal or absolute rights belong individual endowments, both physical and moral—"his right to life, liberty and free use of his faculties in the pursuit of happiness."[72] Raymond adds to these personal rights "those which man has in common with his fellow man . . . his right to the light of the sun—to the air he breathes—to such a portion of land."[73]

While a perfect equality of rights exists in the state of nature, Raymond insists that there is not a "perfect equality of *power*."[74] By this Raymond means that individuals have different strengths and talents which enable some individuals to amass a greater portion of the earth's bounties than others. To put this somewhat differently, while nature distributes equally the right to self-preservation and the pursuit after happiness, nature does not ensure the outcome of that pursuit to be a perfectly equitable distribution of property. Raymond, however, emphasizes that nature did not intend for that inequality to leave one portion of humanity in luxury at the expense of another. It is this initial condition of equality and inequality that structures the human being's entrance into a social compact.[75]

Since human beings have a propensity to avoid work, they enter into groups, hordes, city-states, and nations either to subdue others or find protection. By entering into this social compact, they establish another set of rights which Raymond classifies as conventional rights. These rights, when perfected, imitate nature's design, at least within the limits of human fallibility. If these conventional rights secure the right of each to pursue personal economic ends and the inequality that results, then the social compact will enhance the well-being of its members even if some benefit more than others. Under these conditions Raymond can argue that rational individuals would be willing to alienate their natural rights to the state and to accept the priority of conventional rights over natural ones. However, when the conventional rights permit laws that violate the original conditions, then these are unjust and must be abolished. The laws of primogeniture, entail, private monopolies, etc. fall into this category since they enrich the few at the expense of the many.

The exclusive right to private property is also modified once the individual enters the social compact. A person's right to private property can be rescinded when it interferes with the object of the association, so that the greater good will not be harmed by individual interest.[76]

> Individual right to property is never absolute, but always relative and conditional. . . . The right to property, is merely conventional or conditional, subject to such regulation as may be made respecting it, with a view to the general interests of the whole nation. . . . The public right to every piece of property in the nation, is superior to the private right of the individual owner. Hence, the right of the public to take any man's property from him, whenever it becomes necessary for the public good.[77]

In the third edition of his *Elements*, Raymond extends his theory to institutional or constitutional matters. Although he limits his analysis to the categories of majority versus minority rights, which are immediately pertinent to the tariff debates, the result is consistent with his general theory of natural and conventional rights. In a later book, *The Elements of Constitutional Law* (1845), Raymond systematizes his rebuttal to free-trade constitutional objections to the tariff. There he argues that in contemporary political theory, the people establish governments for their own benefit, and that the majority has the right to determine the form of the government and the extent of its power. The only restrictions placed on that will are those explicitly cited by the constitution of a nation.

Raymond concedes that majority rule could abuse minority rights. However, he gives two reasons for believing that to be unlikely in the case of the United States. First, he cites the presidential veto, the Bill of Rights, and the "double majority" required for Congress to pass legislation as "ample security against hasty and inconsiderate legislation."[78] Second, he assumes the majority to be perfectly reasonable and just, since the opposite assumption would negate for him the very possibility of constitutional (republican) rule.

Given Raymond's theory of natural rights and his economic reasoning, it is safe to say that the majority's morality, or, to use classical republican language, the majority's virtue, depends on its propertied condition and on state policy, which perpetuates the material conditions of freedom—even though Raymond argues that legislation will change from generation to generation. For example, circumstance has dictated the advisability of the protective tariff, but the principles for its adoption find their justification in natural law deduced by political economy.[79]

In order to achieve its interest, the majority can justifiably consolidate power in the legislative branch. Whereas free-trade economists object to consolidation as an example of the government's violation of restricted powers, Raymond views the process as necessary to the majority's interest. In other words, the absence of consolidation is symptomatic of a growing state crisis that can have catastrophic consequences.

The tariff and a broad interpretation of the United States Constitution are, therefore, explicitly linked in Raymond's theory. These concepts produced the most irate response from Southern free-trade thinkers, for whether framed in constitutional language or in that of conventional rights, Raymond's political economy not only challenged free-trade theory but simultaneously offered a possible challenge to slavery, as Raymond himself illustrated.[80]

Raymond's economic defense of the protective tariff develops, for the most part, from a rebuttal of Smith's belief that a tariff can generate state revenue but is economically destructive when used for protective purposes. Raymond responds that "the object of the restrictive system [is] to encourage the industry of the nation, and augment the product of labour."[81] Raymond disagrees with Smith's rejection of the tariff as a form of monopoly. While Raymond admits that the protective tariff is monopolistic, he differentiates between private and public monopolies; the latter, he says, benefit the entire nation by eliminating foreign competition but not internal competition, on which growth is predicated.[82] Raymond is aware that the distinction between public and private monopolies does not fully exonerate the protective tariff because Smith admits the distinction; yet Smith continues to challenge the value of a "public" monopoly by observing that (1) it cannot increase capital, which employs productive labor, and (2) it diverts more capital into areas that are less beneficial to a nation's development than a free-trade policy does.

Raymond takes care to address both criticisms. Regarding the first, he once again dissents from Smith's definition of capital, asserting that Smith has confused capital with labor.[83] For Raymond, capital does not employ labor; on the contrary, labor employs or, more exactly, "manages" capital. Here again, Raymond uses "capital" to refer to property (specifically to the means of production), rather than to money or to commodities produced for profit. He can then argue that "the quantity of labor required to manage a given quantity of property, depends entirely on the state of improvements the property is in—on the use that is made of it, and the manner in which it is managed."[84] According to him, these variables make it impossible to determine the exact proportion that exists between labor and "capital." In fact, these variables suggest that employment is not limited by the amount of "capital" in a nation.[85]

He can reject this proposition only by now conceiving of the economy in terms of commodity production originally linked to the world market. For by requiring the nation to produce more of its own products, Raymond believes the protective tariff will improve the efficiency of the variables enumerated above, thereby employing marginal and underutilized labor.[86] Thus, Raymond's belief that the protective tariff can increase "capital's" employment of labor rests on his shifting between two conceptions of economic activity: one based on self-sufficient producers and another based on exchange values of commodities.

Raymond uses these two contradictory economic conceptions in order to discuss the tariff in terms consistent with his concerns. Commodity production explains why the tariff stimulates more efficient use of labor; such a deepening of the market would lead to a concentration of property and the formation of a working class.

Raymond's theory, however, limits the tariff's effect on the home market. He observes that the extent of the market depends on the number of propertyless laborers who have to purchase their means of subsistence.[87] Given the state's commitment to preserve independent labor, there is a defined limit to the number of propertyless workers and hence to demand. Raymond can thus conclude that the protective tariff increases commercial activity enough to utilize labor but not enough to strip commodity producers of their independence, that is, so long as the state successfully resolves the contradictions in the accumulation process.

Raymond begins his rebuttal of Smith's second criticism of the protective tariff by agreeing that free trade enhances economic growth because a nation can purchase commodities at their lowest prices. However, for Raymond, this is neither the only consideration nor the most important one a nation must weigh in adopting a free-trade or restrictive system. Unemployment is far more important for Raymond, although Smith does not treat this issue. Raymond asks whether a nation experiencing protracted unemployment should import commodities worth one million dollars or produce them for two million.[88] Free traders would import, but Raymond thinks the results would be disastrous. A nation must guarantee employment and consumption despite the additional cost at home. To make this point, Raymond formulates the following analogy, which he must have thought particularly powerful against the objections of his Southern opponents.

> It is the duty and interest of the planter to find employment for all his hands. . . . So it is the duty of the legislator to find employment for all the people. . . . He is not to permit one half of the nation to remain idle and hungry, in order that the other half may buy goods where they may be had cheapest.[89]

According to Raymond, consumers do not pay for the entire rise in the price of commodities. Merchants must lower their prices to some extent if they wish to sell all of the commodities in their possession. In this way the merchant and the consumer share the hardships brought about by increasing prices. Furthermore, these prices are not permanent. As home production increases, prices fall. In fact, Raymond asserts that high prices actually stimulate improvements in production.

More important, the restrictive system improves the condition of the propertyless laborer. Besides ensuring employment, protective tariffs eventually increase real wages as labor becomes more scarce.[90] Even when tariffs are placed on the importation of corn, as in England, labor benefits because wages rise faster than the price of food. Finally, the protective tariff benefits labor by insulating the home market from international fluctuations and from the competititon of goods produced by pauper labor (that is, from English labor) and by prohibiting foreign powers, especially England, from dumping surplus goods on the American market. Such competition would drive down American wages and eventually threaten employment.[91]

In addition to directly benefiting labor, the tariff indirectly advances the nation as a whole in two ways. First, full employment resulting from the protective system enhances the moral fiber of the population and brings the material consequences of increased scientific inquiry that eventually raise productivity.[92] Second, in establishing a protective system, legislators can correct any imbalance among agriculture, manufacturing, and commerce by favoring the weak branch over the strong. According to Raymond, a proper balance among these spheres, in particular between agriculture and manufacturing, is essential to a healthy economy since each contributes to the other's well-being.[93] Because of the direct and indirect benefits of the protective tariff, Raymond is quite confident in asserting that it should be adopted by a nation, although individual interests might temporarily be hurt.[94]

Despite the tariff's integration into his theory, Raymond leaves the actual decision to implement the tariff dependent on the historical circumstances of a nation. In assessing the economy of the United States as he knows it, Raymond concludes that a system of protective tariffs is required for the following reasons: (1) the United States suffers from both unemployment and underutilization of labor; (2) agriculture predominates over manufacturing, creating serious economic imbalances—although Raymond prefers agricultural life for moral reasons; (3) unless the United States adopts a protective system, it will have to compete with English pauper labor by reducing American labor to a comparably degraded level.

The State's Guardianship of Independent Labor: A Natural Distribution of Property

The second set of legislative measures proposed by Raymond is meant to contain the concentration of wealth and to preserve labor's freedom without creating an egalitarian society. Raymond stresses his differences from radical "utopian" thinkers. Inequality and private property are, for Raymond, the foundations of economic growth and of civilization. His restrictions on accumulation are meant to protect property against economic and political instability resulting from aristocratic or capitalist greed. And even here, Raymond does not sanction intervention without sufficiently warning legislators of potential dangers. Any action against the unnatural concentration of property has to be grounded in the preservation of the natural distribution of property and the inequalities it implies. Raymond roundly rejects the "utopian" schemes of Condorcet and Godwin and the fanciful notions on which agrarian laws are based. These schemas, he insists, lead as inevitably to social dissolution as does aristocratic greed.

> Nature, therefore, never intended, that there should be perfect equality among men; and the chimerical theories of Godwin, Condorcet, and other visionary dreamers about a state of perfect equality, are in as direct violation of natural law as those existing systems, which place strength in subjection to weakness, talents in subjection to imbecility, and secure to one portion of the community in perpetuity, all the property, to the total exclusion of a more numerous and equally entitled portion.[95]

Raymond's program to restrain capitalist behavior is somewhat more ambiguous than his easy suggestion to repeal the "aristocratic" laws of inheritance and to replace them with laws that divide property equally among each surviving child. He does not offer specific measures to resolve the contradictions inherent in economic growth, and so indicates his lack of clarity about this process. Even his more rigorous analysis of money is not wholly satisfactory.

Raymond's initial response to concentrated wealth arising from capitalist activity is to attack private monopolies and corporations.[96] Yet a careful reading shows that he is actually ambivalent toward such attacks, at least with regard to corporations. According to Raymond, monied interests unhappy with the private power of money seek to form corporate associations such as banks, insurance companies, and transportation companies. These organizations free individual capitalists of financial responsibility for any venture while multiplying the actual power of their individual sums of money. The net result of such organizations is to magnify the dangers inherent in money. Thus it seems that Raymond would discourage the state from promoting the formation of corporations. But he hesitates because he recognizes that they actually benefit the nation by pooling large sums of capital, which are necessary for the construction of roads, canals, and other large projects. Consequently, Raymond recommends that corporations be judiciously encouraged.

Raymond selects banks for special consideration probably for two reasons.[97] First, banks represent capital in its most evident form, and second, they are the subject of heated political debate. We have seen that while Raymond thought banks useful, he considered them potentially dangerous because of their combined functions of printing and lending money.

Raymond offers three reform proposals. The first would completely prohibit banks from manufacturing money. Only the state would retain this power. The federal government would issue paper currency in direct proportion to the amount of specie it held in reserve. Since Raymond doubts that so drastic a reform would find much support, he includes two other measures, neither of which totally eliminates the power of banks to issue notes. In his second plan the federal government would be granted the exclusive right to engrave and print bank notes; because of this power the federal government could establish the ratio between loans and specie held in reserve. If this plan were held to be impractical, Raymond feels that his third proposal might find less resistance. In this last plan, banks would be permitted to manufacture money, but the state would limit the amount of interest a bank could receive on its specie. The banks would therefore have the power to manufacture money but would lack the motivation. Through any one of these plans, Raymond argues, it would be possible to eliminate the wild fluctuations and speculation caused by the banks' authority to lend and manufacture money. Raymond wants to regulate, not eliminate, capitalist activity.[98]

Raymond's Anticapitalist Thought

In light of the preceding analysis it would be absurd to consider Raymond an anticapitalist thinker, although he might insist on such a characterization. At most, we can concede that he attempts to resist the development of industrial capitalism by encouraging legislation intended to protect independent labor. The glaring difficulty in his program results from his reluctance to perceive that the independent producer is in fact tied to a capitalist circuit. In his discussion of capital, he does admit that the independent producer is connected to the capitalist market and, further, that, once so connected, this producer functions as a merchant or, more generally, a capitalist. Later, in discussing the tariff, Raymond recognizes the dependence of those producers on the world market. Thus capital or, more specifically, commercial capital affects the basic elements in his theory and the general economic laws which he discovered. Capital's influence, in fact, is so pervasive that propertyless labor itself appears as a basic category in his theory.

Raymond's conscious failure to treat independent producers consistently as capitalists can be attributed to his rejection of Smith's theory. Although ideological factors (as discussed in the next chapter) contribute to this rejection, Raymond's dissatisfaction with *The Wealth of Nations* was also shaped by differences between the class structures which radically separated England and the United States. The major difference is the degree to which a working class had developed. Because Raymond's prescriptions are directed toward restricting the development of a working class rather than controlling an existing one, the anticipated similarities from a functional perspective between his theory and Ricardo's, both "spokesmen" for industrial capital, necessarily break down. Similarly, despite the surprisingly frequent concurrence between Raymond and Malthus, their theories diverge significantly over the role of labor.

Raymond's optimism derived from the ambiguity of the period. While the home market was already organized under capitalist principles, it was still restricted, and manufacturing was based on craft technology, giving labor the semblance of independence. It was not clear that labor was participating in capitalist production and that it would be subsumed under industrial capital. Furthermore, the frontier permitted a continual revitalization of the small farmer. Capitalist accumulation on the land might concentrate wealth in one area, but cheap land was always available so that the farmer might avoid being forced into the ranks of propertyless labor. Raymond, as a good American Whig, never perceived the western lands as a solution to the problem of the working class.[99] For him, the state, not the frontier, functioned as the safety valve for capitalist accumulation. Therefore, the incontestable evidence for capital's supremacy had not yet presented itself. The signs are more subtle and studiously misrepresented by Raymond. Consequently, his legislative recommendations had the intention of limiting the home market and the formation of a working class while, in fact, they promoted the development of capital by seeking to increase national wealth.

4. DANIEL RAYMOND *on Protecting the Republic from Slave Capital*

The American slavery and anti-slavery question, is about as important to the working classes of this country, as the great division of British politics, "the landed interest and moneyed interest," is to the operatives of Great Britain; which, in plain English, means this: which shall have the power best secured by law, to plunder the producers of wealth to the greatest extent: the LANDLORD OR THE MONEY LORD?

A very important matter, for the poor, plundered victims to contend about!! Equally so is the slavery question to the working classes of the United States. In this chapter we have shown that there is no such thing as active or productive capital, but in the form of chattel slavery. The pseudo free labor and chattel slavery systems have been compared—the advantages and disadvantages of them considered. It now remains for the working man to decide which system is the best to suffer under, *or to be free.*—John Pickering, *The Working Man's Political Economy*

Raymond's *Elements* builds up to the discussion of slavery, the most serious challenge to America's economic and political viability. Like aristocratic privileges, Raymond argues, slavery has to be completely removed from the body politic. To do otherwise is to permit unnatural growth to infect the nation with a disease causing irreparable damage. An additional excursion into the messianic aspect of Raymond's thought is necessary before focusing directly on slavery.

Raymond's Concept of History

Raymond agrees with Smith that history is an extension of human nature, that its end is freedom, and that its course can be best understood by an analysis of wealth. Yet there are striking differences between Raymond and his English counterparts regarding the actual composition of human nature, the precise mechanism of historical motion, the rules for historical periodization, and the moral significance of expanding wealth.

My analysis has already revealed several features pertinent to a study of Raymond's theory of history. In rejecting the immediate relevance of Malthus's theory of population, Raymond simultaneously rejects the notion that historical movement is the result of the antagonism between human and natural fecundity. Instead, Raymond's theory of historical change develops from his theory of value.[1] This theory rests on the proposition that desires, not needs, always exceed productive capabilities. It is the human being's continual struggle to satisfy these desires that causes economic and, consequently, historical motion. At first sight this may sound like Smith. However, as noted earlier, Smith's theory encourages human acquisitiveness while Raymond prescribes measures to constrain it. In fact, where Smith makes the passions the guide to human action and pride a positive attribute, Raymond condemns both, particularly pride, as the cause of all social ills. Unlike Smith, then, Raymond subordinates the passions to reason; only reason can truly comprehend nature's laws and establish the proper moral basis for the technical mastery of nature.

To explain the persistence of this pre-Smithian interpretation of reason, we must consider the religious dimensions of Raymond's thought. Unlike classical political economists, Raymond does not structure his political economy solely by scientific reasoning that requires experimental proof and empirically verifiable assumptions. Religious reasoning—in particular, biblical exegesis—is used extensively in Raymond's intellectual universe. In fact, Raymond opens his *Elements of Political Economy* with a hermeneutic analysis of Genesis 4, Adam and Eve's expulsion from the Garden of Eden. Through that exegesis Raymond defines fallen human nature and the dynamics of history.[2]

Raymond accepts the view that pride caused Adam and Eve's fall and their banishment from Eden to live by the sweat of their brow. But being proud (depraved), the human race refused to heed God and sought to avoid labor by subjugating others. This act of rebellion, in Raymond's opinion, is the source of all human history because it promoted the formation of tribes, city-states, and nations to avoid labor and subjugation.[3] Defiance of God has condemned the human being to misery and damnation.[4]

Raymond thus explains through religious reasoning both humanity's natural and unnatural acquisitiveness and the dynamics of history. Natural law becomes the will of God as revealed in the Bible. Raymond's legal and economic theories are attempts to understand God's will in order that social conduct may be organized in accordance with God's plan, which, understood in Raymond's Calvinist terms, makes material success a sign of God's approval. Increasing wealth, therefore, attests to a nation's morality and hence to its probable redemption. Consequently, the state has a moral imperative as well as a material one, and "statesmen" are, for Raymond, "the viceregents of God on Earth" who must discipline the unnatural acquisitiveness of their subjects.[5]

When we view Raymond's theory in terms of his religious paradigm, it becomes easy to understand the peculiar moral quality of his condemna-tion of English political economy. His religious interpretation of republi-can doctrine also helps explain his retention of the traditional relationship between reason and the passions, even though his theory makes the econ-omy the sphere of moral improvement.

But his Calvinst criticism does not determine the way Raymond con-structs an alternative economic theory. The proposition "from the sweat of the brow" tells little about the relationship of labor to the means of production, nor does "man's price" necessarily inform us that wage labor is a form of subservience. For different ideological reasons, the English economists also opposed subservient relationships; yet wage labor in their opinion cannot be included in that category. As already suggested, the structure of Raymond's economic thought is principally structured by the development of the social relations of production.

Raymond's Periodization

Smith has two methods for periodization: an analytic distinction between an early state and an advanced state, used to highlight the economic prob-lem of production and distribution, and historical periodization that em-ploys modes of subsistence to designate different states of history.

Raymond's theory is likewise bifurcated. His analytical periodization separates societies into two categories: (1) those in which depraved human beings rebel against natural law and are damned and (2) those in which human beings conform to natural law and are redeemed. From a material viewpoint the two are separated by the degree of property concentration and the size of a pauper class. The unifying feature is the constant pursuit of individual wealth. Exchange and capital also appear in both periods, since they are means by which individual wealth may be acquired. In the second or redeemed state, exchange permits independent producers to dis-pose of surplus products and to acquire use values which they are unable to produce. Money facilitates exchange by storing the value of perishable commodities and providing a universal equivalent that permits producers to sell and buy at their convenience. However, the first or unredeemed state takes on a perverse character because money is used as a means to accumulate and to concentrate wealth.

If capital appears in both states, so does profit or saving price. In Ray-mond's system, the appearance of these categories is perfectly consistent with natural law, for property may be concentrated to the extent that dif-fering talents, skills, and morals are naturally distributed among the indi-vidual producers. Thus, propertyless labor is also to be found as an ele-ment in a society organized under natural law.

As in Raymond's analytic periodization, labor's status defines histori-cal periodization. Seen transhistorically, labor is either dependent or independent, either pauper or proprietor. The various forms that dependent labor assumes and its relationship to a propertied class constitute the elements of Raymond's periodization. Thus, the lord-serf, master-slave, and capitalist-pauper relationships all distinguish different types of societies.

> The subject of controversy is not pauperism in any particular form and shape, for its mode of existence, depends entirely upon the institutions of the country. In one country, it may exist in the shape of strolling mendicity; in another, in the shape of a sort of pensioned poverty; in another, in the shape of retainers, clients, dependents, in various shapes; in another in the shape of feudal vassalage; and thus it may be modified indefinitely, according to the nature of the government, and the provision made for its support.[6]

However, Raymond is forced to qualify his definition when he confronts the disconcerting phenomenon of pauperism in an economy functioning according to natural law. In this case, he uses the conventional definition of paupers as laborers unable to support themselves. In a "natural society," the paupers, including the disabled and aged, are "obliged to rely upon the bounty of individuals or the public, for the whole or some portion of their subsistence."[7] Hence, employed propertyless labor in a natural (redeemed) state is not defined as dependent labor.

Raymond therefore offers two definitions of pauper labor. Concretely, this allows Raymond on the one hand to label a feudal knight as a pauper, despite a knight's probable prosperity and despite his willingness and ability to work and, on the other hand, to exclude propertyless labor from the category of pauper in a regenerated state, even though the laborer is dependent on another's will. Raymond's theory necessitates this contradiction since the theory's object is to condemn as degraded all dependent labor outside an economy based on natural law.

Of the unnatural societies mentioned by Raymond, he concentrates his attention on England. Its extraordinary wealth seems to verify Smith's assumption that a working class is a natural phenomenon. Raymond attacks this correlation by pointing out that the unnatural distribution of property in England results from aristocratic laws and from capitalist behavior. Raymond suggests that the latter predominates in England and distinguishes it from other "fallen" nations.

Although exchange may exist in all other societies, the development of market relationships is most advanced in England in Raymond's system. This historical interpretation is consistent with Smith's, to whose authority Raymond defers in this matter.[8] However, whereas Smith posits that full employment of market relationships is consistent with natural law, Raymond argues that this development is the most extreme symptom of the human being's rebellion against natural law.

The full development of the market breaks the organic connection between the propertied and propertyless classes which characterizes all other unnatural economies. Bonded English labor may now become free labor but not independent labor, since aristocratic laws and capitalist accumulation still preserve the unequal division of property. Once the organic ties are broken, the paternalistic spirit that has prevailed among the propertied class disappears. The pauper class now depends on an impersonal market for employment. And, as the capitalist ethic of accumulation spreads even into the aristocratic class, the market functions less and less smoothly, causing vast unemployment and misery for the propertyless laborer.[9] The continual introduction of machinery, another feature of English society, only exacerbates the situation since it is used to reduce labor costs and to further concentrate wealth.[10] Faced with starvation, a large portion of the English pauper class turns to crime.

For Raymond, this degradation of labor is without precedent in human history. Although he concedes that several degrees of degradation coexist and that not all English paupers are criminals, he nevertheless asserts that the economic tendency is to reduce the entire class to criminality. In their most depraved condition, the paupers, according to Raymond, are incapable of establishing stable families and reproducing themselves.[11] Where the market does not dominate the economy, labor possesses a greater semblance of humanity because paternalistic attitudes among the propertied classes ensure the employment and material well-being of dependent labor.

> The knights, squires, and dependents, of the old feudal barons, were, no doubt, a much higher order of beings than present paupers of England; but this was owing to the character, manners, and occupations of the times, and not to those circumstances which constituted them paupers or dependents. This also shows, that there is some radical vice in the English government, or their system of civil polity.[12]

As this passage suggests, Raymond does not confine his criticism of the effects of capitalist accumulation to the propertyless class; he is also concerned with the propertied class and the state. His indictment of English aristocrats and capitalists over others derives from the English proprietors' refusal to guarantee employment or provide charity for the dependent class. Because market relationships and capitalist ethics prevail in England, full employment is not possible there, but charity remains an option and a responsibility of the wealthy even in an unnatural society. However, the English propertied class is so morally corrupt that it has proposed legislation to dismantle the poor laws, which were a minor compensation, in Raymond's opinion, for the wrongs committed against English labor.[13]

It is interesting to note that Raymond offers an alternate remedy for the English situation which is not so drastic as his proposal to redistribute property, namely that the aristocracy abandon the market and retain the poor as it did before the market's full development. In other words, Raymond thinks that feudalism is more humane than full-blown capitalism.

> Let the rich men in England divide the paupers among them, in proportion to the magnitude of their estates, and they will, for their support, render them as much service, as was rendered by the feudal vassals to their lords. If they refuse to do this, let them not complain of compulsory assessments for the support of the poor.[14]

For Raymond, the pauper class is not only piteous, it is dangerous and capable of "destroying the body politic."[15] Since English society extends rather than limits pauperism, Raymond argues that a foreign war, an exceptionally sharp economic downturn, or some other calamitous event would be sufficient to precipitate a working-class insurrection.[16] This would be disastrous in Raymond's view because the paupers' degenerate character would cause them to follow demagogues and seek utopian fantasies.

America's Historical Mission

Unlike Smith, Raymond does not arrange the societies he identifies in any order of chronological succession. Since his comments on them are scattered in digressions and historical asides, it is hard to determine whether his silence on the concept of linear progress means that he believes history does not follow a predetermined path. In any case, we can be quite certain that he does not believe history will automatically redeem human beings. Their redemption needs continual striving to constrain human pride and to construct social institutions that will be beneficial.

Ideally, for Raymond, mental and moral faculties would develop in concert with God's will, as revealed in the Bible and confirmed through the human being's mastery of natural law. The means of mastery are the production of wealth and the establishment of a just and stable political order. However, since the world is corrupt, scientific knowledge may advance independent of a movement toward redemption and cause a disjuncture between mental and social development.

Given this possible disjuncture, a historical accident can initiate a great leap in the historical process by incorporating the moral lessons of accumulated scientific knowledge, as for example the unusual relevance of the United States in Raymond's panorama of history. For him, the accidental discovery of America had a paradoxical effect on human history; it encouraged human pride and disrupted the balance of political powers established during the Middle Ages by the rise of the nation-state. That balance had tempered the violence in human nature that now broke out into wars between rival commercial powers which required additional sources of labor and found them in Africa.[17] The African slave trade and slavery itself are, in Raymond's mind, the most heinous violations of natural law committed during those turbulent years of exploration and settlement in the New World.

> Unfortunately for our country, and long and deeply shall we deplore it, we are not free from the deadly sin of having participated in the violence and outrage committed upon the African race. Our fathers and ourselves have tasted the forbidden fruit, and the *curse* resteth upon us.[18]

Despite these crimes, Raymond believes that America offers Christendom a vast continent for a great moral experiment to found a society on natural law. In his estimation, that potential has been realized by the American Revolution and the founding of a republican government. Chance allows for the settlement of a nation freed from the corrupted European institutions. But only virtue can ensure the natural foundations of the new nation. Raymond uses "republicanism" as a synonym for "righteousness." A republican government corresponds to the political tenets of natural law, which are the preconditions for a moral economic order. Republicanism is, therefore, the political vehicle for redemption.[19]

Slave Capital's Threat to the Republic

Like English pauperism, American slavery presents two problems: (1) a depraved and potentially dangerous population now complicated by the issue of race and (2) a degenerate propertied class of masters who corrupt national politics.

While Raymond is aware that the horrors of slavery are the subject of philanthropic criticism, he is the first to be concerned with slavery's harmful effect on national wealth, thus correcting the omission.[20] He lists three adverse effects of slavery on national economic and political life. However, the unequal division of property so central to his theory is conspicuously absent. A possible reason for this exclusion might be an equitable distribution of property in the South. But this is not the case. In several passages Raymond remarks that the South suffers from the malaise of unequal distribution of property more than any other region of the nation. The reason for his omission becomes apparent once we examine the adverse effects Raymond does enumerate.

Slavery's influence on America's national wealth "is to be considered mainly with a view to slavery's influence on population."[21] Population is a measure of a young nation's economic prosperity since it is correlated with an increasing demand for labor by proprietors. Raymond examines the census and discovers that "the white population increases about twice as fast in the free states . . . as in the slave states."[22] The census also reveals that the gross population, black and white, in the South increases at a slower rate than the population of the Northern states. Since the Southern states have geographic and climatic advantages, Raymond concludes that slavery must be the reason for this disparity.[23] He proceeds to argue that the differences reflect relative levels of industriousness and adds that slaves reproduce faster than Southern whites. He attributes this disparity to a greater demand for the products of slave labor than for those of free labor, which makes it advantageous for the master to raise slaves "as an article for profit and traffic, the same as cattle and horses."[24]

The second adverse effect he mentions is a corollary of the first. Slavery degrades labor—used synonymously with free white labor. Raymond acknowledges that slavery's first effect is the degradation of black labor; however, that degradation assumes significance for him only because of its consequences to free white labor.[25]

He includes Southern slaves in the category of morally depraved labor exemplified by the criminal sector of England's pauper class, even though the causes of depravity differ. Significantly, Raymond does not compare the consequences of Southern paternalism with those of feudalism. The systems are indeed very different. Medieval feudalism had a limited market in which the laborer was in immediate control of the tools and the process of production. Southern slavery, in contrast, profitably participated in a world capitalist market. Slaves neither possessed tools nor controlled the labor process. The master organized and dictated production. Raymond implies these differences when he insists on the slave's total moral dependence on the master.

In contrast to the negative comparison between serf and slave developed by my analysis, Raymond offers a positive one between slave and prison inmate: neither makes decisions; the organization of duties lies entirely in the power of others. The forced lack of responsibility for organization and direction of work results in the inability to perform these functions, and finally in total moral and social dependency.[26] This implies that neither recovers social responsibility when freed.

Since slave labor is used in the South to perform most of the required menial tasks, the depraved moral state of slavery is associated there with labor in general. Consequently, propertied white labor attempts to avoid work by owning slaves, and thereby perpetuates and exacerbates the unnatural basis of Southern society. The effect is to further degrade free propertyless labor in the South, for "if a white man or woman has the misfortune to possess no property, and is under the necessity of going into service," he or she is viewed as a member of an "inferior order of being" and lives as wretchedly as a slave.[27] In short, Southern antipathy toward work restricted its economic power.

Slavery's Effect on White and Black Labor

In his assessment of the differing growth rates between black and white labor, Raymond evinces his primary concern with politics. As the excessive increase of paupers in England threatens the body politic, so too the rapid growth of slave labor endangers the political stability of the Southern states. Raymond predicts that if blacks continue to reproduce faster than whites, the situation "will terminate in insurrections and servile wars, shocking even in imagination."[28]

Even though white labor, except for that of planters, is increasingly degraded by slavery, propertyless whites are not among the insurrectionists described by Raymond. He conceives the principal antagonism as white versus black rather than labor versus slavery. This formulation is certainly consistent with his theory about the effects of slavery on national wealth. However, the primary division of labor into the categories "black" and "white" is not consistent with his overall theory. In general, his theory asserts that the unequal division of property creates dependent labor no matter what it is for; an unequal division of property structures political conflict. There is no category in Raymond's theory that can alter this basic division in society. Thus, for Raymond to conclude that the Southern states are primarily divided between free labor and slave labor, between black and white, is to introduce an unstated or assumed concept, namely a division by race.

Raymond's work contains theoretical propositions and historical commentaries that help to reveal his unacknowledged theoretical conception of race. He employs the term "race" in describing black laborers as members of the "African race" merely to distinguish the ancestral origins of black labor from those of white labor, and insists that race has no further implications. He holds firm to the proposition that "men are created equal" and maintains the natural equality of the African race against assertions to the contrary.[29] Raymond does believe that black slaves are of an "inferior order of being," but he explains that their depravity is a consequence of an unnatural economic order and not of lineage.[30]

Furthermore, race and nation-state are not synonymous in Raymond's thought. His formal definition of a nation is a legal one based on the legitimacy of a state and its sovereignty over a territory. The inclusion of the inhabitants of that territory in the state is also a legal question regarding the rights of citizenship. Since Raymond subscribes to the modern republican theory of government, slavery is an aberration because it denies freedom and citizenship to a sector of the population.

An ambiguity, however, emerges from Raymond's often unclear separation between the concepts of lineage or race and the nation-state. In describing the establishment of colonies, Raymond asserts that they cannot become nations "until a race of men have grown out of the soil—who know no other country, and whose affection and attachments are all centered in the colony. . . . The emigrants to a colony must be planted in the earth, and from their bones must spring up a race of men, armed too they must be, before that colony can be considered as firmly established."[31] Here Raymond suggests that a nation might develop from the emergence of a common lineage or race rather than from the creation of a state. Irrational factors, such as familial ties, custom, and myth seem to be prerequisites to the legal establishment of a state. The United States is a "white man's country."

Manumission as Genocide

Raymond's inexplicit concept of race makes itself felt in his consideration of various plans to end slavery.[32] Those considerations begin from his general ideas regarding the adverse effects of a pauper class on the body politic; then he examines competing strategies to offset rebelliousness and to alleviate oppression by including the pauper class in the body politic. However, because of the racial factor involved in the American pauper problem, Raymond prefers to be rid of the free slave population.

The first schema he considers is colonization in Africa. He rejects this plan because slaves reproduce faster than the possible rate of forced emigration to Africa.[33] Raymond believes that an alternative plan to transfer the slaves to the Caribbean is more realistic. It can only succeed if that area becomes a free territory for blacks. The plan, therefore, is based on a vague hope, and Raymond concludes that "the African race is effectually planted in this country."[34] From this, he comes to a second proposal to end slavery and the fifth column that free black labor will present. If blacks cannot be transported out of the country, they perhaps can be eliminated in another way: "The only way in which the country can be entirely cleared of them, is by a general massacre—a measure not very likely to be resorted to."[35] It is an inappropriate solution because it would violate natural rights. As Raymond puts it, "We have no more right, because blacks are an evil, to take violent measures against them, than the people of England have, to adopt violent measures towards the paupers of that country, because they are an evil."[36] Such action would only condemn the United States to God's retribution.

The third schema that Raymond considers, and the one he adopts, is manumission. On first appearance this solution seems a benevolent one, consistent with the fundamental propositions contained in Raymond's theory. Manumission conforms to natural rights and is in agreement with Raymond's formal definition of a nation as a corporate entity whose inhabitants are its citizens. Finally, manumission is an act of Christian charity in which the wrongs committed against an innocent people would be righted and the curse of slavery ended. However, Raymond's proposal is not designed to incorporate blacks into the nation but is calculated to decrease the black population to a point of virtual extinction without, according to Raymond, violating natural law:

> Manumission presents a simple, natural and practical mode of remedying the evil of slavery; and although it does not present a mode of getting rid of the black population entirely, yet it presents a mode by which the number will be more effectually prevented from increasing, than any other that has ever yet been proposed. It is also more consonant to the principles of justice and humanity, than any other that has every been suggested.[37]

How is it that manumission will "humanely" and effectually rid the United States of its blacks? Although Raymond considers the African race naturally equal to any other race, he believes that those blacks who have lived under slavery are thoroughly depraved. If freed, nine out of ten blacks will become paupers and criminals, incapable of establishing families and reproducing themselves. Manumission will have the same practical effect as wholesale massacre of the black population. The few slaves who are morally fit and survive freedom may be given citizenship;[38] yet these fit blacks cannot finally be incorporated into the nation since intermarriage between the races is inconceivable to Raymond. Perhaps it was this "humane" schema for manumission which led George Fitzhugh, the archconservative of the Southern cause, to comment in the 1850s that, since the abolitionists intended genocide, the planters were truly the slaves' protectors.

A comparison between Raymond's proposal for eliminating slave labor and Malthus's recommendation for controlling pauperism further clarifies Raymond's thoughts on race. Malthus's plan for repealing the poor laws rests on two assumptions which Raymond rejects: (1) that human misery caused by the antagonism between human and natural fecundity is unavoidable and (2) that this antagonism can be resolved if the laboring population—inherently inferior—is better trained morally and mentally. Without the poor laws Malthus believes nature will improve the class by selecting the morally sound and eliminating the unfit.

Raymond objects to Malthus's reasoning since it violates natural law by abrogating the proprietor's responsibility of providing charity to the needy. Raymond, however, cannot object to the final consequence of Malthus's plan, namely the extinction of the poor, for Raymond's proposal regarding slavery has a similar effect on blacks. What differentiates the two programs is the means, not the ends. Within Raymond's paradigm, Malthus's schema is flawed in yet another way. He cannot isolate the depraved sector of the working class, since the poor laws are applicable to the entire working class; no "radical" characteristic distinguishes the depraved from the morally sound laborers. English propertyless laborers are all members of the same lineage sharing a common culture in Raymond's terms.

Raymond's theory avoids the conflict of immediate interests between proprietor and propertyless implied by Malthus.[39] Although other factors contribute to the harmony of interests in Raymond's theory, race plays an important role with regard to Southern labor. Race permits the depraved portion of propertyless labor to be isolated and its existence to be seen as potentially dangerous to both propertied and propertyless labor. Furthermore, the planters may be identified as a corrupting element in the state which creates the potential for an alliance of white laborers and yeomen to retard the disastrous effect of slave power. Raymond's use of race, therefore, forces a wedge between black and white labor.

Raymond's suggestion for alleviating English pauperism further illustrates the racial component of his thinking. In the case of England—that most debased and evil country in his view—Raymond suggests a general redistribution of property. He does not fear that the pauper-criminals will be unable to manage their new-found prosperity.[40] On the contrary, he has every confidence that the English poor will be revitalized by their possession of property.

Raymond never conceives of the same solution for the American blacks, perhaps because it is not immediately applicable to redressing the evils committed against black labor. Unlike English paupers, blacks have not been robbed of their land, but of their freedom. Hence manumission seems to rectify the violation of natural law. Although plausible, this argument is rather weak. There is another explanation which follows from Raymond's assumed distinction between nation and state: he does not consider blacks as part of the American nation.

Slavery's Effect on the Planters and the State

In Raymond's view, slavery must be categorized as a perverter of the state. The Southern representatives in the federal government are torn, in Raymond's view, between their responsibilities as viceregents of God and their responsibilities to their slave-holding constituency. Raymond consequently fears for the state's divine mandate.[41]

The problem, in Raymond's general analysis, is the concentration of property. Since primogeniture and entail are nonexistent in the antebellum South, by default capitalist accumulation becomes the only explanation. Raymond indirectly suggests this in the discussion on the planters' relationship to the world market. First, he observes that employment is more stable in the South than in the North because of the world demand for Southern products. Second, he notes that slavery's products are so profitable that slave labor itself has become a profitable commodity.[42] Finally, the responsibility of the planters to provide employment for their slaves is fulfilled only after considerations are made for capitalist gains; the masters employ slaves to produce commodities that will sell on the world market. If one commodity fails, the slaves are redirected to produce another: "It is the duty of the planter to find employment for all his hands, and if this cannot be done in one branch of *business*, to seek another" (my emphasis).[43] Therefore, although Raymond locates the origin of slavery in the unnatural human desire to avoid laboring by subjugating others, Southern slavery, as presented in his work, is maintained and perpetuated through "unnatural" capitalist activity.

The capitalist nature of the Southern economy points, for Raymond, to several similarities between the South and England: both participate in the most degenerate form of the unnatural state; they promote a dangerous pauper class and self-serving ruling class; and each advocates the economics of Adam Smith. In practical terms, Raymond fears that a free-trade policy will affect more than the South; it will also reduce Northern labor to a level comparable to that of the slave. Universally to adopt the free-trade policy of the South, whose statesmen have relinquished their responsibility as God's viceregents, would be to doom the United States to material and spiritual perdition.[44]

If the slave masters cannot perceive the dangers associated with the iniquitous institution of slavery, Raymond believes it necessary for the state to act by manumitting the slaves. To meet the planters' objections that the policy would violate private property, Raymond offers a defense of national wealth and the general welfare analogous to his justification of the tariff:

> The advocates of slavery reason much in the same manner respecting slavery, that the English property-holders do respecting pauperism. The property-holders in England . . . take it for granted, that their right of property is absolute and unconditional; . . . The property-holders have not an absolute, unconditional right to their property—their right is subordinate to that of the nation.[45]

Raymond's condemnation of the South through a critique of free-trade policy might seem rather banal when it is recalled that the South, too, had a protariff "party"; Southern sugar and hemp producers as well as incipient manufacturers lobbied for economic protection.[46] And even under the Confederacy, which constitutionally prohibited a protective tariff, there was ample provision for sheltering economic interests from the world market.[47] But it should be kept in mind that the tariff was a means, not an end. For all of Malthus's differences from Raymond in objectives, both men recognized that restriction was but one policy among many that could be used by the statesmen to achieve desirable ends. Their agreement on this means certainly does not trivialize their fundamentally different ends in defining the good society. To further illustrate the contingency of a position in favor of or opposed to the tariff, it may be pointed out that, in Fitzhugh's proslavery writings, Raymond's answer to the threat of national decline is as fanciful as those of the radical socialists whom he dismisses as utopian. Unlike Godwin's or Condercet's, Raymond's utopia is defensive; he wants to perpetuate the petty bourgeois relationships that characterize the Northern economy of his period. His program makes the unrealizable and contradictory promises to preserve the supremacy of the small producer and to ensure the economic stability of propertyless labor. At the same time, his entire program permits and unintentionally encourages capitalist accumulation. In exchange for slavery, which affords the planters only individual gain, Raymond magnanimously offers them freedom from the curse of slavery and of moral degradation. The only sector of America's population that will not gain from Raymond's plan is black labor, which, conveniently, he does not consider American at all.

It may be tempting to conclude that Raymond's position is petty bourgeois at the service of industrial capitalism; but this would be a reduction in retrospect, mistaking results for intentions. This kind of functional explanation, in other words, obscures the real power of Raymond's writings, which derives from human agency (i.e., that free individuals determine the validity criteria for political association) in the process of legitimating the state and perpetuating the conditions for continued accumulation.

To be certain, Raymond's theory does not hide its economic conditioning, but it goes beyond economics. Through a complex interaction of religious and secular concerns, Raymond helps to systematize a political discourse that attempts to reconcile precapitalist relationships with capitalist growth, and particular interests with the general welfare. While Raymond perceives the antagonism between precapitalist and capitalist interests, his definition of economics in terms of individual freedom, perpetuated through state intervention, permits the antagonists to recognize one another's rights and to entertain Raymond's theory that would reconcile growth with the perpetuation of the independence of yeoman farmers and artisans. Since the state guarantees the conditions of freedom, the individual owes allegiance to it and is expected to subordinate personal interests to the general welfare. Thus, economic calculations, whether from an individual or national perspective, will not in themselves determine the efficacy of one policy or another; growth rates do not present the qualitative conditions for the good society.

In addition to constructing a language that mediates opposing economic forces through ethical-political concepts, Raymond's theory offers a safety valve should the predicted American utopia falter. His excuse would be the villainous planter class, which corrupts the state and leads to labor's degradation. Paradoxically, that degradation is in fact an inevitable consequence of the expanding home market which Raymond recommends and which is inimical to the plantation system. Yet in Raymond's system it is the planters who are the capitalist menace to the Republic, so an alliance of industrialists and independent laborers is not only reasonable but necessary if the planters refuse self-negation through manumission.

5. THOMAS RODERICK DEW *on*
Accommodating the Republic to History

As riches increase and accumulate in few hands; as luxury prevails in society; virtue will be in a greater degree considered as only a graceful appendage of wealth, and the tendency of things will be to depart from the republican standard. This is the real disposition of human nature: It is what, neither the honorable member nor myself can correct. It is a common misfortune, that awaits our state constitution, as well as others.—Alexander Hamilton, *Papers*

Pessimist Planters and Utopian Plain Republicans

During the period between the presidential election of 1824—when the second party system originated—and the election of 1848—which marked the demise of Whig/Democrat politics—the American System defined the terms of political discourse for the nation.[1] Its corporate definition of government and the interventionist character of its policy recommendations shaped the controversies and the national elections of the twenty-four-year period. Yet despite its influence in the Whig Party, the American System never dominated, nor did any of its advocates become president except John Quincy Adams. And, it was his presidency that initiated the opposition to the American System in party politics.

Opposition coalesced around Andrew Jackson, whose laissez-faire politics blocked the interventionist recommendations of the American System and who temporarily succeeded in forging an alliance between—in Van Buren's terms—the Planters and the Plain Republicans. But the pragmatic ideological evasions that favored the alliance could not continue to bind the nation indefinitely, especially after Jackson dismantled the Bank of the United States and alienated states' rights advocates by vigorously opposing nullification. The dissenting sectors, on whom Jackson had relied, formed an unlikely alliance of planters, American System sympathizers, and "Plain Republicans" in the Whig coalition of 1834.[2]

Because of its disparate interests, the coalition politics of the Whigs was especially inhospitable to its own American System leadership. In contrast, the Democratic Party's principles of laissez-faire were theoretically congruent with the particularist demands of coalition politics which interpreted "consolidation" as special privilege for a new aristocracy of money and/or industry.[3] Despite the Democrats' noninterventionist policy, nationalism was an important force in their party; like its antagonist the Whig Party, the Democratic Party accepted the notion of American exceptionalism and of the nation's historic mission.[4]

Although the Jacksonian alliance successfully curtailed the implementation of American System recommendations during the 1830s and 1840s, the coalition of Planters and Plain Republicans splintered in the election of 1848 and finally collapsed as a national party in the election of 1860.[5] While generally accepting the rhetoric of laissez-faire economics, the Plain Republicans in the North never adopted the pessimism inherent in classical political economy and in the thought of the South, because they believed that America's unique institutions and its abundance of land would prevent the formation of a privileged, decadent aristocracy and of a propertyless, depraved laboring class.

This sort of political optimism was manifested in the radical wing of the Jacksonian movement, which developed utopian schemes—whether of land redistribution or taxes or inheritance—in an attempt to preserve the independence of labor while the production of limitless wealth continued unhampered.[6] For the mainstream Plain Republicans, deliberate economic theory was replaced by a naive faith in the independent producer and a hope that corrupt forces that selfishly manipulated the state could be subdued.[7] To be sure, the state was manipulated at times to further particular interests in the Jacksonian coalition (internal improvements and a tariff), but these measures were discreet and never amounted to a systematic program for the development of the economy. Systematic change favorable to capitalist development did occur within the American legal system, but since this transformation remained outside politics, its effects did not immediately threaten the Jacksonian coalition.[8]

The Planters did not enjoy the same blithe faith in the inevitability of American progress. They, along with free-trade Northern mercantile interests, developed a rather rigorous position on economic theory, for the most part adopting the terms and often the conclusions of classical political economy. Alterations were unavoidable since the United States lacked a landed aristocracy, but the classical definition of a natural society and its economic dynamism pervaded the Southern literature. Thus, the Planters differed from their Northern allies and from the American System over the survival of yeomanry; the Planters scoffed at the idea. For them, a working class was an inevitable component of a natural economic order. Therefore, in the Planters' theory universal white manhood suffrage and majority rule (the keystone of Jacksonian nationalism) were problematic for the propertied classes.[9] Furthermore, the Planters saw the left of the Jacksonian movement as supportive of agrarianism and correctly sensed the antislavery tendencies among Northern Democrats.[10]

Because of their projections for economic and social development, the Planters' interpretation of constitutional rule differed fundamentally from that of their Northern allies in the Jacksonian coalition. Their differences sharpened during the nullification controversy of 1832, temporarily splitting the Democratic Party, and the nation in general, along sectional lines.[11] For the Planters, the constitutional question was in fact a class question, since class mediated their conception of economic development and constitutional rule. Calhoun's writings attest to the Planters' conscious association of class and constitutional rights. According to Calhoun, the process of capitalist accumulation would eventually transform the United States citizenry into two antagonistic classes: a propertyless majority and a propertied minority.[12] He viewed this development as pernicious to the republican character of American politics since the majority could legislate against the propertied minority. As a result, he believed that a natural unity existed between Northern and Southern propertied classes. In fact, he believed that Northern property owners should advocate nullification because it provided the minority with the only true constitutional check against the tyranny of the majority. Consequently, Calhoun could warn the Northern property owners that their endorsement of abolitionist demands was actually an endorsement of majoritarian tyranny, for if the abolitionists could legislate against the property rights of the Southern slave owners, a majority could eventually outlaw private property altogether. From this perspective slavery became the immediate issue historically, while theoretically it assumed secondary consideration as only one particular form of property.

Many Northerners viewed Calhoun's basis for national unity with scepticism, for they failed to see how the right to private property (i.e., in things and animals) could be extended to human beings. Didn't the human will, or spirit, represent the dividing line that separated human beings from the realm of material objects to be owned by others? Although these critiques pointed to a fundamental fallacy in Calhoun's reasoning, he did not believe that his proposal for an alliance of Northern and Southern property owners was based on a fraud. Throughout the period Southern thinkers, particularly those who followed classical political economy, had offered theoretical justifications for black chattel slavery. By developing racial theories which legitimated the hierarchy of paternalism on the Southern plantation, these thinkers attempted to demonstrate the compatibility of black chattel slavery and freedom. Their success was of course flawed, whether examined in economic, political, or legal terms, but these deficiencies only posed intellectual ambiguities for which Southerners sought solutions.

Even if important sectors in the North had accepted the right to hold human beings in property, Calhoun's plan for national unity could not overcome the differences arising from the sectional institution of slavery, which effectively prohibited a unified vision of national development. Slavery undermined the South's integration into the emerging national home market—although not because the slave system was inimical to commercial expansion. On the contrary, slavery was commercial, and the South's commitment to commercial activity was evident both in the Old South and in the New South. While fostering paternalism and while legally justified by racism, slavery was nonetheless viewed as a profit-maximizing institution comparable in that respect to English wage labor.

Free white labor in the South was another issue that fueled the sectional conflict. Following the logic of classical political economy, the Planters perceived the yeomen farmers as problematic to the republic, unlike Northern thinkers who viewed them as the foundation of the republic. If the Southern economy followed a natural course of development according to free-trade principles, some yeomen would pursue commercial gain and compete with the established slave owners or even challenge the economic viability of the slavocracy. The majority of the yeomen would lose their property in the increasing competition and become a degraded laboring class.[13] However, the Southern economy could not develop naturally in terms of classical political economy because slavery inhibited the division of labor and the formation of a home market. Large sectors of the Southern yeomanry remained "subsistence" farmers susceptible—so the Planters believed—to agrarianism and to abolitionism.[14]

During the 1820s and the early 1830s the democratic demands of the Southern yeomanry in the Old and New South threatened the economic and political hegemony of the "aristocratic" seaboard planters. The Planters' fears of democracy seemed well founded when, in the aftermath of the Nat Turner rebellion, yeomen from western Virginia forced the legislature to debate the future of slavery. For these reasons, the Planters could perceive the yeomen as a more imminent danger than the Northern opposition or even than the slaves themselves. But the Planters could not entirely disassociate their interests from those of the yeomen in order to effectively participate in national political parties and to maintain regional stability.[15] Indeed, the maintenance of the Planter/Plain Republican alliance depended on continued support from the yeomen.

Opposition to a tariff and commitment to cheap western lands were fundamental to the Planter/Plain Republican alliance.[16] These attitudes were conceived of either as a means by which to shield independent labor from the corrosive effects of time, i.e., capitalist development, or as the proper course by which the nation would eventually be transformed into an industrial power. Yet the demands of national politics and the fears of majoritarian rule created sharp divisions within the Jacksonian coalition.

The Jacksonian leadership endorsed the Tariff of 1828 in order to guarantee a coalition of sufficient strength to send Jackson to the White House.[17] But the price was a major crisis in the coalition and in the nation, for it caused South Carolina to exercise states' rights and nullify the "Tariff of Abominations."

A commitment to cheap lands was complicated by conflicting interests. The apparent universality of the appeal to Western yeomen and Southern planters did not convince many for very long. The illusion was dispelled when the specific components of the protariff strategy were understood. Defenders of the tariff would support cheap western lands as long as a distribution clause was included in any legislation.[18] The immediate effects would be advantageous to state governments because revenues from the sale of lands would be redirected from the federal treasury into the state coffers. The impoverished federal government would have little choice but to institute a tariff.

For Plain Republicans and Planters, for the West and the South, the issue of the tariff acquired different meanings. Since Western interests conceived of the tariff as merely an economic question, they could support a distribution plan and a subsequent tariff as long as the benefits outweighed the costs.[19] The South, however, interpreted the tariff issue more broadly. As a result of the debate on the Missouri Compromise, the Denmark Vesey conspiracy, the Negro Seaman controversy, the Ohio resolution for emancipation, and the appearance of radical abolitionism, the Planters began to perceive a constitutional threat to slavery. Majoritarian rule—a concept of a general welfare—offered the possibility of a national coalition which could attack the South's peculiar institution.[20] Consequently, the South interpreted the tariff as the first stage of a process whose ultimate result would be the abolition of privilege.

Such fears were not only consistent with the peculiarity of the South's slave property but were also inherent in its theoretical stance, which predicted both the inevitable rise of a propertyless class and the excesses of democracy. Thus, the tariff became transformed from an economic to a political-constitutional issue in the minds of the Southern planters. Despite the support of many Southerners for western expansion, cheap lands, and even a homestead policy in the 1850s, the South consistently found itself unable to support land legislation advocated by the yeoman wing because such legislation violated constitutional principles vital to Southern interests—that is, slavery—and to national interests—that is, the preservation of private property.[21]

While the Southern conception of national development is evident in the debates within Jacksonian democracy, the body of theory that informed the South's position cannot adequately be reconstructed from these debates. Rather, the body of theory necessary for understanding the South is developed in the texts in political economy. Despite the particular party allegiance of their authors, the treatises establish the parameters of Southern discourse and indicate the dilemmas that the advocates of slavery confronted in attempting to realize their vision of American republicanism. Thomas R. Dew's critique of the American System and his response to Southern critiques of slavery pushed the elements of proslavery thought to their logical limits and consequently indicated the contradictory foundations of Southern life.

Thomas Dew: Defender of the Republic

In the summer of 1836, the William and Mary Board of Visitors chose Thomas Roderick Dew to succeed Adam Empie as president of the college. Dew, only thirty-three years old, was already the senior professor of the college with years of service and had distinguished himself both as a scholar and a spokesman for Southern interests. His inaugural address was a display of erudition and dedication to Southern institutions and political sentiment. In that address, later published in the *Southern Literary Messenger*, Dew argued that slavery was more than compatible with the ideals of the American Revolution; it was virtually indispensable to their realization. For this reason, Dew could assert that the future slaveholders in his audience bore a considerable responsibility in plotting the future of republicanism. The years spent at William and Mary were to train them in the intellectual skills needed in fulfilling that historic duty.[22]

Dew's conclusion concerning the peculiarity of his native region did not derive solely from academic investigation,[23] but also from participation in public life. His debut was at the Charlottesville Convention, which was concerned with promoting statewide internal improvements, where he was instrumental in drafting the first position paper. Three years later he attended the Free Trade Convention in Philadelphia as a Virginia delegate. Although Dew collaborated on the report of the convention, he found it necessary to submit, with Chancellor Harper of South Carolina, a more radical memorial to Congress. The Nat Turner rebellion and the subsequent debate on slavery in the Virginia legislature interrupted his preoccupation with the tariff and resulted in his writing the South's classic defense of slavery. In the years directly preceding his presidential appointment at William and Mary, Dew engaged in polemics concerning national banking policy and continued working to promote internal improvements in Virginia. In later years Dew became associated with the Whig Party, partially because of family ties and his dislike for Van Buren's treasury plan; yet like many other Southern Whigs, his philippics against the protective tariff and majority rule were not blunted by his contact with the Clay party.[24] He defended his notion of the American republic until his early death in 1846.

The Tariff Controversy: Economics as Social Reproduction

Dew's baptism into sectional politics took place in the fire of the tariff controversy. The conflict over a restrictive system posed questions similar to those of the English Corn Law debates, with which Dew was familiar. Both debates marked a transition from commercial to industrial capitalism. In England, the controversy ostensibly focused on the effects of the Corn Laws on distribution. In fact, the debates attempted to define the proper relationship of each class to the accumulation process and to the state.

Similarly, the immediate concern of the tariff debates from 1819 to 1848 was the effect of the restrictive system on distribution.[25] Yet the technical arguments that were devised to show either a positive or negative result from the protective tariff did not remain confined to questions of distribution. The contemporary treatises on political economy established a discourse and sought to ground technical arguments in a concept of the natural economic order. Identifying the elements of that order, the consequent laws of development, and the proper organization of political life, as well as the true relationship between the state and the economy, became the treatises' extended intellectual terrain.

The Corn Law and tariff debates can, in fact, be identified as nodal points of conflict between the contending dominant classes as England and America moved in their respective paths from a preindustrial to an industrial capitalist order. However, the shared generalities concerning the characteristics of these transformations, whether conceived from the vantage point of economics, politics, or ideology, give way to differentiating specifics as the developments are considered in their historic settings. Although England and the United States had a common intellectual tradition emphasizing the establishment of "natural" elements in the construction of theory, the particular features of these nations determined the specific content of that tradition as each developed it, creating a series of contrasts between the debates on the Corn Laws and those on the tariff.

Despite the apparent precapitalist character of the English landlords, the debate over the Corn Laws openly sought capital's most conducive path of development. To be sure, aristocracy persisted in securing its monopoly on land through laws inconsistent with the abstract laws of capitalist development. Yet the aristocracy itself was tied directly to the capitalist accumulation process, for its rent was dependent on the dynamism of that process. Consequently, though the landlords stood outside capital's circuit, their monopoly on land made it possible for them to secure a portion of the surplus accrued in that circulation process.[26] For this reason, a solid defense of the aristocracy and its Corn Laws had to be constructed in terms consistent with capitalist accumulation. Malthus, among others, assumed this task. By viewing rents as a natural surplus, Malthus could argue that the landlord's nonproductive consumption habits were the actual source of capitalist profits so that the Corn Laws and the landlord class were the pivotal elements in the process of accumulation. Ricardo, the foremost theoretician of capitalist production, challenged that conception, arguing that the landlords' wealth, inflated by means of the Corn Laws, had a harmful effect on the capitalists' profits and, consequently, on economic growth. For this reason, Ricardo condemned the Corn Laws and advocated free trade. While the precise effects of rents were questions in the course of the Malthus-Ricardo controversies, the opponents agreed that the natural order was composed of three classes—the capitalist, landlord, and working classes. Disagreement continued on the proper means of dealing politically and ideologically with the working class, which represented for Malthus and Ricardo degraded humanity capable of irrational behavior. But here again, while political economy could not agree on a political formula for including the working class in the nation, the basic parameters of the problem were accepted by both sides of the debate.

This was not the case in the United States. Although Northern "industrialists" and Southern "planters" espoused the notions of the commercial nature of the human being and the republican ideals of the revolution, they could not agree on the elements of a natural order, on the foundations of a republican government, and on the proper role of the state. The Northern "manufacturers" did not adopt a free-trade outlook, as did their English counterparts. America's relative "underdevelopment" compared to England, as well as its scarcity of labor, prompted the incipient industrialists to advocate a protective tariff rather than free trade. But their dissent from the English tradition went further as the economic demand became systematized in Northern protectionist theory.

Daniel Raymond, the inspired founder of the American school of economics, constructed a political economy that promoted wealth while preserving independent labor. He believed that the resolution of the contradiction between limitless wealth and the continued presence of a propertied laboring class could be effected by means of the state. Protection, internal improvements, a central bank, etc. became measures which assured the preservation of yeoman and artisan laboring class that created the foundations of the American republic. Under these conditions majority rule could be synonymous with constitutional rule. In fact, it was not the working class which would become the principal danger to the natural order for Raymond, but rather the capitalist class whose Ahab-like drive could distort the balance in economic and political life.

As if to make the inversion of the Corn Law debates complete in the United States, Dew adopted Ricardo's proindustrial system to combat the restrictive policies that the English landed gentry favored. In so doing, he accepted two important propositions: (1) that the natural order is indeed composed of capitalist, landlord, and working classes and (2) that agriculture itself has no special role in the accumulation process. An attack on the protective system from such premises did not need to replace the capitalists as the dynamic class in a theory, as Malthus's attack did. To defend laissez-faire, Dew had to demonstrate its advantages over restrictions to natural economic growth.

The espousal of free-trade theory may not seem appropriate for the slave South's most articulate spokesman. Yet it is a conception consistent with the Scottish Enlightenment tradition that informed Dew's thought and so much of the general intellectual life of the South.[27] Freed from the artificial constraints of feudal Europe, planters and yeomen could pursue the "natural" inclination to truck, trade, and barter. For this reason, Dew could consider the laws of classical political economy applicable to America and equate the pursuits of yeomen and planters with those of mature capitalists.

Reconciling a tradition which claims that human freedom is the logical end of historical development with a social system which in practice denies freedom forces Dew into logical inconsistencies from which he desperately attempts to escape. Dew's theory futilely attempts to resolve the antagonisms introduced by the contradictory tendencies between the precapitalist and capitalist aspects of the South. Although he recognizes black slavery's economic limitations, he insists that slavery is advisable in the modern world because it can offer a reasonable solution to the inevitable conflicts between propertied and propertyless classes.

Proceeding from the abstract principles of classical political economy and his conviction that the United States is in fact a natural economy, Dew explains its agrarian character by its abundant supply of land. Dew reasons that, as accumulation proceeds, population will increase, making land scarce and creating the three-tier class structure of an advanced society. In the interim, yeoman and planter classes will dominate. These will not hamper economic development, but they represent a temporary form required because of the peculiar circumstances of American settlement.

But such an abstract analysis becomes unmanageable when Dew addresses the specific questions of slavery and republican government in a mature economy. In his *Lectures on the Restrictive System*, Dew is not immediately concerned with slavery; his analysis of that institution comes in response to Virginia abolitionists. Dew finds that while the planter pursues limitless wealth, the master-slave relationship actually inhibits the full development of capitalist accumulation. In this respect, slavery retards historical progress. However, Dew can remold this retrogressive feature of slavery into a positive feature of his political analysis.

He has to agree with the American school that an agrarian stage of development resolves the political conflicts inherent in capitalist production. In his estimation, this resolution is temporary; time will reshape the American economy, altering the agrarian classes into capitalists and workers. Ricardo's principles about a deadly conflict over scarce resources will then be applicable to America. The final outcome will be decay and social retrogression, hardly a propitious situation for Dew's ideal of democratic republicanism. The solutions offered by Raymond are of course rejected since they are utopian; likewise, Dew rejects the English utilitarian solution because it relies too heavily on the virtuous behavior of an unvirtuous class.[28]

Instead, Dew seeks a resolution to the problem in legal constitutional checks against majority rule and in slavery itself. Slavery possesses two properties that can neutralize the politically corrosive effects of economic development: it excludes black laborers from the political community while racism fosters an identity between the masters and the free laboring classes. As the rate of profit plunges society into economic decay, slavery can have yet another positive effect: that of ensuring employment. As Dew recognizes, slavery need not be a capitalist relationship, so as profits diminish, the masters will not refuse to engage their slaves in the production of the means of subsistence. Under the conditions of decay, therefore, slavery becomes a solution to both the problem of economic motivation and that of political conflict, as long as slavery is extended to the entire working class. Slavery cannot revitalize the economy, but it can halt its social decay.

Thus, like Raymond, Dew raises the precapitalist relationship peculiar to his region to a theoretical element of the "natural" order. And like Raymond, he thereby creates theoretical ambiguities that could not be easily resolved. In this regard, the U.S. debate on the transition from preindustrial to industrial capitalism differs from England's. In England the working class has already been formed and recognized, and so has the need to be incorporated into appropriate political and ideological structures. The Malthus-Ricardo debates testify to that concern. On the other hand, while the United States is committed to production for limitless wealth, it has not yet developed a recognizable working class. For the accumulation process to mature into a fully capitalist economy, it is necessary to dispossess the laboring classes of the means of production. This process will itself be protracted, but both Raymond and Dew see it as inimical to the republic. Hence their efforts to reconcile the precapitalist relationships of their respective sections in order to avert the recognizable danger of the working class.

Free Trade: National Wealth at the Expense of Independent Labor

Dew's *Lectures on the Restrictive System* is divided into four parts. The first describes the development of political economy and establishes the true principles of the subject. The second examines the erroneous arguments of the protective system. The third considers the subject of protection in relation to "morals, health, happiness, and politics." And the fourth attempts to explain the continued success of the protectionist argument despite its obvious fallacies. As this organization indicates, Dew's method is systematic and his argument is carefully considered, unlike the polemical treatises of other Southerners, most notably Thomas Cooper's *Principles of Political Economy*.[29]

Dew turns to Ricardo's theory of trade for a defense of laissez-faire's positive effect on national development. According to Ricardo, labor time is the determining element in the cost of production. Since Ricardo assumes that capital and labor do not move across national boundaries, wages and profits are not equalized internationally. Consequently, international trade is not predicated on differences in value or price between two nations but instead on a comparison of the labor time required to produce commodities within a nation.[30] Dew offers an example to demonstrate Ricardo's principle: Virginia is well suited for the production of tobacco and wheat, while South Carolina has a climate and soil conducive to growing corn and rice. A farmer laboring in Virginia can produce as much tobacco and wheat in one day as he could produce rice and corn in two. The opposite situation prevails in South Carolina, so the two states find it advantageous to engage in trade; it enables both to acquire more goods with less labor as measured by their own standards of labor time.

Dew extended this principle to trade between the United States and Great Britain, in which American agricultural goods are exchanged for English manufactured products. There is one alteration, however.[31] America's comparative advantage in agricultural production and Great Britain's advantage in manufacturing do not derive from geographic considerations, as in the Virginia–South Carolina example. Instead, social circumstance, or level of development, dictates each nation's specialization.

In an advanced society price consists of wages, profits, and rents. However, Ricardo's system permits Dew to argue that the cost of production is actually determined by the amount of capital employed on the least fertile land, with only wages and profits entering into cost. Corn produced on the least fertile land regulates agricultural prices, permitting the establishment of rents on the more fertile lands. The level of wages and profits set by production on the least fertile land also determines the wage and profit rates in manufacturing. If this were not the case, Dew notes, agriculture and manufacturing would have their own wage and profit rates.

Following Ricardo's assertion that, as society advances, less fertile lands are brought into production, Dew constructs a two-stage model of development for a nation assumed to be commercial—that is, free of any aristocratic privileges or monopolies which would prevent the market from operating naturally. In its first stage the nation is characterized by its colonial or agrarian status, so soil is abundant and population scarce. Since monopoly on land is impossible under these conditions, the entire proceeds of production belong to the workers and capitalists. Thus, wages and profits are high whether measured in corn or money, because there is no rent and only the most fertile land is in use. During this stage, Dew argues, capitalists can rapidly augment their capital, and workers can save since wages exceed subsistence. Soon a worker's savings become sufficient to allow the worker to purchase land and thereby become a capitalist. This rapid accumulation of capital spurs population growth, causing less fertile land to be cultivated. Eventually, land becomes scarce and a landlord class emerges, which claims a share of the total product as rent. Wages and profits necessarily fall. In Dew's theory, the relative share of the product which remains to be divided among the capitalists and the workers once rents are deducted depends on the supply of labor and capital and the demand for them. In the long run, however, Dew agrees with Ricardo that the rate of profit tends to fall and presages inevitable economic decay.

For Dew, this dynamic constitutes the movement from a colonial-agrarian state to an advanced state, as society divides into a rigid three-class system. Furthermore, investments shift from agriculture to manufacturing as the former becomes less profitable than the latter.

Through this dynamic model of a commercial nation's metamorphosis from the agrarian to the advanced stage, Dew can posit that it is better for an agrarian-colonial nation to import manufactured goods from an advanced nation since the prices are determined by low wages and profits; on the other side, it is advantageous to the manufacturing nation to import agricultural goods. With international trade, the price of agricultural products will be determined by the price of corn produced on the least fertile land in that country specialized in manufacturing, since the market in corn is international. However, the introduction of corn from an agrarian nation disrupts the existing equilibrium of supply and demand in the manufacturing nation. When a new equilibrium is established, the quality of land used in the advanced nation will have improved since less land need be cultivated. This cheapens the general price of corn, but still keeps it above the cost of production in the agrarian society. In this way the agrarian nation actually receives the displaced rent, which is distributed among its capitalists and workers in the absence of a national landlord class. Under these favorable conditions, population in the agricultural nation will rapidly advance, and land will become scarce. A landlord class will in turn emerge as wages and profits fall. Under these new conditions, domestic manufacturing will develop and ultimately be competitive with foreign industry. When the agrarian-colonial nation becomes advanced, natural differences in the climate, the soil, the supply of raw materials, water power, etc. will determine the comparative advantage of each nation in producing specific agricultural and manufactured commodities.

Dew's elaboration of Ricardo's theory suggests differences in intention and further illustrates the historical specificity of their respective nations' transitions to industrial capital. Ricardo's theory of comparative advantage, as developed in his *Principles*, not only functions as a general justification for free trade but also offers a practical though temporary solution to the falling rate of profit which plagues the mature economy. By means of free trade, an advanced society may cheapen the price of its foodstuffs, thereby reducing the value of wages and bolstering profits. Armed with these notions, Ricardo launches his assault on the English Corn Laws, which he feels restrict the importation of grains and fatten the landlord class at the expense of continued capitalist accumulation.

The central problem facing Dew is not that of a mature economy, but that of establishing the most advantageous program for the development of an agrarian economy. Dew's theory has to demonstrate that free trade would most efficiently transform an agrarian-colonial nation into a manufacturing nation. Ricardo's theory of comparative advantage does not account for the transforming mechanisms. In fact, it can be argued from Ricardo's theory that an agrarian nation does not necessarily diversify if it does not have the necessary capital—that is, the productive resources—by which to make the transition.[32] In other words, the international division of labor based on comparative advantage does not ensure that each nation will develop into a mature economy. Because Dew believed in the inevitability and the desirability of an advanced economy, he is forced to extend the notion of comparative advantage.

Dew's two-stage model implies several other important features of his thought. In making an analytic division between an agrarian-colonial state and an advanced state, Dew accepts the formation of a three-class society. In this respect, Dew concurs with Smith and dissents from the Northern protectionists. Dew's intellectual universe, in fact, is fundamentally drawn from Smith. Even when Dew defends slavery—as discussed later—he employs, ironically, concepts developed by Smith, who condemns slavery.

The notion of a natural course of development from agriculture stemmed directly from Smith's discussion of the transition of European society from feudalism to modern commercialism. Smith uses this theory of natural development against the mercantilist policies, which favor monopolies and restrictive trade legislation to prematurely promote manufacturing over agriculture. Like Smith, Dew argues that a natural course of development exists, but, unlike Smith, he rejects the idea that agriculture is inherently more productive than manufacturing by adopting the Ricardian notion that rents do not represent a natural surplus. But the exception to Smith is only a technical one. Dew accepts Smith's "natural" course of development and the efficacy of free trade. The advanced state, therefore, represents in Dew's theory, as in Smith's, a truly "free" realm where the individual and society are in harmonious relationship.

Seen from this perspective, a restrictionist policy can only stunt a nation's natural development. Dew attacks the protectionist policy by countering the arguments used to justify it. Employing the two-stage theory of growth and international trade, Dew argues against restrictionist claims that a tariff will increase the home market, improve existing technology, guarantee national independence, reduce business cycles, and function as a general panacea for a stagnant economy. On the contrary, Dew contends, the tariff benefits one class, the manufacturers, at the expense of the nation. Citing Smith's critique of the mercantilist system, Dew argues that a tariff cannot increase a nation's capital, as the protectionists claim, but can only redistribute it from the unprotected to the protected industries. The favored industries can raise the cost of production above the world market price for their commodities, so the community subsidizes the protected industries.[33]

Dew applies this analysis of the class bias in protectionist policy to its differential effects on sections. While he admits some controversy on the subject, he believes that in a large country, such as the United States, a tariff will exacerbate uneven development among regions. Dew notes that such factors as familial ties and regional loyalties retard the movement of capital and labor across geographic sections. Consequently, unequal wages and profits in the United States create different regional rates of growth. Certain northeastern sections are more advanced—that is, they have lower wages and profits—than those in the southwest and northwest, so there is a tendency for population to move to the West, where wages and profits are high. A tariff protecting northeastern manufacturers would maintain high wages and profits in that region, curtailing migration to the West. Thus, the advanced sector would experience unnatural growth, in which wages and profits would be high despite the dense population, while the agrarian sectors would remain stagnant despite their favorable economic conditions.[34] Instead, Dew affirms the desirability of free trade, which permits rapid growth benefiting all the sections and classes equally.[35]

Dew, therefore, does not consider the protectionist promise for preserving independent labor while promoting production for limitless wealth to be utopian but merely selfish. He believes that the Northern protectionists could indeed have their way if the South would be sacrificed. In exposing the sectional bias of his Northern counterparts, Dew offered to the South and West, to the planter and yeoman, an alternate policy designed to further their interests. However, that promise also predicted inevitable doom since the advanced state transformed the citizens into capitalists, landlords, or workers.

The Natural Order: Self-interest as Virtue

Although Dew interprets the economic consequences of the restrictive system to be "unnatural," he does not attribute the legislation of the tariff to a malignancy in the economy or to a poorly designed political system. In Dew's opinion the American Revolution erected a political structure adequate to the preservation of wholesome economic conditions. The revolution further cemented the legal egalitarianism of the republic through the Constitution, which invests sovereignty in the people and which is designed with a system of constitutional checks to prevent tyranny. Despite this republican foundation, it appears to Dew—and to the South in general—that monopolies and their oppressive consequences have been introduced by the Tariff of Abominations.

Dew can explain this economic and political aberration only through the fundamental antagonism in his conception of the natural order, whether expressed in the terms of laissez-faire economics or of the political science of the American republic: individual freedom can indeed result in the oppression of some individuals by others. This contradiction defines for Dew, as well as for classical political economists in general, the political dilemma of their contemporary world. For them, the purpose of economic activity—and of history itself—is the achievement of individual freedom. It can be realized only in the advanced stage of history. This conclusion derives from the assumption in classical political economy that the human being is naturally propelled into commercial activity. In the process of production, exchange, and accumulation, human beings both concretize their individuality and realize their relationship to others as social beings. The individual interacts with nature through the labor process and creates a product which becomes a commodity through exchange. Thus, the individual commodity owner confronts a universe of commodity owners whose individuality is established through the specific qualities of their products. In the interaction, individuals assert their freedom, since they can exchange the products of their labor for any other commodity they wish. Individuals find themselves free and equal "citizens" in a world of commodity production and exchange. Furthermore, as human beings are by nature acquisitive, they realize their limitless potentiality as producers.

This structure of freedom creates a dichotomy between private and public interests. Commodity owners enter into exchange relationships in order to satisfy their private needs and desires and so deny the possibility of establishing any truly common interest.[36] Smith attempts to resolve this dilemma by positing the hypothesis of the invisible hand, which converts private interest into social good. The market forces commodity producers to operate efficiently by lowering prices and thereby augmenting the wealth of the nation. This transformation of private interest into social welfare can only occur so long as each individual respects the rights of others—that is, respects the "natural" laws of the market. However, since individual gain motivates the economic agents, there is little reason to believe that the commodity owners will necessarily respect the rules of the marketplace. Dew formulates this problem in the terms of the classical tradition.

> But it may be asked, may not the interests of individuals be at war with each other? May it not be the interest of the blacksmith to make the shoemaker contribute to his gains? And may not the manufacturer be interested in making the farmer contribute to his gains? and vice versa. And in the same manner, may not individual interest be opposed to national interest? To this I answer, that our assertion always supposes fair play, and equal justice, to all parties.[37]

A war against all is prevented, according to Dew, when each member of society adheres to the rules of the marketplace. To ensure that adherence, Dew argues for the legal mechanisms of the state.

> Government is formed from necessity and mutual advantage. Without it, the strong man on all occasions would be tempted to oppress the weaker, and a combination of weaker would in turn oppress the stronger. Government is intended to remedy this individual oppression, and to defend the society from the aggression of foreign force.[38]

Therefore, the state establishes and perpetuates individual rights, including the right to property, and preserves the marketplace.

In his *Digest of the Laws, Customs, Manners and Institutions of the Ancient and Modern Nations*, published posthumously in 1852, Dew traces the development of subjective freedom from society's early and rude state to its advanced, commercial stage.[39] As in Smith's theory, Dew believes that the demise of the feudal manor, the liberation of the peasantry, and the expansion of commerce provided the conditions for humanity to freely pursue the passions and to construct a government premised only on self-preservation and inhospitable to monopolies. From this, Dew can justify the right to revolution in two situations: (1) when a government is not based on the joint agreement of individual producers, as under feudalism, and (2) when contractual government no longer fulfills its legitimate end, to preserve life. Thus, when Dew resorts to nature to justify his claims regarding legitimate rule, he does not refer to an original state of nature but to nature directly, since it dictates human beings to be social and the good society to be a system of rights that permits human beings to pursue their individual interests.

For this reason, Dew asserts that legislative acts should be negative in content; positive interventionist laws like those recommended by the American school benefit a particular economic interest. Dew specifically criticizes Raymond for granting the state a positive or corporate identity and for advocating legislation contrary to the natural free-market principle.

Dew's objections imply a political dimension to the contradiction between private and social interest. Given the acquisitiveness of human nature, what prevents those who govern from constituting a separate and oppressive interest, or a particular economic interest from gaining control of the state and using it for its own ends? This acquisitive nature may precipitate governmental abuses that have political as well as economic dimensions. For Dew, these are not academic questions; the Tariff of 1828 made them immediately relevant.

Republican Government: The Lawful Limits of Self-Interest

In order to curtail governmental abuses that derive from acquisitiveness, Dew appeals to republican political theory, since it defines good government as that government in which the interests of the individual and the state are identical. For Dew, this equation between ruler and ruled is the necessary solution of conflict.[40] In adopting republican theory, Dew draws particularly on the American variant, as developed through the drafting of the Constitution, which he feels has relinquished the classical ideal of immediately forging individual interest into the social good and creating, in the process, a truly civic human being.[41] Instead, American political science has converted the classical conception of self-interest from the irrational and corrosive force undermining republican governments to the elementary premise of political theory and practice.[42] The object of political theory becomes the construction of mechanisms which, on the one hand, will permit human beings to pursue their self-interest along lines consistent with natural law while, on the other hand, providing institutional structures or checks to prevent government from favoring some interests over others.[43] As the pursuit of self-interest becomes identified with proper conduct, the term "virtuous citizen" loses its meaning and is replaced by a "utilitarian" definition, providing the appropriate political focus for Dew's conception of the natural order.[44]

According to Dew, popular sovereignty constitutes the necessary, although not sufficient, condition for the resolution of the contradiction between ruler and ruled, between the interests of government and the interests of the people. Dew thus reaffirms the principles of the American Revolution and necessarily rejects the theory of constitutional monarchy as espoused and practiced in England, where sovereignty is assigned to a parliament that recognizes the feudal estates of monarchy, nobility, and people.[45] So long as a privileged regal or aristocratic entity is included in political sovereignty, Dew sees an inevitable contradiction between the government and the people, between the state and the natural economic order.[46] If, however, sovereignty is located exclusively in the people, government functions only as long as the people desire. Should the interests of the two diverge, the people retain the right to dismantle the government and reestablish another on principles conducive to their interests.[47]

Dew, like the founding fathers before him, breaks the substantive link between economic privilege and the functional aspects of government. For Dew, the conditions that create monarchic and aristocratic classes give them no inherent virtue or suitability to perform the functional duties of government. In fact, in Dew's theory the opposite is the case, since privilege, even if legitimate solely on political grounds, is inimical to the interests of the people. Thus, for Dew, the ideal government should be purely mechanical, functioning to articulate the people's will.[48] To strengthen the mutuality of interests between the ruler and the ruled, Dew endorses the election of public representatives. Through an electoral process, power is "lodged but a short time in the hands of the public agents, whose interests could never be separated from those of the society which they represent, and who are thus, too, made directly responsible for their conduct, and made for it as the bar of public opinion."[49]

In defining democracy as popular sovereignty and election of representatives, however, Dew does not overcome the federalist mistrust of unbridled majoritarian rule.[50] Electoral representation, a bicameral legislature, the indirect election of the upper house and the president, and the system of checks and balances among the branches of government are all assumed in Dew's theory as the means for selecting a talented minority to assume the more responsible roles of government. While Dew calls the hierarchy of the constitutional monarchy artificial, he defends a natural hierarchy based on degrees of talent that must be reflected in the structure of government. For this reason, Dew does not advocate democracy in its classical sense, where political rule is direct, or even in its radical contemporary sense, in which all social distinctions are leveled by the creation of a unicameral legislative body. Instead, Dew accepts the principal definition of the founding fathers, which conceives of politics in terms of minority and majority rights.

But preventive mechanisms like those in the United States government, he goes on to say, are not always sufficient to avert the manipulation of government by a particular interest emerging from the people. Thereby, the government's legitimacy is abrogated, or in Calhoun's language, constitutional rule becomes absolute rule. Dew describes this kind of abuse in the traditional language of minority and majority political constituents.

Majority versus Minority Rights: Fair Play among Capitalists

In addition to representation and a system of checks and balances, Dew proposes majoritarian rule in the legislature to counter tyranny by the few. But this circumvention itself bares a new difficulty. Coalitions can form a majority which may oppress a minority economic interest:

> But even here [in a democratic republic] great dangers appear: the majority, on all occasions rule, and they frequently have interests opposed to the interests of the minority, and whenever the former is without control, abuses will arise; man will be governed by his interest. The majority will oppress the minority, and perhaps such oppression may be even worse than the oppression which arises under a monarchical government.[51]

By stating the problem in this fashion, Dew denies that the general welfare can be conceived of in terms of simple majority rule and argues for a definition in terms of countervailing forces in which individual interests are not sacrificed for some notion of a higher good.

Dew's illustration of the political dangers associated with the rule of the majority is the tariff, which he feels must be abolished to preserve the republic. This issue brings up a new qualification to the problem of majority and minority rights. Because of the geographic size of the United States, Dew argues that legislative majorities may be formed on the basis of sectional alliances which can push through laws that may oppress the minority section. This clearly disrupts the equivalency between ruler and ruled, since the rulers may enact laws from which they are exempt for practical purposes.

According to Dew, the Tariff of Abominations is the work of just such a sectional coalition of diverse interests which has forged a majority. Through "artificial combination," Dew believes these interests have devised a plan in which the losses sustained will be more than compensated by the gains appropriated from the minority. Although the majority benefits, Dew calls attention to the oppression of the significant minority living in the district of country "stretching along the Atlantic frontier, from the Chesapeake to the Gulf of Mexico, and reaching far into the interior."[52]

Majoritarian abuse can be contained, according to Dew, by states' rights, originally constructed by the founding fathers to resolve difficulties in the federalist and antifederalist debates on the Constitution.[53] Dew's interpretation of the states' rights doctrine combines both the antifederalist fear of consolidation and the federalist desire to protect minority rights. The United States Constitution, in Dew's opinion, derives its power from the people through the ratifying conventions of the states, which are the direct representatives of the people's will.

As a handmaid to the states, the federal government fulfills essential functions in the preservation of republicanism in North America by coordinating economic activity in a large geographic area and by maintaining a national army to prevent interstate rivalries from turning into serious conflicts that would make republicanism impossible.[54] However, Dew maintains that the federal government's power to intervene in local matters should be restricted. In this way he restates his defense of individual rights over majority rule in a broader context of state versus federal authority.

The illegitimate use of power by the federal government is described in antifederalist terms as consolidation, even though the usurpation of power is by a majority rather than an aristocratic minority. When the federal government exceeds its legitimate power and subsequently oppresses a state or section of the nation, the injured state or states, according to Dew, must demand redress. Should the appropriate channels prove ineffective, Dew proclaims that the states must assert their rights—if necessary, by secession.[55]

Majority versus Minority Rights: The Limits of Fairness

The dichotomy between the propertied and propertyless classes further complicates the issue of majority versus minority rights. For classical political economists, the concentration of the means of production is both just and rational since it allegedly results from differing talents and increases national wealth. Smith argues that it is rational for the working class to accept its subordinate position because the advanced stage offers the laboring population an improved standard of living when compared to previous periods. Ricardo and Malthus likewise argue that the increased productivity of capitalist society sets the basis for the political obligation of the working class, even though they are more pessimistic regarding the limits of growth. The difficulty, according to the English economists, is that the division of labor, which increases a nation's wealth, stunts the rational development of the working class and makes it possible for the working class to act in ways that are not in its best interest. Hence, the dilemma over the political role of the working class.

The rapid emergence of democratic—i.e., universal white male—suffrage in the U.S. compounded Dew's theoretical problems. The democratic movements of the 1820s and 1830s sought state constitutional and electoral reforms that were to lead to the world's first mass democratic party system. Dew concedes to these forces reluctantly by pointing to the potential danger than an enfranchised working class presents to a propertied minority. He foresees this as a major problem when the United States becomes a mature society. However, Dew does not develop a cogent constitutional argument to check the working class, since it remains a distant problem. But his suggestions for circumventing the immediate threat of majoritarian tyranny are applicable to the problem of the working class.

Dew appears to substitute sectional for class conflict as the inherent antagonism in American society. That substitution, however, arises from the historical contingency of America's vastness that results in geographic and climatic differences among state governments. Dew's general concepts convert those geographic differences into economic antagonisms and lead him to accept federation as a method of avoiding sectional conflicts.

Geography and climate create a natural economic division of labor, which creates competitive regions. For this reason, Dew associates states' rights with minority economic rights in his attempt to preserve the South's economic interests against the encroachment of a legislative majority. In fact, Dew derives the right to secession from the fundamental right of an oppressed economic minority to withdraw from the conditions of government.[56]

Since Dew's argument for states' rights depends principally on economic notions, it may be logically applied to majority versus minority rights, the ultimate contradiction during the advanced stage. Unlike the tariff controversy, in which propertied economic interests contend against one another, in the advanced stage propertied and propertyless classes conflict. According to Dew, as a result of the national division of labor, this conflict has emerged more rapidly in the Northern manufacturing areas; states' rights will offset any political gains the Northern working class might make which could have national impact. However, states' rights can be only a temporary strategy because of the inevitability of economic progress in Dew's schema. Eventually a working class will emerge in each region and nullify states' rights as a constitutional check against the will of a propertyless majority.

The South would have to wait until Calhoun's conception of the concurrent majority for a political theory which proceeded consistently and effectively from minority rights to constitutional checks. The concurrent majority would be more than a mere numerical coalition; it would give interest groups and/or sections the right to veto legislation that they found prejudicial. While Dew failed to establish a legal restraint on the potential power of the working class, he did pose the problem clearly and did find a check outside of the legal framework of constitutional rule. That check was chattel slavery based on race.

Free Trade's Bittersweet Promise

Dew's line of reasoning follows a crooked path. He begins by arguing that free-trade policy will economically liberate agrarian interests from an economically and politically oppressive tariff. Yet in Dew's theory, free-trade policy finally promises the forfeit of agrarian and artisanal property into the hands of landlords and capitalists and presages the tyranny of a propertyless majority in the advanced stage.

Consequently, in the last chapter of the *Lectures* Dew makes a conservative defense of the agrarian stage as more conducive than advanced commercialism to a nation's well-being, since the equitable distribution of property in agrarianism unifies society by an organic bond that bridges social differences and eases political tensions. In comparing the agrarian stage to the commercial stage, Dew discusses each stage as two discrete societies and thus contradicts his original contention that each is a phase of commercial development. His confusion may result from the partisan demand of cementing a coalition of agrarian interests in opposition to the manufacturers' interests.

He does this by abstracting from the dynamics of the process and by solely focusing on the laborer's relationship to the means of production in each stage. Within this framework, Dew could agree even with Raymond's claim that the issue of property rights poses no fundamental problem so long as society remains in the agrarian stage. Why would a propertied majority universally abolish private property? Yet even this ambivalence does not dissuade him that the transition to the advanced stage is an economic necessity which conforms to nature's moral order. It is no wonder he was less optimistic than the utopian Raymond.

6. THOMAS RODERICK DEW *on Black Slavery as the Republic's Check on the Working Class*

When a majority is included in a faction the form of popular government, on the other hand, enables it to sacrifice to its ruling passion or interest both the public good and the rights of other citizens. To secure the public good and private rights against the danger of such a faction, and at the same time to preserve the spirit and the form of popular government, is then the great object to which the inquiries are directed.—James Madison, *The Federalist Papers*

Abolitionism at Home

As an economic question, the protective tariff did not immediately challenge the efficacy of Southern slavery. From the planters' point of view, the tariff oppressed them not as slave owners but rather as agricultural producers; this helps explain their political alliance with the Plain Republicans. Within the economic limits of the threat, a simple reaffirmation of free-trade theory seemed the most appropriate response. And since the issue at hand was not the substantive definition of freedom but rather the role of international trade in economic development, the contradiction between free-trade doctrine and slavery could simply be ignored.

The tariff, however, did pose a political threat to slavery. If a majority could legislate against the interests of a minority, as did the Tariff of 1828, it might be possible for a national majority to abolish slavery. While this possibility was inherent in Dew's defense of minority rights, he did not explicitly relate majoritarian tyranny to abolition.[1] He would make that connection several years later in his famous analysis of Southern slavery, *Review of the Debate in the Virginia Legislature of 1831–1832*.

The Nat Turner rebellion forced Dew's attention from the tariff to slavery;[2] the entire white population of Virginia put aside other economic and political issues. The Virginia House of Delegates debated the question from January 16 to January 25. Although technically the debate was confined to a select committee report which found it "inexpedient of the present legislature to make any legislative enactment for the abolition of slavery," the discussion that ensued gave antislavery forces the opportunity both to condemn slavery and to offer proposals for its abolition.[3] The abolitionists won a major point when the legislature agreed that slavery was an evil, but the defenders of slavery won the debate and succeeded in maintaining the evil as a necessary one.

The antislavery sentiment expressed in the House debate had a long and respected history in Virginia. From the time of the revolution, prominent Virginians like Richard Henry Lee, Patrick Henry, George Washington, James Madison, and Thomas Jefferson had spoken against slavery for moral, economic, or political reasons.[4] When the American Colonization Society was founded in 1817, other reputable Virginians such as James Madison and John Marshall gave their endorsement of the society's goal of repatriating free blacks to Liberia. Only two months before the Nat Turner rebellion, Chief Justice Marshall, acting as executive of the Virginia branch of the society, lauded the organization's progress and its effect of healing differences between Northern and Southern states. However, as strong as these antislavery sentiments were, the economic and sectional factors proved stronger.

Following the national economic crisis of 1819, Virginia suffered a downturn that was to last for twelve years. Western expansion to fertile soils had created a period of protracted price depressions in Virginia's marketable agricultural products.[5] Its soil, depleted from years of intensive farming, could not produce competitive crops. The U.S. census of 1830 documented Virginia's declining economic position. As late as 1810 Virginia was the most populous state in the nation; by 1830 it had fallen to third.

These figures also imply its deterioration as the nation's leading political force.[6] Congressional reapportionment would inevitably follow with subsequent reduction of power in both the House of Representatives and in the electoral college.[7] Aware of the danger and determined to retard migration from the state, Virginians developed an agricultural reform movement dedicated to promoting scientific cultivation and to improving Virginia's internal transportation system.[8] They also felt obliged to find an explanation that could offer social and economic reasons for Virginia's inability to meet the challenge of western lands. As we will see, two opposing paradigms emerged, one blaming the tariff and the other blaming slavery for the continued stagnation of Virginia's economy.

The effects of the economic downturn were, of course, not experienced uniformly throughout the state. Geographic conditions influenced both the effects of increasing competition and the responses to it. Nature had divided the state into three regions: the sea and the fall line marked the boundaries of the tidewater region; the fall line and the Blue Ridge Mountains delimited the piedmont region; the valley between the Blue Ridge Mountains and Allegheny Mountains designated the third section.[9]

The mountain ranges also divided the state between east and west, while the river system in the east integrated the piedmont and tidewater regions. The east can be characterized as a plantation economy specializing in tobacco. In contrast, the west was primarily cultivated by yeomen farmers producing wheat and livestock for local markets but isolated from larger regional or international markets. The 1830 census reflected these divergent economies in the number of slaves located in the two sections of the state. In the tidewater and piedmont regions the black population accounted for 56 percent and 54 percent of the total population respectively. However, only 23 percent of the valley population and a mere 10 percent of the trans-Allegheny population was black.[10] The eastern section of the state was harder hit during the years of economic depression and lost nearly half of its white population between 1810 and 1840.[11] A decline in the white population meant an increase in the black/white ratio. Whites had exceeded blacks by 25,000 east of the Blue Ridge in 1790; by 1830, however, blacks outnumbered whites by 81,000.[12] This fact was noted with alarm by antislavery advocates, who prophesied that the Nat Turner rebellion was only a foreshadowing of general revolt.

Easterners responded to their economic plight in two ways. Some adopted a thoroughly commercial approach to farming as advocated by the agricultural reformers; others retreated from commercial life, using slaves merely to reproduce the conditions of the plantation. Here, too, geography was associated with the alternative responses, although the division ran east and west, with the James River demarcating two sections known as the Northern Neck and the Southside. The Northern Neck, which had been a federalist stronghold and was to become a major source of Whig support in the elections between 1836 and 1840, experimented more heavily in new agricultural techniques and crops as a means of revitalizing the economy. Slavery itself receded in importance as oats, grasses, peas, wheat, and even truck farming became more popular.[13] The new policy resulted in a quantitative and qualitative division of labor that established conditions favorable for sustained economic growth on a capitalist basis. In this respect the Northern Neck region resembled the Northern states, which provided a model for Virginia reformers.

In contrast, the Southside remained tied to the traditional pattern of slave production. Except in the wealthy tobacco counties of the piedmont region, the soil of the Southside was exhausted from the overcultivation of tobacco. Like the Northern Neck planters, those of the Southside were forced to turn to cultivating more grains. However, unlike their northern neighbors, the Southside planters remained loyal to an agrarian tradition inherited from their antifederalist fathers and from the democratic tradition of John Taylor of Caroline.[14] By refusing to adopt more "rational" economic attitudes, the planters retained their entire slave force even though their new production required less labor. The region consequently became overcapitalized in labor and remained "slave poor." The limitation of a home market, therefore, curtailed the accumulation process among planters and ultimately led plantation production to be transformed into "household" production.[15]

In the western part of the state a similar dichotomy existed between commercial and independent farming. Without proper transportation facilities to connect these regions to broader and even international markets, self-sufficient farming persisted. Ideological differences resulted between commercial farmers who supported economic development and independent farmers who favored the status quo.[16]

These internal issues conditioned the Virginia debate on slavery, which was, in general, split along sectional lines, with western representatives opposing the institution and eastern representatives defending it.[17] The antislavery advocates did not condemn the institution principally because of its injustice to blacks, although this was mentioned, but because of its adverse effects on whites. Slavery, the abolitionists argued, destroyed the morality of Virginia and undermined the economy because slaveholders were forced to drive yeomen off their land to fully engage the planters' slaves. Without this hardy and industrious class, Virginia could not hope to improve economically. Furthermore, the small slaveholders unable to compete with the more powerful ones "were forced to sell out and remove, until in the course of some twenty or thirty years, the disproportion between the blacks and whites, would become so great, that slaves would attempt to recover their liberty."[18] Thus, for the antislavery faction, slavery was itself responsible for Virginia's continued economic decline, and for reasons reminiscent of Malthus, slavery presaged political chaos in the minds of the Virginia abolitionists.

The proslavery response, with rare exception, agreed that slavery itself was morally culpable. But these eastern representatives dismissed the allegation that slavery ruined the economy by simply observing that Virginia compared favorably to other sections of the country. The advocates of slavery seemed convinced that Virginia's economic decline was due to the tariff and not slavery.[19] (These contending explanations for the economic downturn of Virginia and the Southeast in general found their way into the national debates on the tariff.)

As for the potential political danger of slavery, the defenders ignored it by saying that the antislavery forces were idly crying wolf.[20] Blacks, in the opinion of the proslavery advocates, were better cared for and better managed than the laboring poor of Europe and so were less likely to rebel.[21]

Finally, the proslavery representatives relied on a single proposition to ward off the abolitionist attack, namely that abolition violated property rights. They considered these rights to be the very basis of government and any violation of them to be an abuse. Did the majority have the right to abolish slavery even if financial compensation was provided? For eastern planters, the success of such a proposition would signal not only their demise but also the demise of constitutional rule.

In continually raising the issue of democratic abuse, the proslavery forces revived the antagonism of the 1829–1830 Virginia Constitutional Convention, where a similar split had occurred between east and west as the western forces, under-represented in the legislature, sought to democratize the state constitution. While the democratic forces won small gains, including an extension of the franchise for white males and limited reapportionment, Virginia politics—unlike that of most states during the period—remained thoroughly "aristocratic."[22] The eastern planters opposed democratic reform since they feared the west would legislate internal improvements for which they would pay disproportionately and which would benefit their western competitors. Moreover, the east feared that democratic rule would lead to an attack on property, whether from the abolitionists or from an agrarian movement for a redistribution of property. Abel P. Upshur, an eastern representative, a judge of the general court, and later secretary of state in President Tyler's administration, stated the problem as follows:

> There are two kinds of majority. There is a majority in *interest*, as well as a majority in number. If the first be within the contemplation of gentlemen, there is an end of all discussion. It is precisely the principle for which we contend, and we shall be happy to unite with them in so regulating this matter, that those who have the greatest stake in the Government, shall have the greatest share of power in the administration of it. But this is not what gentlemen mean. They mean, for they distinctly say so, that a majority in number only, without regard to property, shall give the rule.[23]

The debate on slavery, therefore, revealed social antagonisms based on class. The opposition between planters and yeomen was muted, among other things, by divergent attitudes toward internal improvements and the formation of a home market in general, concerns which to some extent cut across economic lines. Nonetheless, Virginia distinguished itself among Southern states in its growing conflict between planters and yeomen that finally resulted in the western region's independence from Virginia during the secession crisis.[24]

Dew's Treatise on Black Slavery

For the most part, the proslavery argument failed to develop a moral basis for the economic and political defense of slavery in the legislative debates.

Dew altered this situation in an article which appeared in the *American Quarterly Review*; later he expanded the essay in his *Review of the Debate in the Virginia Legislature*, published in 1832. Subsequently this work was included in the handbook of Southern radicalism, *The Pro-slavery Argument*, published in 1853. Unlike the proslavery legislators, Dew boldly asserted, despite his own earlier views, that slavery was a positive good.[25] He admitted that the international trade in black labor was itself an evil, but that once black slavery had been imposed on the colonies by England, the institution had been transformed from an evil to a virtue of natural law.

Dew's polemical concerns are defined by the Virginia abolitionists, who recommended either repatriating American slaves to Africa or emancipating them and settling them in North America. As Dew perceives it, such proposals raised the following questions: "Can the black be sent back to his African home, or will the day ever arrive when he can be liberated from his thraldom, and mount upwards in the scale of civilization and rights to an equality with the white?"[26] For Dew, consideration of these questions necessitates

> profound knowledge of the nature and sources of national wealth and political aggrandizement,—an acquaintance with the . . . spring of population [and] a clear perception of the varying rights of man . . . and a powerful knowledge of all the principles, passions, and susceptibilities which make up the moral nature of our species . . .[27]

In Dew's opinion the viability of abolitionist schemas must be assessed by political economy, and it is here that he confronts a perplexing problem.

According to classical political economy, history moves toward ever greater freedom. Dew's primary theoretical task, therefore, is to reconcile black slavery to historical progress; otherwise he will be unable to convert political economy into a weapon against the ideological offensive of the abolitionists.[28] He attempts to reconcile the South's peculiar institution with the natural order, first, by identifying labor in the civilized stage as dependent or slave labor and, second, by positing that the natural relationship between the white and black races is that of master and slave. He further insists that in addition to being consistent with the natural order, black slavery is also essential to preserving America's republican government.

Despite his belabored effort to make black slavery compatible with capitalism, Dew finally admits that the master-slave relationship produces different social effects and corresponds to a different stage of historical development than the capital/wage-labor relationship does. Consequently, he notes ironically that as Southern society advances, black slavery must recede.

It is not surprising that Dew's attempt failed. What is striking about his effort, however, is that he correctly perceived the contradictory directions of Southern economic development. As recent scholarship has shown, the Southern family farm, when organized as a plantation, was internally structured by precapitalist—that is, non–wage-labor—relationships.[29] Yet, since the cotton plantation produced for the international market, the cotton-based plantation economy was regulated by capitalist production. The dependency on the world market determined the nature of the commodity circuit in which the cotton plantation participated.[30] As a product destined for industrial capitalist consumption, cotton functioned as commodity capital.[31] Since cotton dominated the Southern economy, its economic growth became regulated by capitalist development and the planter, as an owner of capital, became entitled to an average rate of profit.[32] Included within the general circuit of capital, the plantation became infused with a capitalist ethos in the production process and in the management of the plantation.[33]

Despite these capitalist aspects of the slave South, the plantation itself limited the development of capitalism by inhibiting the formation of the home market, both extensively and intensively. The plantation invested in slaves, who were calculated as fixed capital. To maximize this investment, the planter had to employ this labor force continuously.[34] However, since the seasonal production of cotton did not require the constant use of the slave labor force, planters directed their laborers in tasks neither directly associated with cotton nor with the market. For this reason, many average and large plantations achieved self-sufficiency in areas such as food production.[35] The effect of this self-sufficiency was to restrict the regional division of labor, which initiated the formation of a capitalist home market.[36] As a result, pockets of "subsistence" yeomen farmers remained outside of an emerging market structure.[37] The situation dramatically differed from that in the North, where an extensive market developed and the family farms introduced machinery as a means of overcoming labor's scarcity.

The plantation remained integrated into the market structure, not because it depended on the market for commodities required for the plantation's physical reproduction, but because of debt. During the course of a year the plantation required money for "purchases of basic plantation supplies: marketing expenses for the planter's cotton or sugar (transportation, storage, processing, insurance commissions and fees) and purchases of land, slaves or other improvements."[38] A factor supplied the planter with the needed cash through commercial notes (bills of exchange) guaranteed against the future crop. The long line of credit that supported the factor reached back to England and to a capitalist system of finance.[39] Thus, the planter was doubly tied to the capitalist world market: through the production of goods that entered the circulation of commodity capital and through the financing of the plantation.[40]

As long as the demand for Southern goods remained strong, the system could grow quantitatively, even though it did not produce an internal dynamic capable of industrial expansion. With a restricted home market, the potential for conflict remained between the planters and the "self-sufficient" yeomen, as well as between the planters and those yeomen promoting capitalist development. As the economy diversified in the non-cotton areas, capitalist development became more feasible and politically more necessary given the growing Southern nationalist movement.[41]

Dependent Labor

Dew's first task in attempting to make chattel slavery compatible with the advanced state is to reconcile slavery with political economy's interpretation of human history as progress toward individual freedom. He admits that at first glance chattel slavery appears inimical to freedom. However, he argues that a study of history shows that slave labor—that is, dependent labor—is with rare exceptions a condition of civilization in which freedom is equated with property and dependence with propertylessness.

Dew's concept of dependent labor derives from classical political economy's notion that civilization is distinguished by private property and the social division of labor. In the civilized stage, wealth is natural and social: it is natural in that it is unequally distributed according to the individual's varying abilities to truck, barter, and exchange; it is social in that it is a result of the division of labor, which produces beyond the bare biological requirements.

Dew defends this conception of history and individual freedom even more wholeheartedly than Smith himself by making explicit the latent contradictions in Smith's notion of freedom. Smith is well aware that the advanced state frees the capitalist while condemning the worker to the rule of capital. He accepts this juxtaposition of freedom and dependency because he believes economic growth will eventually improve the living standards of the impoverished laboring class.

Dew develops Smith's negative remarks on the status of the working class in two ways. First, he argues that the worker is dependent on the capitalist class. He admits that, by being legally free, the worker possesses more possibilities for individual autonomy than the chattel slave or serf, but Dew maintains that this freedom is limited because the worker must rely on the capitalist for a livelihood. Dew concludes that the real condition of the working class is one of practical, if not legal, enslavement. Second, because he accepts Ricardo's ideas of diminishing returns in agriculture and the falling rate of profit, Dew's theory, unlike Smith's, condemns the working class to perpetual poverty. Their miserable circumstances lead Dew to compare the workers in the advanced state with the pitiful chattel slaves in the first stage of civilization. Consequently, he asks if the worker is not indeed a slave of capital.

With this evaluation, Dew challenges Blackstone, the noted British legal authority, who denies the propriety of workers' selling themselves into slavery.[42] In Blackstone's opinion, liberty has no equivalent for which it can be exchanged. Dew's objection is quite simple. Given the dire material conditions of the working class, he suggests that the guarantee of material nourishment is a suitable equivalent for an individual's liberty. But he laments that the capitalist, with an eye on profits, will never accept the exchange. Thus, while praising the advanced state as the highest achievement of humanity, Dew is aware of its cost to the working class. He consoles himself by emphasizing the achievements of the period and blaming the misery of the laboring class on its immoral and irrational nature.

After rejecting the notion of wage labor's freedom, Dew heightens the contrast between the free propertied classes and the dependent laboring class by arguing that chattel slavery is a natural development and the very foundation of civilization. According to Dew, the early and rude state is torn by perpetual tribal war.[43] Vengeance perpetuates these wars, in which the desired end is the complete extermination of the vanquished. Only when it is discovered that enslavement of one's victims can be economically advantageous is the ferocity tempered. In other words, when interest has succumbed to the passions, slavery arises and, with it, civilization.

By instituting chattel slavery, Dew argues, the human being advances from barbarism to civilization.[44] He offers two reasons for this development. First, slavery is allegedly the initial form of private property; therefore, chattel slavery can be linked with the earliest form of the social division of labor and to the formation of a social surplus. Dew designates this level of historical development as the pastoral stage. Second, since the vanquished are enslaved rather than annihilated, Dew views slavery as a civilizing force. With chattel slavery, the human being's animal need for immediate gratification in warfare is replaced by a desire for economic growth and accumulation. The masters will develop these new drives as property owners. They will impose the discipline of labor on their slaves in order to benefit rationally from their property. The indirect result, in Dew's analysis, is the moral improvement of the laborers themselves. In sum, Dew makes chattel slavery consistent with civilization by making it responsible for the general characteristics that distinguish civilization from barbarism.[45]

"Biological Determinants of Black Slavery"

In identifying civilized labor with slave or dependent labor, Dew does not, in fact, make chattel slavery an element of the natural order, for he distinguishes between "slavery" as a general term and "chattel slavery" as a specific one. Throughout his discussion, he recognizes differences among the various forms of dependency: wage labor, serfdom, and chattel slavery, each of which has distinct effects on the economy.

As noted above, he finds it difficult to argue that chattel slavery is as profitable as wage labor, because slave labor is supported by the master's paternal responsibility rather than by the natural law of supply and demand. Since profitability is the mechanism by which economic efficiency is measured, Dew cannot justify slavery in the advanced stage unless he shows that this form of labor, although not designed to maximize wealth, is necessary for other natural reasons. To justify chattel slavery in the advanced stage, Dew adds the variable of race to his discussion.[46] Even so, his tacit reconciliation of chattel slavery with the commercial stage falls apart.

As a general historical rule, Dew asserts that two races cannot live together in equality. He does not precisely define "race" but merely uses it as a color code referring to the "natural" differences among the red, black, and white populations in the United States.[47] According to Dew, each race possesses a particular potential that is manifested in its historical achievements. He observes that "the red man" is by nature a savage incapable of advancing beyond barbarism. He is more generous to "the black man," who is by nature capable of civilization but only the semibarbarous or pastoral stage. Unlike either the red or black race, the white race, according to Dew, can progress through each stage of history and eventually reach the advanced stage of civilization.

Where the races coexist, Dew conceives of their relationship as a confrontation between different levels of historical development. Since the white race, in Dew's opinion, represents the highest form of civilization, it should dominate the others. Interestingly, Dew argues that the confrontation between the red and white races, between the savage and advanced stages of history, leaves no alternative but physical annihilation of the "inferior" race. Only through chattel slavery, he asserts, could the red race be incorporated into white civilization, but because "the red man" is naturally incapable of achieving even a rudimentary level of civilization, he naturally resists slavery and makes his extermination by the white race necessary. Fortunately, says Dew, the black race is independently able to attain a pastoral stage of development so that the whites need not annihilate them but merely enslave them. This allows a harmonious relationship between the two races which raises the black race from a rudimentary to a more sophisticated civilized condition.

Although slavery is generally not as profitable as wage labor, Dew insists that black slavery is economically feasible because it raises the productive powers of laborers who would otherwise function at a pastoral level. The master can utilize black labor to produce commodities to be sold for a profit on the world market and thereby raises the slaves from their relatively underdeveloped economy to a commercial one, for which Dew expects the slaves to be grateful.

But here Dew confronts a serious contradiction, for chattel slavery, when considered as a system of production, is incapable of creating a dynamic advanced economy. The restrictive characteristics of chattel slavery are apparent in the pastoral stage, where both the division of labor and the growth of the market is restricted by the demand of a small propertied class. With the size of the market thus limited, not all the use values produced by chattel slavery are commodities. In fact, most of the use values produced in the pastoral stage are destined for immediate domestic consumption, leaving only a relative few that actualiy circulate as commodities.

From the perspective of the advanced stage of development, this non–commodity-producing aspect makes the pastoral stage and its use of chattel slavery irrational. In other words, the master who employs capital in a fashion that does not produce commodities is not using capital to its full capacity. The potential profits on capital are lost, so Dew can argue that these use values represent a deduction from capital even though they permit the reproduction of both master and slave.

The equivocal nature of chattel slavery as both labor and property obstructs the natural pursuit after profits. Because chattel slavery, in Dew's conception, is fixed capital costs, the masters will attempt to maintain the value of their laborers rather than reduce it in the pattern normal to the capitalist wage-labor relationship. Also, it is possible for nonmarket attitudes to develop among the masters so that they will not use their laborers in the most economically rational way. Both of these factors keep wages from falling to their lowest level and thereby limit the amount of profits that can be realized. For these reasons, the existence of chattel slavery in an advanced state, even when justified on racial grounds, can potentially cripple the economy. Consequently, Dew relegates black slavery to a secondary position in the Southern economy and defends wage labor as the primary motor force.

Dew emphasizes the nonrational character of slavery in the advanced state when he predicts slavery's receding importance in the South as the economy matures. He foresees that within fifty years Americans will settle the western territories and propel the nation out of its agrarian state. If the fetter of the tariff can be removed, Dew predicts, Virginia will develop into a manufacturing center which will increase the demand for white labor and offset the migration of Virginia laborers. Dew argues that, until that time, internal improvements should be undertaken to promote Virginia's division of labor both quantitatively and qualitatively. Manufacturing, towns, and the rise of garden farming will result from such a program which will reverse Virginia's decline.

Under these conditions black slavery will increasingly lose importance for two reasons. First, the plantation's dependence on black slavery restricts the division of labor. Thus plantations become economically less feasible as a more efficient form of agriculture, namely garden farming, emerges. Second, Dew believes, black labor cannot be employed either on garden farming or in manufacturing since, he claims, these forms of production require semiautonomous laborers. For this reason, Dew can taunt the abolitionists by observing that they would best serve their interests if they paid more attention to political economy and less to abstract morality, for as Virginia's economy improves, the plantation will decline in importance and the slave population would diminish significantly.[48] Therefore, despite his concept of race and regardless of his emphasis on chattel slavery's ability to produce commodities, Dew cannot maintain black slavery as a long-term force in the Southern economy.

Dew's ambivalence toward slavery recurs in his attempt to resolve the antagonism between the western and eastern sections of Virginia through his system of internal improvements that will, he claims, bridge the economic gap. The eastern section will develop a manufacturing population while the west will specialize in agricultural production to meet the growing needs of the eastern towns. The consequent formation of a home market will negate the potential danger of the west's agrarianism but will not necessarily reduce its abolitionist tendencies. In fact, given the admitted constraints of slavery on economic growth, these tendencies may increase as a result of the burgeoning economy.

Dew addresses this objection to slavery in an article entitled "The Improvements of the James and Kanawha Rivers: Mischievous Effects of the Immigration to the West," published in the *Farmer's Register* in July of 1835. Here Dew argues that, as the economy develops in the west, the growing demand for labor can be met in the short run only by slavery. Thus, east and west should become slaveholding sections equally benefiting from slavery.[49]

In arguing that the spread of slavery will resolve the split between slaveholder and nonslaveholder, Dew reasons that slavery is a transitory institution: experience has already shown it to be receding in the east as garden farming gains ground from the plantations. Slavery will logically recede in importance in manufacturing, too, although it may be useful in facilitating the initial stages of industrialization.

There are two possible objections to Dew's prediction that slavery will decline in economic importance. First, the world market demand for cotton could reinforce the plantation economy and inhibit the "natural" formation of a home market. For Dew, the contradiction between internal capitalist development and the world market poses no real problem, since he believes that his two-stage model demonstrates the link between an agrarian nation's industrial growth and its involvement in the international market. We have already noted Dew's thinking on this matter in his writing on the tariff and have observed that the theory of comparative advantage does not guarantee the full development of an economy, as Dew asserts. Second, as Dew recognizes, the master-slave relationship might lead to nonmarket behavior. Dew has no developed response to this objection, but perhaps he would reply that the "whiteness" of the master class ensures civilized behavior. The actual developments in the South during the 1830s, 1840s, and 1850s proved Dew's vision of economic growth false and created a crisis for those who, like Dew, had looked forward to Southern economic growth.

But Dew may have anticipated the historical failure to reconcile slavery and capitalist production when he considers the long-term tendency of the rate of profit to fall. Because he follows Ricardian economics, Dew foresees the inevitable stagnation of the economy and prescribes slavery to remedy the moribund economy and contain the conflict between labor and capital over scarce resources. The catch in this solution, as Dew formulates it, is that the entire working class, regardless of color, will be enslaved, so that the capitalist will be transformed into the benefactor of the laborers. Under these conditions chattel slavery will be geared toward domestic production rather than commodity production. Instead of engaging in the most profitable endeavors, the slave masters will provide labor with the means of subsistence even if it has to be deducted from their capital. Although Dew does not elaborate the implications of such recommendations, it is evident that, although they resolve the falling rate of profit, they produce a movement toward barbarism.

Dew's failure to reconcile slavery to capitalism may be seen in two incompatible equations. In the first, Dew equates black chattel slavery with the "natural" order because race dictates the subordination of black to white. In the second, Dew maintains the major tenet of classical political economy, which identifies capitalism as the "natural" order. However, he is forced to admit that black chattel slavery and capitalism are not compatible. Otherwise he would be obliged to conclude absurdly that the "natural" order (black chattel slavery) is not equivalent to the "natural" order (capitalism). Smith can link the natural and the social (or advanced stage) through the human propensity to truck, barter, and exchange. Dew, in contrast, cannot connect the natural biological state and the natural advanced state. Human nature, which mediates between the poles of Smith's concept of nature, is obstructed in Dew's system by the "biologically" determined subordination of the black race to the white.

Dew's concept of the different moral aptitudes of white and black labor also obstructs his effort to make slavery compatible with the natural order. Although he denies it when addressing the abolitionists, Dew fundamentally believes that black labor suffers by comparison with white labor in the natural endowment of morality. Hence, black labor—regardless of its legal status—is unfit for the more autonomous work of manufacturing and garden farming. For this reason, black slavery has to be eventually relegated to a minor role if the economy is to advance. Even if Dew could accept black labor as morally competent, his condemnation of the international slave trade forfeits a pool of labor sufficient to meet the demands caused by America's high land/labor ratio and the constraints that plantation production has placed on the development of labor-saving machinery. Therefore, Dew's concept of black chattel slavery inhibits his general theory of accumulation and accounts for much of his profound pessimism about the future of the American republic and of civilization in general.

Black Slavery and the Republican Ideal

The attempt to reconcile slavery with the economic structure of the natural order is only part of Dew's theoretical task. He also has to demonstrate that slavery is compatible with American republican government. The conflict between majority and minority rights represents the central dilemma, according to Dew, in republican thought. The aspects of the conflict, as we have seen are (1) the conflict among propertied interests and (2) the conflict between propertied and propertyless classes. Of these two, Dew considers the latter the more long-term problem.

Dew's rebuttal to the Virginia abolitionists illustrates his underlying fear of majoritarian rule by a propertyless class. Although the abolitionist schemas pose an immediate threat to one particular form of property, Dew's counterattack moves from a specific defense of slavery to a general defense of private property and an assertion of the consequent need to restrain majoritarian rule.

> The doctrine of these gentlemen (abolitionists), so far from being true in its application, is not true in theory. The great object of government is the protection of property . . .
> . . . Now, only sanction the doctrine of the Virginia orators, let one interest in the government (the west) rob another at pleasure (the east), and is there any man who can fail to see that government is systematically producing that very oppression which it is intended to remedy. . . .[50]

In Dew's theory, constitutional checks are "the most efficient mode of protecting property" from the tyranny of the majority. The most important of these, as noted above, is states' rights. However, this check is incapable of preventing a majoritarian tyranny of the working class, since in the advanced stage wage laborers will form the majority in both the North and South. Dew does not reformulate the concept of states' rights in light of this structural weakness; instead, he offers slavery as the appropriate means of retarding the growth of a politically dangerous working class.

Classical political economy includes morality and education in addition to legal channels as safeguards against a tyrannical government. The logic of this position is that an educated and moral working population will not challenge the sanctity of private property; workers will realize that nature itself has established private property as the basis of society and as a condition for the laboring populations to advance out of barbarism.

Dew adopts a similar stance. He, too, believes that checks against governmental abuse may lie outside the formal boundaries of government in the realm of civil society. However, Dew does not stress education as the most significant moral check but again defends slavery—that institution apparently most antithetical to freedom—as the most appropriate means of convincing a working class that its best interests are associated with capital's rule.

Dew begins his defense by countering the abolitionist claim that slavery is antithetical to republicanism with the simple observation that ancient Greece, where republican government was first developed, was a slave-based society. Next, he asks what the essential condition of republicanism is in the modern world and answers that it is a sense of equality among the social orders. Without this sense of equality, animosity and conflict between the social classes would be inevitable. Dew can claim that black slavery is well suited to provide this kind of "equality."

> Jack Cade, the Irish reformer, wished all mankind to be brought to one common level. We believe slavery, in the United States, has accomplished this, in regard to the whites, as nearly as can be expected or even desired in this world. The menial and low offices being all performed by the blacks, there is at once taken away the greatest cause of distinction and separation of the ranks of society. . . . Color alone is here the badge of distinction, the true mark of aristocracy, and all who are white are equal in spite of the variety of occupation. . . . And it is this spirit of equality which is both the generator and preserver of the genuine spirit of liberty.[51]

Unlike the equivocal results of his writing on states' rights, Dew's treatment of slavery's conservative effect on the Southern working class has a certain internal consistency. Although he does not fully elaborate his notions, Dew does suggest that, in addition to solving the racial question, slavery provides the South with a social institution that diminishes the class struggle between wage labor and capital in two ways. First, he argues, slavery provides a source of productive labor which allows capital to expand and excludes the laboring population from the body politic. Second, slavery, or more precisely racism, serves as an ideological mechanism which unites the interests of the white population, whether propertied or propertyless.

Indeed, this ideological check on the conflict between the majority and minority is simpler and more complete than the moral instruction proposed by the classical tradition. In the English model, formal instruction is required for the laboring masses to comprehend nature's logic; whereas in Dew's theory, nature's hidden hand reveals itself by color-coding "natural" social relationships. Whites, whether yeomen or masters, workers or capitalists, supposedly have an interest in preserving the "natural" subordination of blacks. In so doing, the mutuality of white interest affirms chattel slavery specifically and private property in general, and establishes the ideological foundations of white republican government.

Dew is so confident of this solution that in an article entitled "An Address on the Influence of the Federative System of Government Upon Literature and the Development of Character," published in the *Southern Literary Messenger* in 1836, he proclaims the South to be a tranquil land, enjoying the spirit of equality and the "true spirit of genuine republicanism." In contrast, he draws the reader's attention to the North, where the "almost unlimited extension of suffrage in the most populous states, the frequent appeals made to the indigent and the destitute by demagogues . . . [and] the lawless mobs of the north which . . . have pulled down and destroyed the property of the citizen . . . are but the rumbling which precedes the mighty shock of the terrible earthquake."[52] For Dew, black slavery is the guarantor of the South's harmony, so he, like Raymond, elevates a precapitalist relationship to the level of theoretical necessity in guaranteeing the preservation of the "natural"—that is, the capitalist—order. By substituting the historical accident of black slavery for a universally valid "check," Dew treats the antebellum South as if it were the most significant development in the tradition of political experiments to establish a republican order.

Even if one interprets Dew's argument as a historically contingent solution to the problem of the working class, the fundamental justification for slavery in the natural order remains problematic. In this regard, Dew's logic is riddled with contradictions, so the political argument totters on an uneasy foundation. Those thinkers who followed Dew's lead had to reconcile the economic contradiction of slavery in a capitalist world market. Two avenues of investigation emerged: one attempted to make slavery more like capitalism and the other sought to make capitalism more like slavery.

Although the first school, associated with thinkers like James DeBow and Leonidas Spratt, accepted for the most part Dew's justification for slavery and its political implications, they reformulated elements of his economic reasoning. First, they argued that blacks were capable of working in manufacturing and, second, that the reopening of the African slave trade would eliminate labor constraints in an expanding and diversifying economy dependent on black slave labor. By asserting that the African slave trade is moral, these disciples of Dew could petition for its reopening to satisfy capital's need for a cheap and flexible labor force.

The other school, whose most articulate spokesman was George Fitzhugh, also attempted to reconcile the poles of capital and slavery but shifted the emphasis from economic development to the preservation of privilege based on the labor of slaves. In its most extreme form, this position was willing to forfeit the development of the advanced state by substituting a general form of chattel slavery for wage labor, which it considered a decadent form of slave labor. Despite the transition from wage labor to slave labor, commodity exchange would still structure the relationships among masters who entered the market to maximize their personal wealth. Constraints on that process were accepted by these theorists for the sake of social stability and a natural order firmly rooted in agriculture.

7. JACOB N. CARDOZO *on*
Making Slavery Work

When the causes now in operation have produced their full effect, and inventions and discoveries shall have been exhausted,—if they may ever be,—they will give a force . . . difficult to be anticipated. . . . The first effect of such changes, on long established governments, will be, to unsettle the opinions and principles in which they originated . . . The interval between the decay of the old and the formation and establishment of the new, constitutes a period of transition, which must always necessarily be one of uncertainty, confusion, error, and wild and fierce fanaticism.—John Calhoun, *A Disquisition on Government*

Radical Politics and Conservative Economics

In systematizing the proslavery argument, Dew's treatise revealed the two distinct lines of argumentation to which I have referred.[1] The position which has achieved most attention, particularly as a result of Eugene Genovese's ground-breaking essay on George Fitzhugh, is the more conservative view which attempted to demonstrate the incompatibility of slavery with capitalism since capitalism was characterized as an aberration of the natural order.[2] Because my study is limited to the pre-1848 period and because the conservative wing of the proslavery argument has already received serious treatment, I will explore the defense of slavery that attempted to make slavery compatible with capitalism. The relevant material is supplied by South Carolina, the hotbed of Southern nationalism. While South Carolina's radical nullification movement produced cogent political and economic writings in defense of free trade, slavery, and minority rights, they confined their economics to a "conservative" Ricardian interpretation and so did not provide the most significant advances in reconciling slavery to capitalism. The core economic arguments were formulated by Thomas Cooper, the spirited and unpredictable theoretician who also contributed to the theory of states' rights and to the defense of slavery. Yet his writings dutifully followed Ricardo's model and never achieved the intellectual rigor of Dew's treatises.

To remain in the Ricardian camp, Cooper had to concede that nature was itself limited and that no form of production could affect the inevitability of economic demise. Thus, Cooper, like Dew, was burdened with the arduous knowledge that the pursuit after the natural order carried the seeds of its decay. The radicalism of South Carolinian nullifiers remained confined to political doctrine and to practical activities; in the realm of theory the doctrine of Ricardo and Malthus remained sanctified but not invulnerable.

Nullifiers All

By the mid 1820s South Carolina had distinguished itself as the South's intellectual leader in the doctrine of states' rights. The tariff controversy sharpened the issue during these years, but it was not the only motivating factor in South Carolina's efforts to establish a political doctrine capable of checking majority rule. The debate on slavery that emerged as a result of the Missouri Compromise, the Negro Seaman controversy, the Ohio resolution for emancipation, and of course the Denmark Vesey conspiracy indicated the need to check majoritarian rule in order to contain the political power of the young but dangerous abolitionist movement.[3]

An additional danger to slavery was apparent in the conflict between Southern agrarian and Northern manufacturing interests. For South Carolina, it pointed to the more fundamental political antagonism between minority and majority rights. If the majority could legislate a tariff that damaged minority interests, it could also legislate against slavery and eventually against property itself.

The nullification movement was composed of planters from two geographic sectors of South Carolina. The major slave holdings were located in the southern portion of the state along the Atlantic Ocean where large plantations predominated and produced crops of rice and the sea island cotton used in manufacturing only the finest luxury garments. These lowland planters dominated state politics not only because of their extraordinary wealth but also because of their "aristocratic" manners and education, which set the cultural and ideological standards for the state. In contrast, the central region of South Carolina, the piedmont district, had less fertile soil, suitable only for the production of short-fibered staple cotton. Settlement in this region occurred later than in the low country, and while fortunes had already been made in the 1820s, the section retained much of its frontier character. Small plantations were common, as well as yeomen, who in many instances were antagonistic to the planters but nonetheless strove to enter the elite circles of plantation life.[4]

Although divided by these geographic and economic factors, the planters were unified by their common interest in slavery and by an intricate web of familial, social, and educational ties and thus provided a contrast to Virginia's radically divided east and west. In approaching the tariff issue and the doctrine of nullification, the two groups of South Carolina planters found common ground in ideology rather than in immediate economic concerns. Economic stagnation, which persisted in Virginia after the financial crisis of 1819–1822, did not affect South Carolina with the same force. From 1822 to 1829, the piedmont planters suffered decreasing prices because of an overproduction in short-staple cotton and consequently faced continued economic pressures in meeting their outstanding debts; for them the tariff appeared as an additional economic burden that could possibly mean bankruptcy. Those pressures were not felt by the owners of large estates in the low country because the specialized markets in rice and sea island cotton were unaffected by the increasing competition from western lands.[5]

The hatred for the protective tariff was more than matched in the low country. Here, however, it was not economic necessity that prompted the planters to abandon the aesthetic life for the practical requirements of forging a political movement. It was ideology that propelled them into the tasteless world of party politics. Since the low country had the highest concentration of blacks in the Old South, the "aristocratic" planters carefully scrutinized any political tendencies that might endanger the stability of their region. They considered the antislavery agitation of the 1820s mild as it was when compared to that of the post-1840 period, a potent social force, capable of either building an abolitionist movement or inciting slaves to rebellion. The tariff opened the route for the emerging abolitionist movement by testing the right of a majority to institute laws harmful to a minority under the constitutional guise of the general welfare. As a combined force the planters of South Carolina forged a movement that literally challenged the political bonds of the Union in the Nullification Crisis.

In general, South Carolina politics reflected the aristocratic bent of the lowland planters. Personal ties and loyalties rather than party machinery structured the political process while democracy remained an incendiary word. The constitution had been reformed to permit a broad franchise, but most officers from the governor to the tax collectors were appointed by the legislature. To ensure the continued control of South Carolina politics by the worthy, there were high property qualifications for legislators.[6]

Ideological differences rarely shaped politics in this homogeneous world between 1819 and 1827, with one important exception. Considerable controversy developed over the Constitution's implied powers to grant extended authority to the federal government. In these years the nationalism that resulted from the War of 1812 still informed the political ideals of many prominent South Carolinians, including future nullifiers such as John C. Calhoun, James Hamilton, Jr., and Robert Hayne.[7] They, among others, established a distinct faction within South Carolina politics which argued that national defense demanded a national bank, internal improvements, and a protective tariff. However, they always qualified their support for these policies by insisting that any protective tariff or the construction of any highway be truly national, i.e., that it benefit the entire republic rather than a particular interest. This tendency did not go unopposed. Centered around the political career of William Smith, a states' rights faction formed which opposed Calhoun and his nationalist coterie's broad interpretation of the Constitution.[8]

The year 1827 marked a turning point in South Carolina politics. The tariff became clearly related to abolitionism and forced the Calhoun nationalists into a sectional position. In that year the American Colonization Society requested aid from Congress; the woolen manufacturers sought higher duties; and protariff forces convened in Harrisburg to chart future action. The connection between abolitionism and the tariff found further clarification with the appearance of Robert Turnbull's pamphlet *The Crisis*. This work complemented Thomas Cooper's influential political piece, *Consolidation*, which soundly condemned the tariff and the growing power of the federal government. The proslavery and nullification philosophies had practical consequences in the desertion by many nationalists, such as Hayne and Hamilton, of nationalist politics in favor of states' rights.[9]

Finally, the Tariff of 1828 shattered the nationalist tendency in South Carolina and reshaped its politics, dividing the state between nullifiers and unionists in alignments that defied predictability. The Nat Turner rebellion and the subsequent debate on slavery in the Virginia legislature intensified the anxieties of the South Carolina planters about the potential dangers of abolitionism and majoritarian rule. Through the exigency of crisis, the nullification forces sharpened their theoretical arguments both in support of nullification and in defense of slavery. After the tariff crisis had been resolved through the Compromise Tariff of 1833, South Carolina prepared itself for the protracted struggle to champion minority rights and to defend slavery as a necessary element in the American republic. Nationalism was now exclusively associated with the American System.[10]

Opposition did emerge during this metamorphosis, but it merely catalyzed the conversion of South Carolina politics. The pro-Union forces derived their social strength from two classes outside the influence of the planter hegemony—namely, the merchant class on the East Bay in Charleston and the yeomen in the northern regions of the state. But they were neither unified in their economic interests nor particularly cohesive as a social force. To underline the political impotence of the South Carolinian pro-Union forces, it should be noted that their leadership was composed of wealthy planters who agreed with the nullifiers that the tariff was an evil and that abolitionism had to be stopped, but who differed with them about how to repeal the Tariff of Abominations. For the pro-Union forces, a majoritarian repeal of the tariff still seemed possible, and even if it was not possible, the benefits of continued participation in the Union outweighed the potential dangers of nullification. Among those dangers the mass support for nullification seemed especially threatening to the "aristocratic" planter leadership of the pro-Union faction.[11]

Jacob Cardozo belonged to that faction. From a Sephardic mercantile background, Cardozo was essentially self-taught, having left formal education at the age of twelve.[12] In 1816 he entered a career in journalism, in which he was able to keep abreast of the important issues of the day. Although never a statesman himself, Cardozo was frequently consulted by politicians on matters concerning the tariff, internal improvements, banking, and slavery. His arguments against Ricardo in *Notes on Political Economy* (1826) established Cardozo as a first-rate political economist. In 1828 he applied these arguments in a critique of Cooper's *Lectures on the Elements of Political Economy*.

During the tariff controversy, Cardozo was a strong advocate of free trade.[13] He implicitly agreed with Dew that laissez-faire presented the most advantageous policy for transforming an agrarian society into an advanced one. But in keeping with his conservative bent, he confined his criticism to the class rather than the sectional aspects of the controversy. In highlighting the class bias of the tariff, Cardozo criticized Calhoun's and McDuffie's writings on the subject and opposed nullification. Furthermore, following Cooper's lead, Cardozo calculated the costs and benefits of South Carolina's membership in the Union. Where Cooper found the Union harmful to South Carolina, Cardozo reckoned it beneficial.[14] In making this calculation Cardozo agreed with Cooper that the Union was premised merely on economic gain. In so doing Cardozo opened the unionist position to statistical criticism of which the Fire-Eaters were to take advantage in the 1850s.

Having shown that the tariff was not the cause of South Carolina's economic malaise, Cardozo turned his scrutiny to the state itself and blamed a lack of diversification for its sad economic condition. Manufacturing seemed to Cardozo the most promising solution to South Carolina's economic difficulties.

The Compromise Tariff of 1833 and an improvement of economic conditions delayed the debate on the urgency of immediate diversification. By 1841, however, South Carolina and other Southern states perceived that the persistent abolitionist agitation and the economic downturn of 1839 would cause a crisis. More and more Southerners desired economic independence from the North, and the debate on diversification was renewed.[15] In South Carolina such prominent figures as James Hammond, William Gregg, C. G. Memminger, and William Harper engaged in a continuing dialogue on the suitability of black slave labor for manufacturing and on the proper relationship between white free labor and black slave labor.[16] In 1842 Cardozo contributed to the dialogue with a series of articles in the Charleston newspaper *The Southern Patriot*, in which he endorsed the use of slave labor in manufacturing. As the conflict between North and South over slavery deepened, Cardozo became more committed to Southern economic independence and was forced from his moderate pro-Union position into a call for secession.

Nature's Bounty versus Society's Poverty

Cardozo's polemics against the Ricardian system did not question the basic elements of the "natural" order as described by Ricardo—namely, the division of society into landlord, capitalist, and working classes. In this respect, Cardozo concurs with Ricardo and his Southern advocates. Cardozo dissents on technical questions regarding value, rent, and the falling rate of profit. For him, the Ricardian system's discussion of these categories is "unnatural" since their existence is dependent on English social structure, which is itself distorted by the presence of an aristocracy and mercantile monopolies. These unnatural institutions create the perverse conclusions found in Ricardo's work; they need to be expunged if political economy is to be truly scientific.[17]

America presents, in Cardozo's opinion, the perfect situation for scientific investigation. From his study of the United States Cardozo develops a theory which removes the barriers to accumulation alleged by Ricardo and thereby makes limitless accumulation and increasing wealth possible for all classes of society.[18] Hence, Cardozo removes the "natural" or biological economic necessity for conflict which plagues Ricardo's, Dew's, and Cooper's works and wholeheartedly endorses the rise of manufacturing. Unlike Dew, he has no need to hesitate in his endorsement since, for him, the advanced stage of development only promises rising living standards for the whole population.

Despite his economic optimism, Cardozo concedes that the advanced state exacerbates the political contradictions between private and social interests even though a propertyless class can be promised rising wages. In his mistrust of the working class, Cardozo concurs with Dew, and he similarly turns to slavery as an appropriate check against the irrationality of the masses. In fact, Cardozo advances Dew's proslavery argument by partially resolving the theoretical contradictions between slave labor and capitalist development. The particular and retrogressive features of contemporary Southern slavery do not necessarily damn, for Cardozo, the entire institution as incompatible with economic progress.

Cardozo does, however, develop substantive criticism of Ricardo's concept of nature, in which the productive powers are finite and limit economic growth, thus making class struggle and the inevitable demise of the economy and society inherent in the "natural" order. Cardozo objects to this pessimism. For him, nature's design offers humanity perpetual economic growth if a truly natural order is established.

Fundamentally, Cardozo argues that Ricardo has erred in his theory of rent and that this error affects his general theory of accumulation. According to Cardozo, Ricardo has two contradictory definitions of rent: one corresponding to the "natural" conditions of production, the other reflecting the "unnatural" or social conditions existing in England. In the first, rent has its origins in the indestructible powers of the land. Although Ricardo does not develop the implications of this definition, Cardozo reasons that it establishes rent as an absolute rather than a differential phenomenon. All lands produce a surplus above subsistence (that is, above wages and profits), so that each plot of land is entitled to a rent. Relative or differential rents exist only when varying qualities of land are tilled. Ricardo's second definition, according to Cardozo, attributes rent to the scarcity of land and the advance in the price of raw materials arising from the natural limitations on production.

Of the two definitions, Cardozo believes that the first is correct, since it derives from the physical, material side of production, while the latter presupposes an "unnatural" social structure based on monopoly. Cardozo adopts an absolute definition of rent and develops this theory as an alternate view to Ricardo's concept of differential rents, the diminishing returns of production, and the retrogressive role of the landlord class.

Since the market operates in a natural order independent of special privilege, land itself circulates freely as a commodity, subject to the laws of the marketplace. With this premise Cardozo argues unconvincingly that rents will not exceed the rate of interest because the tenant will find it advantageous to borrow money and purchase land. Therefore, Cardozo can assert that rent is doubly determined by nature: it has its origin in the natural conditions of production, and its particular rate is set by the natural functioning of the marketplace. However, where social convention prohibits the formation of a truly natural market, rents will not be regulated by the interest rates. Cardozo believes that such an aberration exists in England because of its aristocratic landlord class. This class receives rent because it has established a privileged legal sanction to its ownership of land, and its institutionalization of the Corn Laws has forced the rents to rise above the rate of interest at the expense of the capitalist and working classes. Moreover, since the landlord class receives its tribute as a result of the increasing difficulty of production, it has no economic interest in promoting the technological improvement of the soil. Consequently, production on the soil has definite limits in England which appear only "natural," as does the conflict among landlords, capitalists, and workers for scarce resources.

If aristocratic privilege is the source of technical constraints in agriculture, Cardozo can argue that a "natural" order will find no limits to production. Technology can be freely developed in agriculture as well as in manufacturing. When Cardozo applies this notion to the accumulation process, he removes the fetters restricting growth in Ricardo's theory and promises a future of sustained economic advance.

The Beneficent Cycles of Capital

Cardozo begins his own discussion of accumulation by defining profits and wages. He distinguishes between both a money profit and a real profit and between a money wage and a real wage. The money profit he considers equal to the amount of money received by the capitalist as a return on the investment: "real profit is the quantity of produce, whether destined for unproductive or productive consumption, for which this money will exchange."[19] "The *rate* of profit must therefore be in proportion to the difference between the outlay and the returns, not in money, but in what that money will purchase."[20] Cardozo applies the same distinction to money and real wages, so the wage rate "is in proportion to the difference between the money received by the labourer and what that money will command of the commodities necessary to his subsistence."[21] The wage rate has historically determined subsistence levels below which wages cannot fall.

This assertion indicates how much more optimistic Cardozo is than Malthus. Malthus's theory of economic cycles posits that wages can indeed fall below subsistence levels in periods of oversupply of labor; the fall will perform the useful task of eliminating unnecessary laborers until such time as their meager numbers are again needed in the production process. Only then will wages meet the level of subsistence; they will fall again when adequately fed laborers reproduce at a greater rate than the market demands.

While Cardozo accepts the reality of economic cycles in a laissez-faire economy, he believes that the condition of the laboring class varies from tolerable to enviable rather than from unacceptable (indeed, deadly) to tolerable, as in Malthus's theory. Cardozo's reasoning is based on his understanding of the theory of accumulation, which he has constructed from the inverse relationship between real wages and money wages and from the constancy of money profits. According to Cardozo, money wages fall and real wages rise as society progresses economically. Real wages rise "because the price of necessaries falls" as productivity increases so that the laborer is able to command a greater amount of goods with the same or even lower money wages.[22] Money wages fall, since the improved conditions of the working class encourage population growth: consequently, the supply of labor outstrips the demand for it and thereby forces money wages down. Although they fall, Cardozo asserts that they do not fall as fast as real wages rise, for otherwise "the labourer would not be improved, and he would not be induced to marry and increase."[23]

Unlike money wages, money profits in Cardozo's theory "do not fall in the progress of society, for although the price of all commodities declines, their quantity increases in equal proportion, and the capitalist receives as large a money amount as before the decline."[24] Real profits, however, do rise, "for they depend on the amount of the returns *in produce* compared with the amount of the expenditure, and as the quantity of production in the progress of society is multiplied, the real gains of the capitalist must increase."[25]

For Cardozo, the capitalist's expenditures consist of wages and rents. The former is the principal deduction for two reasons. First, in a natural economy rents never advance beyond the interest rate, and therefore they make up a small portion of the capitalist's expenses. Second, following Smith's distinction between productive and unproductive labor, Cardozo views capital's growth as dependent on productive labor. Only it is capable of producing commodities which can replace its wages as well as the capitalist's profits and the landlord's rents.[26]

Having offered these definitions and repudiated Ricardo's theory of diminishing returns in agriculture, Cardozo establishes the basic elements of his theory of accumulation. He develops it from a model which incorporates several distinct stages or moments. Cardozo posits that the introduction of machinery into agriculture increased the output of corn. Because of the increased supply, the price of food falls and real wages rise. The improved living conditions of the working class permit population to expand and eventually force the money wage to fall. Although the declining price of food preserves the improved conditions of the workers, the decrease in money wages allows the capitalist to hire more laborers—that is, to command more productive labor. Additional profits, resulting from the employment of more laborers, cause production to expand rapidly and to absorb the surplus population. As the demand for labor outstrips the supply, wages rise and eventually cut into profits. The reduction of profits forces the capitalist to substitute machinery for labor, which increases productivity and forces money wages down.[27] This substitution of machinery for labor sets the stage for a new round of accumulation.

Cardozo's description of the accumulation process, then, resolves all class conflict over the distribution of income by illustrating that real wages and profits advance with the progress of society. Only rents have a tendency to remain constant since they are fixed by the natural corn rent.

> We thus see how well these principles harmonize with those
> laid down on the subject of rent and the increase of the produce of

the land. . . . Thus is the capital made not more instrumental to the increase of population than population to the increase of capital— thus is the ratio of their increase precisely equal. Wages do not encroach on profits nor profits on wages. All that is necessary to the final results is, that science and skill should be able to overcome the difficulty of production on land of a decreasing fertility.[28]

Cardozo attempts to describe the natural law of economic growth in his theory of accumulation by demonstrating the harmony of interests among the three principal classes in society. Yet, in harmonizing society— that is, in naturalizing society—Cardozo separates economic growth from any natural determinants and paradoxically socializes production to an extent not found even in Ricardo's writings.

The paradox can best be understood by returning here to Cardozo's theory of population. In his theories of rent and accumulation, Cardozo consistently emphasizes that his theory of population differs substantially from that of Ricardo. For Ricardo—a student of Malthus on this point— population growth is determined by natural biological factors which in turn affect economic life by increasing the demand for corn and forcing less productive lands into cultivation. Cardozo counters Ricardo's theory by arguing that population grows as a result of the land's increasing productivity, which is itself principally determined by the accumulation process.[29]

Cardozo's ostensibly conservative political economy is, therefore, radical in uprooting production from the "natural" limits of human fecundity and agricultural productivity. Ricardo's and Malthus's pessimism no longer has meaning in Cardozo's world, nor does Dew's nostalgia for an agrarian order. Cardozo can endorse manufacturing without believing that the advance brings society one step closer to its inevitable demise. But predictably, by remaining within the discourse of classical political economy, Cardozo is bound by its limitations. His assumptions that society should reflect nature and that nature dictates the coexistence of the capitalist, landlord, and working classes prohibit him from truly overcoming the inherent determinism of laissez-faire thought.

In February of 1842, in a series of articles on manufacturing published in *The Southern Patriot*,[30] Cardozo argues that South Carolina has reached a stage conducive to the immediate introduction of manufacturing. Competition from the more fertile western lands has made agriculture in South Carolina unprofitable in Cardozo's estimation. To revive the state's economy Cardozo advocates the immediate diversification of South Carolina in particular and of the South in general.

Despite the innovation of discrediting the Ricardian pessimism inherited by Cooper and Dew, class struggle remains, in Cardozo's economic thought, a condition of the "natural" order. While Cardozo can dispense with the biological necessity for class conflict, he cannot resolve the contradiction between private and social interests inherent in the conception of classical political economy. This contradiction distorts the mutuality of interests in Cardozo's discussion of the accumulation process and pits worker and capitalist against one another on both economic and political levels.

In considering this impasse, let us reverse the order of investigation applied to Dew and consider first the contradiction between propertied and propertyless classes, then the contradiction among the propertied interests. According to Cardozo, the capitalist in the advanced stage of society seeks to reduce the money wages of the working class even to the point of actually reducing the real wages. While Cardozo asserts that this tendency will not reach such extremes and that the conflict will finally resolve itself through a new phase of accumulation in which real wages and profits advance, the immediate antagonism between capital and labor foments class struggle.

> The capitalist has every interest in that excess of population, which while it tasks the labourer to the utmost of his bodily energies from the pressure of want, keeps down his money wages to the lowest possible limit. The landlord has an equal interest in the depression of his corn wages. The toils and privations of the working classes may not always measure the amount of profits and the value of rents, for wages may advance proportionally with both; but, in the ordinary state of things, the sacrifices of the labourer will very nearly determine the gains of landlord and capitalist.[31]

In fact, Cardozo states in his journalistic writing that the class struggle between labor and capital actually structures the foundation of modern society: "The great social problem of the age is the true relation of capital and labor."[32]

He fears that this conflict over money wages may lead the working class to a revolutionary course against private property. The utopian socialist and communist writings of Owen, Fourier, Saint-Simon, and their ilk only confirm, to Cardozo, the potential threat of the base propertyless classes. The threat is patent in the United States. The Industrial Congress, comprised of agrarians like Arthur Brisbane and William Channing, incites Cardozo to an adamant defense of capital's virtues.

> The Industrial Convention is a sworn foe to all employers. It advocates the cause of the labourer, but it denounces the class who gives the labourer employment. This opposition to employers is founded on the most mistaken view of the principle of equality and justice. Is

the capitalist entitled to no remuneration for this capital invested—
for displays? The world is governed by a system of compensation.
Let each be contented with his allotted station.[33]

Thus, the working class assumes a peculiar status in Cardozo's theory,
as in free-trade thought in general. On the one hand, the working class
forms a "natural" component of society, and, on the other hand, it exists
as society's potential enemy. With this conception of the working class and
its potential political manifestations, Cardozo's writings on universal suffrage are understandably critical. During the Jacksonian democracy, Cardozo warns that an extension of suffrage will be an extension of the masses'
political power and hence a danger to private property.

> The whole current of history shows that there are two leading prin-
> ciples, which in every period of history, are more or less antagonisti-
> cal—namely that of property combined with sound intelligence, and
> of numbers, united with imperfect knowledge. On the due balance
> of these opposing impulses rests social order and prosperity.[34]

The conflict between classes represents, for Cardozo, only one aspect
of the fundamental social antagonism between majority and minority
rights; it emerges as well among propertied interests. The debates over the
tariff give ample illustration. As we have seen, Cardozo condemns the tariff but defends the Union, unlike his fellow South Carolina nullifiers.
While constrained in his rejection of the tariff, Cardozo joins with more
radical nullifiers in soundly attacking the emerging Northern abolitionist
movement.[35] For him, that movement presents a serious threat not only to
Southern slavery but also to the institution of private property in general.
Although the abolitionists are not inspired by working-class visions of a
future utopia, Cardozo foresees that their moral condemnation of slavery
and their call for its abolition can establish a dangerous precedent for the
emerging working-class movement. Thus, his appeal to Northern property owners to join with the South in restraining the fanaticism of the abolitionists is rooted in a logic quite similar to that of Dew. And like Dew's
defense of slavery, Cardozo's contains a sectional bias, for slavery itself becomes identified as a "constitutional" check against the working class for
the preservation of the republic.

The Peaceful Solution: Slavery

Cardozo's views on slavery can now be considered. As in my discussion of
Dew, it has been necessary to address economic and political elements of
Cardozo's theory before the issue of slavery could adequately be appreciated. The particular meaning of slavery has its determinants in general
economic and political concepts.

First, Cardozo seems to take for granted that, because of their "suitability" to the climate, black chattel slaves presented a solution, when the South was originally settled, to the problem of labor scarcity. Second, slavery seems to offer the planter a labor force that is contained politically. Like Dew, Cardozo finds this political solution to the discontents of the working class more satisfying than Ricardo's proposed systematic education of laborers in the principles of respect for property and for class distinctions.

With other Southern theorists, Cardozo argues that a politically impotent black labor force is "natural" by asserting the biological inferiority of blacks and concluding that slavery functions to regulate race relationships. Despite the oligarchic structure of Southern society, which results from the unequal distribution of slave property, Cardozo agrees with Dew that black slavery preserves social peace by creating a democratic feeling among whites, whether propertied or not. With economic development and the rise of a working class, Cardozo foresees that the South's peculiar institution will become even more necessary to avoid the potential political conflicts inherent in the accumulation process.

> The Southern states in form of government are democratical—in internal organization they are oligarchical. . . . Were population at the South wholly or nearly unmixed, as to color and caste, it might furnish more abundant elements of material wealth, or perhaps, a wider range of general prosperity, but it is scarcely questionable whether it would embrace as perfect constituents of stability, order and repose. . . . The effect of this is that we have no mobs, . . . no large popular risings, no agrarianism, no open contempt of law, no violence to those who administer it. . . . All the tendencies of Northern society are destructive.[36]

It should be clear, then, that Cardozo's attack on abolitionism is itself not conceived of as a means to preserve an agrarian society—though Cardozo does believe in a balance between the agrarian and manufacturing sectors. Nor is his polemic against the abolitionists intended to justify black slavery as a peculiarly Southern institution. Instead, his growing fears of a Northern majoritarian coalition bent on destroying the South's guarantor of harmonious democratic government lead him to a deepening commitment to slavery and finally to secession. Cardozo may dissent from Dew about the scientific character of Ricardian analysis, but he concurs in viewing slavery as necessary for republicanism.

On Slavery's Profitability

While Cardozo's theoretical framework resembles Dew's, subtle but significant differences distinguish them. Cardozo espouses the view that slavery and economic growth can be compatible. First, he denies Dew's contention that blacks are fit only for plantation life and not for garden farming or manufacturing. Second, he objects implicitly to Dew's assertion that the master-slave relationship necessarily retards technological growth. Yet, even if Cardozo reconciles slavery to the needs of industrial capitalism, he is unable to overcome the limits which the plantation system places on the home market. Without that internal dynamic, manufacturing is unable to expand; and without a growing industrial sector, per capita income stagnates and in turn threatens Cardozo's harmony of interests.

There is good reason for Cardozo's optimism regarding the employment of black labor in manufacturing. By 1842, the year of Cardozo's articles on manufacturing, black slavery had already proven itself adequate in manufacturing. Cardozo felt that it was suitable not only because black labor was morally prepared for the tedium of manufacturing but also because the master-slave relationship had been restructured.

Cardozo is a witness to the slave's spiritual worth in order to convince Southerners that slave labor is profitable in manufacturing. This moral defense of slave laborers is based on their propensity for self-denial and on their adherence to authority, two qualities that would presumably make slaves both profitable and reliable in industry. Despite the rationality of using slave labor in manufacturing, however, it could hardly enhance the dynamic of accumulation unless it could be conducive to technical change. If it could not, slave labor would be limited to craft manufacturing, where capitalist technology cannot displace labor.[37] Notwithstanding the prevalence of craft manufacturing in the period, Cardozo goes well beyond this restricted use of slaves when he overtly recommends that they be employed in the textile mills.

Cardozo can assume that slavery will function as wage labor in promoting exponential growth because the system of hiring out slaves to industries enjoyed significant popularity.[38] Southern manufacturers and urban employers during this period hired slaves extensively, renting their services from their masters. Usually, the rental of house servants and factory workers lasted for one year. The terms were established by a contract that included the payment to the master—that is, rental rate—and room, meals, and clothing for the hired slave. Cardozo's theory is consistent with this system because it permits economic dynamism as the manufacturers (free laborers) invest in technology to offset rising monetary labor costs when the demand for labor outstrips the supply.

Given Cardozo's confidence in hired-out slave labor, a resultant challenge develops: How are increasing numbers of slaves to be supplied to a growing capitalist economy? He rejects the reopening of the African slave trade, advocated by many radicals during the period. Although Cardozo does not detail his reason for objecting, it can be surmised that he saw no economic necessity for importing more slaves. In his theory of accumulation, as noted, the supply of labor is regulated by the declining monetary profit rate and by the necessary substitution of machinery for labor. Thus, there was no need to resort to an outside supply of labor to keep wages low enough to stimulate investment. The hiring-out system accomodated this process. Furthermore, because Cardozo contends that the transformation of subsistence farmers into wage laborers represents an advance, he can view the white population as a potential source of labor.[39] Competition between town and country for black labor could be minimized through this reserve pool of labor. And while Cardozo makes negative remarks about immigrant laborers because of their alleged socialist tendencies, they remain a theoretical source if accumulation proceeds faster than the supply of labor. The admission of potentially revolutionary immigrant labor is possible, given Cardozo's notion that black slavery ideologically pacifies white labor by uniting it with the propertied classes along racial lines.

The distinction between wage labor and slave labor in manufacturing does not seem to trouble Cardozo, but a more serious difficulty certainly does. It is the planters' resistance to change. For Cardozo, the South's integration into the world market would perpetuate the plantation system and consequently inhibit economic diversification. Even the hiring-out system, which promised economic dynamism, fluctuated with the demand for cotton.[40] Despite incipient manufacturing, the plantation system limited the home market and therefore stunted capitalist accumulation. Cardozo's articles insisted that South Carolina had reached a stage appropriate for diversification. He argues that the unproductive agricultural slaves be sold to the new southwestern plantations and that the capital be invested in textile mills. Yet for the most part, investments are to remain in agriculture throughout the economic lean years and of course in years when cotton is dear.

Cardozo cannot call for a rupture with the world market, for that would run counter to his free-trade position. Nor can he attack the plantation system as irrational, for that system is the foundation of black slavery, which has, in his mind, become the preserver of the republic. His only recourse is to plead for diversification

Cardozo's radicalism in political economy and the suitability of black labor for capitalist production strengthens one pole in Dew's argument: it makes slavery compatible with capitalism. But Cardozo does not finally establish the "correct" relationship between white and black labor in manufacturing, nor even develop a systematic position showing why black labor should be used in the industrial sector at all. These questions were to grow more crucial in the continuing debates on Southern independence. More important, Cardozo's schema inadvertently questions the viability of the plantation system itself and, consequently, further polarizes the defenses of slavery articulated in Dew's treatise. A position like Cardozo's, which sought to make slavery compatible with capitalism, is logically directed toward an almost unspeakable reevaluation of the plantation system. On the other hand, the position that seeks to make capitalism compatible with slavery is finally led to repudiate the dynamics of capitalism in defense of plantation life.

AFTERWORD

If it seems that, by opening up the language of political economy in ante-bellum America, we have brought the focus around to the underlying normative, as opposed to technical, concerns, we have in fact come full circle to Adam Smith's *Theory of Moral Sentiments*. The great difference is that the English economists agreed that "natural" moral behavior created a three-tier society, while the American economists were in conflict over the social results of the "natural" pursuit after wealth; that is, they could not agree on the social constituents of the natural order. Once the competing definitions of concepts like nature, freedom, and the republic are given economic—which is to imply moral—meanings, it should be possible to understand how the economic debates helped structure the political and constitutional crisis of the 1850s. The tragedy of the Union came from the "irreconcilable" clash between those who saw growth and equality as compatible in a utopian ideal of independent laborers, and those who recognized that capitalist growth, by its nature, had to create inequalities between republican free citizens and their laborers, whose political franchise would only threaten freedom and republican government.

NOTES

Introduction

1. For example, see Raymond Williams, *Marxism and Literature* (Oxford: Oxford University Press, 1977); Mark Poster, *Existential Marxism in Postwar France: From Sartre to Althusser* (Princeton: Princeton University Press, 1977); Alvin Gouldner, *The Two Marxisms* (New York: Seabury Press, 1980); and Jürgen Habermas, "Toward a Reconstruction of Historical Materialism," in *Communication and the Evolution of Society* (Boston: Beacon Press, 1979).

2. This interpretation does not follow the traditional one, which argues that contradictions between the forces of production and the relations of production are the motor force of history. G. A. Cohen offers the most rigorous formulation of this position in *Karl Marx's Theory of History: A Defense* (Princeton: Princeton University Press, 1978).

3. Habermas has attempted to integrate a "moral philosophy" into the structure of historical materialism. See *Communication*, chapters 3 and 4, and *Legitimation Crisis* (Boston: Beacon Press, 1975). John Rawls, *A Theory of Justice* (Cambridge: Harvard University Press, 1971) similarly makes use of ethical notions in establishing reasonable conditions for political association.

4. Josh Cohen explicates these ideas cogently in his "Marxism and Politics: or, Trouble in Paradise" (unpublished manuscript, 1980).

5. To state the problem somewhat differently, there must exist in capitalist society some set or sets of ideas that can justify the private appropriation of social production.

6. Louis Hartz, *The Liberal Tradition in America: An Interpretation of American Political Thought Since the Revolution* (New York: Harcourt, Brace and World, 1955). Recent work in American history has challenged Hartz's evaluation of Locke's influence on American political thought. Instead, current research has emphasized the importance of republican theory in the formation and continuing problematic of the American science of politics. For a review of this debate, see Dorothy Ross, "The Liberal Tradition Revisited and the Republican Tradition Addressed" in *New Directions in American History*, ed. John Higham and Paul Conkin (Baltimore: Johns Hopkins University Press, 1979). Garry Wills has explored Locke's influence on Jefferson in *Inventing America: Jefferson's Declaration of Independence* (New York: Doubleday, 1978). Although this essay follows the thinking of current research on the subject, Hartz's work still contains many enduring insights.

7. See Ralph Andreano, ed., *The Economic Impact of the American Civil War*

(Cambridge, Mass.: Schenkman, 1967), and Stuart Bruchey, *Growth of the Modern American Economy* (New York: Dodd, Mead and Co., 1975), chapter 3.

8. For example, see James Randall, "The Blundering Generation," *Mississippi Valley Historical Review* 27 (June 1940): 3–28; Stanley Elkins, *Slavery* (Chicago: University of Chicago Press, 1959); Roy Franklin Nichols, *The Disruption of American Democracy* (New York: Macmillan, 1948); Ulrich Bonnell Phillips, *The Course of the South to Secession* (1939; rpt. New York: Hill and Wang, 1964); Steven A. Channing, *Crisis of Fear: Secession in South Carolina* (New York: Norton, 1974); Eric Foner, *Free Soil, Free Labor, Free Men: The Ideology of the Republican Party before the Civil War* (London: Oxford University Press, 1970); and Eugene Genovese, *The Political Economy of Slavery: Studies in Economy and Society of the Slave South* (New York: Random House, 1967).

9. Rush Welter, *The Mind of America, 1820–1860* (New York: Columbia University Press, 1975), and Major Wilson, *Space, Time and Freedom: The Quest For Nationality and the Irrepressible Conflict, 1815–1865* (Westport: Greenwood, 1974).

10. See note 19.

11. Drew McCoy, *The Elusive Republic: Political Economy in Jeffersonian America* (Chapel Hill: University of North Carolina Press, 1980), especially chapter 3.

12. Alan Dawley, *Class and Community* (Cambridge, Mass.: Harvard University Press, 1976), and Anthony Wallace, *Rockdale: The Growth of an American Village in the Early Industrial Revolution* (New York: Alfred Knopf, 1978).

13. Eugene Genovese, "The Logical Outcome of the Slaveholders' Philosophy" in *The World the Slaveholders Made: Two Essays in Interpretation* (New York: Random House, 1971).

14. McCoy, *The Elusive Republic*, and Paul Conkin, *Prophets of Prosperity: America's First Political Economists* (Bloomington: Indiana University Press, 1980). Unfortunately, both of these texts appeared after I had completed this manuscript, so I was not able to make extensive use of them.

15. Joseph Cropsey, "On the Relationship of Political Science and Economics," *Political Science Review* 54 (March 1960): 3–14; J. G. A. Pocock, *The Machiavellian Moment: Florentine Political Thought and the Atlantic Republican Tradition* (Princeton: Princeton University Press, 1975); and Albert Hirschman, *The Passions and the Interests: Political Arguments for Capitalism before Its Triumph* (Princeton: Princeton University Press, 1977).

16. Quentin Skinner, "Meaning and Understanding in the History of Ideas," *History and Theory* 8 (1969): 3–53, and David Hollinger, "Historians and the Discourse of Intellectuals" in *New Directions in American Intellectual History*, ed. Higham and Conkin, pp. 42–63.

17. Karl Marx, *Theories of Surplus Value* (Moscow: Progress Publishers, 1968). See also David Levine, *Economic Studies: Contributions to the Critique of Economic Theory* (London: Routledge and Kegan Paul, 1979), Part I.

18. C. B. MacPherson, *The Political Theory of Possessive Individualism: Hobbes to Locke* (Oxford: Oxford University Press, 1962), and Elizabeth Fox-Genovese, *The Origins of Physiocracy: Economic Revolution and Social Change in Eighteenth-Century France* (Ithaca: Cornell University Press, 1976), employ a similar technique, only they differentiate between precapitalist and capitalist societies.

19. In a purely formal sense, capitalism is nothing more than the buying and selling of commodities to make profit, or, put differently, to allow the original value of the commodities to expand. Capital can therefore be thought of as self-expanding value. This formal definition implies that any society in which commerce predominates may be considered capitalist. However, such a definition abstracts from the way that production is organized and hence ignores the internal mechanism that sustains the process of self-expanding value, i.e., of continuous economic growth. That process demands that commodity production be generalized, with labor itself transformed into a commodity so that it can be "rationally" employed. For this reason, capitalism, as a system of production, is usually defined by the presence of wage labor. However, this definition is inadequate as well, since it does not include the competitive forces among capitalists by which the commodity labor power and the means of production are continually devalued. Without this devaluation the difference between outlay and return would not be sustained and economic growth would be limited. Thus, a complete definition of capitalist production must also include competition, technological change (the factory system), and industrial crises as opposed to commercial ones.

The predominance of these features indicates that capital has fully appropriated the relations and forces of production, and they are the characteristics of industrial capitalism, which predominates in the United States only after the Civil War. Prior to that time, commercial capital either directly or indirectly (through credit, transportation, etc.) organized precapitalist (non–wage labor) relationships into the existing capitalist world market or the emerging capitalist home market. During this preindustrial phase of capitalist development, the dominant classes resided in the countryside and in the large mercantile houses. This in turn conditioned the state's "inputs" and "outputs" as well as the legitimating discourse, as this study demonstrates.

The predominance of these precapitalist relationships, therefore, preclude any simple characterization of antebellum America, whether considered nationally or regionally, as a capitalist society and point to the importance of public policy debates. These debates indicate the ways that contemporaries wished their society to develop and thus provide for a periodization that necessarily goes beyond economic categories. In Marxist terminology, these debates over the tariff, slavery, and other issues offer material by which the organization and meaning of the political class struggle may be understood and characterized.

The results of this study also show that the ideological structure of those debates are as complex as the economic relationships that conditioned them. With regard to the Northern writings selected for study, a contradictory yet directionally clear formulation emerges: that the United States should promote economic growth, yet do so in a manner that would preserve the region's precapitalist relationships. For the Southerners two positions emerge, one that would encourage capitalist development—although in a manner that would in some fashion perpetuate slavery—and one that would retard capitalism in favor of a "traditional" slave society. Without close examination of the relative importance of each of these positions in the national policy debates and on secession itself, a decisive characterization of that region and its opposition to the Union is difficult to determine.

1. Adam Smith on the Wealth of Nations and the Poverty of Labor

1. For a discussion of the English Revolution and the political, economic, and constitutional issues involved, see Lawrence Stone, *The Causes of the English Revolution, 1529–1642* (New York: Harper and Row, 1972); Lawrence Stone, ed., *Social Change and Revolution in England, 1540–1640* (New York: Harper and Row, 1965); Christopher Hill, *The Century of Revolution, 1603–1714* (New York: Norton, 1966); J. R. Tanner, *English Constitutional Conflicts of the Seventeenth Century, 1603–1689* (London: Cambridge University Press, 1928); and J. G. A. Pocock, *The Ancient Constitution and the Feudal Law: A Study of English Historical Thought in the Seventeenth Century* (Cambridge: Cambridge University Press, 1957).

2. John Carswell, *From Revolution to Revolution: England 1688–1776* (London: Routledge and Kegan Paul, 1973), pp. 23–25; G. E. Mingay, *English Landed Society in the Eighteenth Century* (London: Routledge, 1963), pp. 111–120; Lewis Namier, *Structure of Politics at the Accession of George III*, 2nd ed. (New York: St. Martin's Press, 1968); Peter Mathias, *The First Industrial Nation: An Economic History of Britain, 1700–1914* (New York: Charles Scribner's, 1969), pp. 57–60; J. D. Chambers and G. E. Mingay, *The Agricultural Revolution 1750–1880* (London: Edward Arnold, 1967); and Christopher Hill, *Reformation to Industrial Revolution* (Harmondsworth: Penguin Books, 1969), pp. 142–145, 213–216.

3. This has been a hotly contested subject in English historiography. For views similar to mine, see Lawrence Stone, *The Crisis of the Aristocracy, 1558–1641* (Oxford: Clarendon Press, 1965); R. H. Tawney, *The Agrarian Problem in the Sixteenth Century* (1912; rpt. New York: Harper and Row, 1967); R. H. Tawney, "The Rise of the Gentry, 1558–1600," *Economic History Review* 11 (1941): 1–38; and Robert Brenner, "Agrarian Class Structure and Economic Development in Pre-Industrial Europe," *Past and Present* 70 (1976): 30–75. For the opposing view, see H. R. Trevor-Roper, "The Gentry, 1540–1640," *Economic History Review*, Supplement I (1953), and J. H. Hexter, "Storm Over the Gentry," in *Reappraisals in History: New Views on History and Society in Early Modern Europe*, 2nd ed. (Chicago: University of Chicago Press, 1979).

4. In the third volume of *Capital* Marx demonstrates that rent plays no economic function within capital's circuit. The landlord's claim to a share of the surplus value derives from the landlord's monopoly, which is protected by the sanctity of private property. Marx's analysis in this regard is soundly reasoned; however, the same cannot be said for his proposition that the landlord class constitutes an essential component of the capitalist mode of production. Here Marx confuses the historical peculiarities of the English transition to capitalism with the logical requirements of that mode of production. For an analysis compatible with my own, see Keith Tribe, "Economic Property and the Theorisation of Ground Rent," *Economy and Society* 6 (1977): 69–88.

5. Christopher Hill, *The World Turned Upside Down: Radical Ideas During the English Revolution* (New York: Viking Press, 1973); and Hill, *Century of Revolution*, p. 276.

6. The critique of the traditional view that the enclosures contributed to the formation of the working class and in so doing impoverished the English laboring classes may be found in G. E. Mingay, "The Transformation of Agriculture," in R.

M. Hartwell et al., *The Long Debate on Poverty: Eight Essays on Industrialization and the 'Condition of England'* (London: Institute of Economic Affairs, 1972), pp. 32–34; and J. D. Chambers, "Enclosure and Labour Supply in the Industrial Revolution," *Economic History Review*, 2nd series, 5 (1953): 319–343.

For works defending the traditional view, see E. J. Hobsbawn, "The British Standard of Living, 1790–1850," in *Labouring Men: Studies in the History of Labour* (New York: Basic, 1964); Karl Polanyi, *The Great Transformation: The Political and Economic Origins of Our Time* (1944, rpt. Boston: Beacon, 1971), chapters 6–9; Maurice Dobb, *Studies in the Development of Capitalism*, 2nd ed. (New York: International Publishers, 1970), pp. 6–7; and E. P. Thompson, *The Making of the English Working Class* (New York: Vintage, 1963), Part 3.

7. The following analysis relies heavily on Pocock, *The Machiavellian Moment*, chapters 10–14; Zera S. Fink, *The Classical Republicans: An Essay in the Recovery of a Pattern of Thought in Seventeenth Century England* (Evanston: Northwestern University Press, 1945); and Caroline Robbins, *The Eighteenth-Century Commonwealthman: Studies in the Transmission, Development and Circumstances of English Liberal Thought From the Restoration of Charles II Until the War with the Thirteen Colonies* (Cambridge: Harvard University Press, 1959).

8. Macpherson, *Possessive Individualism*, chapter 4.

9. Pocock, *The Machiavellian Moment*, p. 426.

10. According to Smith, the various systems of moral philosophy were derived from a concept of nature. See Adam Smith, *The Theory of Moral Sentiments* (Oxford: Clarendon Press, 1976), pp. 165, 305; hereafter cited as *TMS*. A discussion of the ancient, medieval, and enlightenment views of nature can be found in Manfred Riedel, "Nature and Freedom in Hegel's 'Philosophy of Right,'" in Z. A. Pelczynski, ed., *Hegel's Political Philosophy, Problems and Perspectives: A Collection of New Essays* (Cambridge: Cambridge University Press, 1971), pp. 135–140; and Charles Taylor, *Hegel* (Cambridge: Cambridge University Press, 1975), pp. 3–11. A discussion of premodern economics can be found in Joseph Schumpeter, *The History of Economic Analysis*, ed. Elizabeth Boody Schumpeter (New York: Oxford University Press, 1954), Part 2, chapters 1 and 2; and Barry Gordon, *Economic Analysis before Adam Smith* (London: Macmillan, 1975).

11. Joseph Cropsey, *Polity and Economy: An Interpretation of the Principles of Adam Smith* (The Hague: Martinus Nijhoff, 1957), pp. 1–5.

12. Smith, *TMS*, pp. 116–117.

13. This interpretation follows Cropsey, *Polity and Economy*, p. 19.

14. Smith, *TMS*, pp. 79–80. In his emphasis on the necessity of society for nature to prevail, Smith differs markedly from Lockean political theory, which posits that the individual stands outside of society as a separate producing being and only enters for protection against external threats. See Adam Smith, *Lectures on Justice, Police, Revenue and Arms* (1896; rpt. New York: Augustus M. Kelley, 1964), pp. 11–13; hereafter cited as *LJ*.

15. Hirschman, *The Passions and the Interests*, pp. 108–110. The relationship between *The Theory of Moral Sentiments* and *The Wealth of Nations* has long been a topic of interest. For a review of the debate, see D. D. Raphael and A. L. Macfie in the introduction to *TMS*, pp. 20–25.

16. Cropsey, *Polity and Economy*, pp. 32–40.

17. Ibid., pp. 94–95.

18. Levine, *Economic Studies*, pp. 33–38.

19. Adam Smith, *An Inquiry into the Nature and Causes of the Wealth of Nations*, ed. Edwin Cannan (1776; rpt. New York: Modern Library, 1937), p. 15; hereafter cited as *WN*.

20. A more detailed discussion of Smith's contradictory reasoning can be found in Levine, *Economic Studies*, pp. 38–58.

21. *WN*, p. 47.

22. Smith's historical writing conforms to neither ancient nor contemporary histories, which he analyzes in his *Lectures on Rhetoric and Belles Lettres*, ed. John M. Lothian (London: Thomas Nelson, 1963), chapters 16–20. Smith compares himself to Machiavelli, who "of all modern historians [is] the only one who has contented himself with that which is the chief purpose of history, to relate events and connect them to causes, without becoming a party on either side" (pp. 110–111).

Ronald Meek has written extensively on Smith's stages of history. See "Smith, Turgot, and the 'Four Stages' Theory," in *Smith, Marx and After: Ten Essays in the Development of Economic Thought* (London: Chapman and Hall, 1977); *Social Science and the Ignoble Savage* (Cambridge: Cambridge University Press, 1976); and "The Scottish Contribution to Marxist Sociology," in *Economics and Ideology and Other Essays: Studies in the Development of Economic Thought* (London: Chapman and Hall, 1967). Also see Andrew Skinner, "Adam Smith: An Economic Interpretation of History," in *Essays on Adam Smith*, ed. A. S. Skinner and Thomas Wilson (London: Oxford University Press, 1975), p. 136. For an evaluation of Smith's historical writings, see A. S. Skinner, "General Introduction," in Adam Smith, *The Wealth of Nations*, (Harmondsworth: Penguin, 1977), pp. 50–57.

23. *WN*, p. 672, and *LJ*, pp. 14–15.

24. *WN*, Book III, chapters 3 and 4.

25. Cropsey, *Polity and Economy*, p. 62.

26. *WN*, pp. 391–392.

27. Ibid., p. 259. Analytically these stages may be distinguished as the simple commodity and capitalist societies. Macpherson, *Possessive Individualism*, offers a useful exposition of this subject.

28. Smith discusses parsimony under the virtue of prudence; see *TMS*, pp. 212–213, 215.

29. An interesting discussion of Smith's views on the division of labor and its contribution to the critique of capitalism can be found in Nathan Rosenberg, "Adam Smith on the Division of Labour: Two Views or One?" *Economica* 32 (1965): 127–139; and E. G. West, "The Political Economy of Alienation: Karl Marx and Adam Smith," *Economica* 31 (1964): 23–32.

30. *WN*, pp. 734–735.

31. Ibid., p. 30.

32. Ibid., p. 65.

33. Ibid., p. 30.

34. Ibid., p. 314.

35. Whether Smith's knowledge of the Industrial Revolution was insufficient

to generate a theory of industrial production has become a controversy between historians of economic thought and economic historians. Much of the debate focuses on Smith's actual familiarity with the technical improvements that have become enshrined as the pivotal forces in the Industrial Revolution. Lists of Smith's references to these innovations, his association with such leading inventors as Watts, and the number of books in his library pertaining to these matters have weighted the debate. Thus, it can be suggested that the debate has proceeded on the assumption that economic theory is directly related to economic organization.

For an introduction to this debate, see C. P. Kindleberger, "The Historical Background: Adam Smith and the Industrial Revolution," and Asa Briggs, "Comments," in *The Market and the State: Essays in Honour of Adam Smith*, ed. Thomas Wilson and Andrew Skinner (London: Oxford University Press, 1976); and Samuel Hollander, *The Economics of Adam Smith* (Toronto: University of Toronto Press, 1973), pp. 236–241. Keith Tribe offers a critique of this debate in "The 'Histories' of Economic Discourse," *Economy and Society* 6 (1977): 314–344; and *Land, Labour and Economic Discourse* (London: Routledge and Kegan Paul, 1978).

36. *WN*, pp. 259–261.

37. Karl Marx, *Capital: A Critique of Political Economy* (Moscow: Progress Publishers, 1965), Vol. I, p. 348.

38. *WN*, p. 344.

39. Ibid., pp. 347–348.

40. For an elaboration of these distinctions, see Etienne Balibar, "The Basic Concepts of Historical Materialism," in Louis Althusser and Etienne Balibar, *Reading Capital* (New York: New Left Books, 1970); and Dobb, *Studies*, pp. 258–260.

41. Hollander, *The Economics of Adam Smith*, pp. 109–113, details these assertions and surveys the literature on the Industrial Revolution. Of particular interest are Dobb, *Studies in the Development of Capitalism*, chapter 4; Phyllis Deane, *The First Industrial Revolution* (London: Cambridge University Press, 1965); and J. H. Clapham, *An Economic History of Modern Britain: The Railway Age, 1820–1850* (London: Cambridge University Press, 1926).

42. E. J. Hobsbawn, *Industry and Empire: The Making of Modern English Society, 1750 to the Present* (Harmondsworth: Penguin, 1970), p. 109; Clapham, *Economic History of Modern Britain*, chapter 5; and Allan Thompson, *The Dynamics of the Industrial Revolution* (London: Edward Arnold, 1973), chapter 2. Econometricians have argued for an earlier date, but these findings do not contradict the basic point that Smith wrote during England's preindustrial period. For example, see Donald McCloskey, ed., *Essays on a Mature Economy: Britain after 1840* (Princeton: Princeton University Press, 1971).

43. *LJ*, pp. 94–96.

44. Ibid., p. 8. See also Warren Samuels, *The Classical Theory of Economic Policy* (Cleveland: World Publishing Co., 1966), chapter 5. Cropsey argues that "Smith's position may be interpreted to mean that commerce generates freedom and civilization, and at the same time free institutions are indispensable to the preservation of commerce" (*Polity*, p. 95).

Hirschman, *The Passions and the Interests*, p. 104, objects to Cropsey's interpretation by arguing that political freedom is not significant for Smith. To the extent that Smith equates political freedom solely with rule by law instead of with republican rule in general, Hirschman is correct. However, this limited political freedom is necessary for commerce.

45. *LJ*, pp. 96–104. In these passages Smith identifies slavery with chattel slavery, serfdom, and indentured servitude. Ironically, Smith notes that where slavery coexists with commercial pursuits, the conditions of life deteriorate for the slaves. See also *WN*, pp. 364–365, 648.

46. Cropsey, *Polity*, p. 72; Lionel Robbins, *The Theory of Economic Policy in English Classical Political Economy* (London: Macmillan, 1953), pp. 55–61.

47. *WN*, p. lviii.

48. Ibid., p. 740.

49. Ibid., pp. 736–738.

50. Ibid., p. 397.

51. As Coats has pointed out, Smith's attitude toward mercantilist policy is not without its ambiguities. Although he believes mercantilist policy restricts economic growth, he nonetheless admits that it has positive effects and that substantial differences exist in its application among European nations. For example, England and France have systems that are far more beneficial than Spain's and Portugal's. See A. W. Coats, "Adam Smith and the Mercantile System," in *Essays on Adam Smith*, ed. Skinner and Wilson, pp. 228–231.

52. Levine, *Economic Studies*, p. 15; Tribe, "The 'Histories' of Economic Discourse." For an introduction to mercantilist thought, see E. A. J. Johnson, *Predecessors of Adam Smith: The Growth of British Economic Thought* (New York: Prentice-Hall, 1937); Dobb, *Studies*, pp. 198–210; and Elie Heckscher, *Mercantilism* (London: G. Allen and Unwin, 1935), Vol. II, Part 5.

53. *WN*, Book III.

54. Ibid., p. 392.

55. Ibid., p. 87.

56. Ibid., p. 250.

57. Ibid., pp. 392–393.

58. Ibid., p. 249.

59. Ibid., pp. 481–482.

60. Ibid., p. 586.

61. Smith discusses the form of government in relation to historical and economic development in *LJ*, pp. 9–46. He lists the political practices that have secured English liberty in *LJ*, pp. 9–46.

62. Duncan Forbes argues convincingly for this distinction in "Sceptical Whiggism, Commerce and Liberty," in *Essays on Adam Smith*, ed. Skinner and Wilson, p. 184: "The true end of government, is liberty, but liberty in the sense of the Civilians and Grotious, Pufendorf, and the authoritative exponents of natural law: the personal liberty and security of individuals guaranteed by law, equivalent to justice, peace, order, protection of property, the sanctity of contracts." This interpretation corresponds with Smith's emphasis on economic freedom as history's end, but still maintains the importance of the state in establishing the conditions of the advanced order. See also *LJ*, p. 52.

63. Forbes, "Sceptical Whiggism," pp. 187–190, and Donald Winch, *Adam*

Smith's Politics: An Essay in Historiographic Revision (Cambridge: Cambridge University Press, 1978), pp. 94–95.

64. *WN*, p. 651

2. Ricardo and Malthus on Who Uses Labor Best, Capitalists or Landlords

1. David S. Landes, *The Unbound Prometheus: Technological Change and Industrial Development in Western Europe from 1750 to the Present* (London: Cambridge University Press, 1970), chapter 2. Reinhard Bendix discusses the changes in industrial ideology during this period in *Work and Authority in Industry: Ideologies of Management in the Course of Industrialization* (Berkeley: University of California Press, 1974), Part I.

2. Donald Grove Barnes, *A History of the English Corn Laws from 1660 to 1846* (New York: F. S. Crofts, 1930); C. R. Fay, *The Corn Laws and Social England* (London: Cambridge University Press, 1932); Norman McCord, *The Anti-Corn Law League, 1838–1846* (London: George Allen and Unwin, 1958); William Grampp, *The Manchester School of Economics* (Stanford: Stanford University Press, 1960).

3. The Corn Laws can be divided into three stages between 1660 and 1846. Until 1660 the Corn Laws sought to protect the consumer by regulating the internal market. After 1660 the interests of the producer became coequal with those of the producer, for the Corn Laws now regulated the exportation of corn. In 1815 the landlords became the sole beneficiary of the Corn Laws, which were designed to prohibit importation. See Barnes, *History of the English Corn Laws*, pp. 285–287.

4. Ronald Meek, "Physiocracy and Classicism in Britain," in *The Economics of Physiocracy: Essays and Translations* (Cambridge: Harvard University Press, 1963), and Bernard Semmel, *The Rise of Free Trade Imperialism: Classical Political Economy, the Empire of Free Trade and Imperialism 1750–1850* (London: Cambridge University Press, 1970), chapter 3, trace the physiocratic influence in British political economy.

5. Samuel Hollander, "Malthus and the Post-Napoleonic Depression," *History of Political Economy* 1 (1969): 306–335, discusses in detail the debate on economic crisis between Malthus and Ricardo in light of the post-Napoleonic crisis.

6. Grampp, *The Manchester School*, p. 45; Harold Perkin, *The Origins of Modern English Society: 1780–1880* (Toronto: University of Toronto Press, 1969), p. 378; and G. E. Mingay, *Rural Life in Victorian England* (London: Heinemann, 1977), p. 26.

7. Mingay, *English Landed Society*, p. 196.

8. F. M. L. Thompson, *English Landed Society in the Nineteenth Century* (London: Routledge, 1963), chapter 9; and Mingay, *Rural Life*, pp. 43–51.

9. James Mill, "The Article on Government, reprinted from the Supplement to the *Encyclopedia Britannica*" in *Essays on Government* (London: J. Innes, n.d.), p. 27.

10. Ibid.

11. Perkin, *Modern English Society*, pp. 373–375.

12. J. H. Plumb, *England in the Eighteenth Century* (Harmondsworth: Pen-

guin Books, 1976), chapter 3; and E. P. Thompson, "The Peculiarities of the English," in *The Socialist Register, 1965*, ed. Ralph Miliband and John Saville (New York: Monthly Review Press, 1965), p. 326.

13. E. P. Thompson, "The Peculiarities of the English," pp. 318–319; and Semmel, *Free Trade Imperialism*, pp. 30–33.

14. Grampp, *The Manchester School*, p. 91.

15. David Thompson, *England in the Nineteenth Century 1815–1914* (Harmondsworth: Penguin Books, 1950), pp. 126–130. Perkin, *Modern English Society*, pp. 401–402, argues that the moderation of the trade unions offered proof of the working class's fitness for enfranchisement.

16. F. M. L. Thompson, *English Landed Society*, p. 272; David Thompson, *England in the Nineteenth Century*, pp. 119–121; and Mingay, *Rural Life*, p. 27. An analysis of the aristocracy's political persistence can be found in W. L. Guttsman, *The British Political Elite* (London: MacGibbon and Kee, 1963), chapter 3.

17. For a discussion of the pamphlets, see Mark Blaug, *Ricardian Economics: A Historical Survey*, (New Haven: Yale University Press, 1958), pp. 12–13; Maurice Dobb, *Theories of Value and Distribution since Adam Smith: Ideology and Economic Theory* (London: Cambridge University Press, 1973), pp. 67–73; and James Bonar, *Malthus and His Work* (New York: Macmillan, 1924), pp. 227–253.

18. Elie Halévy discusses Smith's influence on utilitarian thought in *The Growth of Philosophic Radicalism* (New York: Macmillan, 1928), p. 153. For Halévy, the concept of utility unified the thought of such divergent thinkers as Malthus and Godwin, Burke and Paine.

19. D. S. L. Cardwell, "Science and the Steam Engine, 1790–1825," in *Science and Society, 1600–1900*, ed. P. Mathias (Cambridge: Cambridge University Press, 1972); and A. E. Musson and E. Robinson, *Science and Technology in the Industrial Revolution* (Manchester: University of Manchester Press, 1969), p. 72. Also see Clapham, *Economic History of Modern Britain*, and Deane, *The First Industrial Revolution*.

20. Tribe, "The 'Histories' of Economic Discourse," pp. 326–337; and *Land, Labour and Economic Discourse*, pp. 101–109.

21. For an account of the contemporary moral refutations of the classical position, see William Grampp, "Classical Economics and Its Moral Critics," *History of Political Economy* 5 (1973): 359–374. The debate on the inhumanity of classical political economy continues in modern scholarship; see, for example, A. W. Coats's response to E. P. Thompson's *The Making of the English Working Class*. A. W. Coats, "The Classical Economist and the Labourer," in *Land, Labour and Population in the Industrial Revolution: Essays Presented to J. P. Chambers*, ed. E. L. Jones and G. E. Mingay (New York: Barnes and Noble, 1968).

22. Ricardo summarized the need for sustained accumulation to offset working-class discontent in the following letter written to a friend shortly after the Peterloo Massacre:

> The outrages of which they (the working class) are at present guilty may be sufficiently accounted for from the stagnation in trade which has never failed to produce similar consequences. I am disposed to think that the people are both improved in morals and in knowledge, and therefore that they are less outrageous under these unavoidable reverses than they

formerly used to be. I am in hopes that as they increase in knowledge they will more clearly perceive that the destruction of property aggravates and never relieves their difficulties. (Ricardo to Trower, 15 July 1816, *The Works and Correspondence of David Ricardo*, ed. Pero Sraffa and M. H. Dobb [Cambridge: Cambridge University Press, 1951], Vol. II, p. 49.)

Similar passages can be found in Malthus's work; for example:

> The indigence which is hopeless destroys all vigorous exertion, and confines the efforts to what is sufficient for bare existence. It is the hope of bettering our condition, and the fear of want, rather than want itself, that is the best stimulus to industry; and its most constant and best directed efforts will almost invariably be found among a class of people above the class of the wretchedly poor. (*An Essay on Population* [London: Dent, 1958], Vol. II, p. 143.)

23. For a discussion of Ricardo's economics, see the editor's introduction in *Works*, ed. Sraffa and Dobb, Vol. I, and Blaug, *Ricardian Economics*. David Levine offers an interpretation of Ricardo's work compatible with the one found in this essay in *Economic Studies*, chapter 3. For an excellent discussion of Ricardian economics in the context of utilitarian thought, see Halévy, *Growth of Philosophic Radicalism*, pp. 317–342. I wrote the essay on Ricardo prior to publication of Samuel Hollander, *The Economics of David Ricardo* (Toronto: University of Toronto Press, 1979).

24. David Ricardo, *Principles of Political Economy and Taxation* (Harmondsworth: Penguin Books, 1971), p. 49.

25. The following paragraph is drawn from Levine, *Economic Studies*, pp. 107–117.

26. David Ricardo, *Notes on Malthus' Principles of Political Economy*, in *Works*, ed. Sraffa and Dobb, Vol. II, p. 46, n. 18, and p. 48, n. 20.

27. Halévy, *Growth of Philosophic Radicalism*, p. 154.

28. Ibid., p. 320.

29. Ricardo, *Principles*, p. 91. Ricardo here confuses rent's social determination with the land's physical properties. Cardozo criticized Ricardo for this confusion but never resolved the difficulty. See Chapter 7.

30. Ricardo comments that the "rise of rent is always the effect of the increasing wealth of the country, and of the difficulty of providing food for its augmented population. It is a symptom, but it is never a cause of wealth; for wealth often increases most rapidly while rent is either stationary, or even falling. Rent increases most rapidly, as the disposable land decreases in its productive powers. Wealth increases most rapidly in those countries where the disposable land is most fertile, where importation is least restricted, and where through agricultural improvements, productions can be multiplied without any increase in the proportional quantity of labour, and where consequently the progress of rent is slow" (Ricardo, *Principles*, pp. 100–101).

31. Ibid., p. 170.

32. An examination of Ricardo's plan for gradually "withdrawing" the Corn Laws further indicates his conciliatory position. See "On Protection to Agriculture, 1822," in *Works*, ed. Sraffa and Dobb, Vol. IV, pp. 261–266.

33. Ricardo, *Principles*, pp. 188–189.

34. Say's law assumes that an individual exchanges a commodity (c) on the market for money (m) in order to acquire another commodity with which to satisfy particular needs, creating a circuit of c-m-c, where money is simply a means of facilitating the circulation of commodities as simple use values. Consumption, not profit, is the object of production. If profits are to be included, the circuit must be altered to read m-c-m' where m' represents an increment in the original exchange value or, simply put, profit. Here it is money that opens and closes the circuit rather than two qualitatively different use values. If money were not increased as a result of its circulation, then its circulation would have no purpose in the m-c-m' circuit.

If one assumes that the first circuit is operative, it is quite reasonable to argue that for every increase in supply there is a corresponding increase in demand. If the circuit is interrupted, it is because the use values being produced are not in proportion to the demand for them. A crisis resolves this problem of proportionality by forcing suppliers to produce the commodities that are in demand in the appropriate numbers. If, however, social production is conceived from the perspective m-c-m' then Say's law falls apart, since the possibility of overproduction is inherent in the circuit itself. Capitalists will potentially withhold their commodities from sale if they cannot acquire a price sufficient to realize an average return on their investment. A crisis of overproduction arises when capitalists are unable to sell all of their products at a given profit margin due to inadequate effective demand.

35. Barton corresponded with Ricardo shortly before Barton published *Observations on the Circumstances which Influence the Condition of the Labouring Classes of Society* in 1817. See Ricardo to Barton, 10 May 1817, *Works*, ed. Sraffa and Dobb, Vol. II, p. 157.

The classical economists, e.g., McCulloch and Malthus, were never very pleased with Ricardo's concession to the labor economists. Blaug argues that it was the challenge of the labor economists, e.g., Ravenstone, Gray, Bray, and Hodgskin, that finally caused the collapse of the Ricardian system, for these economists adopted Ricardo's labor theory of value to demonstrate the economic logic of their moral assertion that the entire social product belonged to labor. See Blaug, *Ricardian Economics*, p. 224; and Tribe, *Land, Labour and Economic Discourse*, chapter 7. Pedro Schwartz challenges this view in *The New Political Economy of J. S. Mill* (London: Weidenfield and Nicolson, 1972), p. 16.

36. For a general introduction to Malthus's work, see Bonar, *Malthus and His Work*. Of the many works written on Malthus's economics, a particularly useful one is Morton Paglin, *Malthus and Lauderdale: The Anti-Ricardian Tradition* (New York: Augustus M. Kelley, 1961). Halévy, *Growth of Philosophic Radicalism*, pp. 225–248, offers numerous insights into Malthus's work.

37. Ricardo, *Notes on Malthus' Principles*, in *Works*, ed. Sraffa and Dobb, Vol. II, p. 50.

38. "It follows, that the relation of the supply to the demand, either actual or contingent, is the dominant principle in the determination of prices whether market or natural, and that the cost of production can do nothing but in subordination to it, that is, merely as this cost affects actually or contingently the relation which the supply bears to the demand" (Ibid., p. 47).

39. Malthus redefines natural price in order to disassociate himself from

Smith's distinction between natural and market price. According to Smith, if a commodity actually sells on the market at its cost of production, then its market price is equivalent to its natural price or value. If it sells above or below that price, then its market price deviates from its value as a result of supply and demand. For Malthus, value and market price are identical, so he finds Smith's differentiation between market price and natural price misleading. In this way Malthus alters Smith's reasoning and the significance he assigns to the cost of production.

40. Ricardo, *Notes on Malthus' Principles*, in *Works*, ed. Sraffa and Dobb, Vol. II, p. 49.

41. Ibid., pp. 212–213.

42. Ibid., p. 271.

43. Malthus questions two additional Ricardian propositions regarding technology. In Ricardo's schema the landlord class opposes technological innovation in the short run, since it will stop production on the least fertile land and consequently reduce rents. In the near future, as demand for food increases because of continued accumulation, those lands forced out of production by technological innovation will be brought back into production, and rents will rise to a level exceeding that of the previous period. Malthus objects. Again he accuses Ricardo of not being able to describe reality accurately, for in his proposition concerning technology's immediate effect on rents, Ricardo assumes that technology is suddenly introduced and dramatically alters supply. In the real world, Malthus asserts, technology is gradually introduced so that demand is able to keep pace with supply, thereby permitting continuous use of the least fertile lands. Hence, technology, both in the short run and in the long run, can only improve the landlord's economic position.

The antagonism that Ricardo finds between labor and technology, which results from the substitution of fixed for circulating capital, remains to be treated. Malthus concedes that in individual cases "the demand for labour can only be in proportion to the increase of the circulating, not the fixed capital," (Ibid., p. 234), so labor can be thrown into the ranks of the unemployed as a result of factor substitution. But from a national perspective this can hardly be the case, since it implies that the introduction of machinery will retard economic growth. In defense of his proposition, Malthus merely cites the enormous economic growth Great Britain has experienced as a result of the extended use of machinery. The general trend runs counter to the particular possibility of increased unemployment because as long as "the market for products can be proportionally extended, the whole value of the capital and revenue of a state is greatly increased by [the introduction of machinery], and a great demand for labor created" (Ibid., p. 236).

44. Quoted in Ronald Meek, *The Economics of Physiocracy* (Cambridge: Cambridge University Press, 1963), p. 337.

45. Malthus rules out the possibility that increasing population can create an increased demand. For a new population to be able to sustain demand, it requires the power to purchase goods. It can only acquire that power if it is employed. But no matter how plentiful, labor will only be employed if capital is capable of earning a profit. If capital is producing commodities in excess of demand, its potential for realizing a profit is diminished, thereby limiting employment. Malthus therefore concludes that an increase in population cannot serve as a stimulus to production.

46. Consequently, Malthus believes that "thirty or forty proprietors, with incomes answering to between one thousand and five thousand a year, would create a much more effective demand for wheaten bread, good meat, and manufactured products, than a single proprietor possessing a hundred thousand" (Ricardo, *Notes on Malthus' Principles*, in *Works*, ed. Sraffa and Dobb, Vol. II, pp. 384–385).

47. Ricardo summarizes his views on the role of unproductive labor in the accumulation process in this way: "A body of unproductive labourers are just as necessary and as useful with view to future production, as a fire, which should consume in the manufacturer's warehouse the goods which those unproductive labourers would otherwise consume" (Ibid., p. 421, n. 284).

48. Malthus further disguises his physiocratic bent by altering his view on productive labor from the first to the second edition of the *Principles*. In the first edition Malthus argues that labor employed in agriculture is more productive than labor employed in manufacturing. In the second edition, he omits this passage, most likely because of Ricardo's criticisms. See Ibid., pp. 18–19, n. 6.

49. For the most part, productive labor's wages come out of the landlord's rents. The landlord's revenues, therefore, are the basis for the increased power by which the prices of commodities are maintained at the necessary price. This power, of course, is a gift of Providence, representing a surplus of the necessaries required to physically sustain agricultural capitalists and laborers. The aristocracy's propensity to consume and the state's responsibility to ensure the smooth functioning of the economic machine constitute the principal mechanisms by which this gift is transferred to the capitalists. In other words, the will to purchase goods resulting from increased accumulation is provided directly by the landlords and indirectly by the state, and the power for these purchases is afforded by Providence. Through its desire to accumulate, the capitalist class reinvests this gift in productive activity, thereby increasing society's wealth along with rents. The landlords, on the other hand, continue to spend, ensuring profits and establishing the foundations for the higher pursuits of the arts, letters, sciences, and politics. With the exception of Malthus's opinion on profits, this schema is in keeping with Quesnay's *Tableau Economique* in that it is the landlords' expenditures that guarantee the operation of the system.

50. Malthus's somewhat confused defense of the Corn Laws begins by asserting that from an individual capitalist's perspective this policy may not seem beneficial. However, when considered from the standpoint of the nation, a protective policy offers the following economic benefits. First, the extra capital sunk into the land reaps extra profits, since the farmer must be reimbursed for the capital invested. At the end of the lease these additional profits become part of the landlord's revenues. Second, the capital invested in the soil is a permanent improvement to the nation. Third, the Corn Laws force investment in agriculture, which yields a rent as well as a profit. Fourth, if the Corn Laws did not exist, corn would be cheaper in money terms, but additional capital and labor would be required for its production, since technological innovation would lag. The increased productivity resulting from the technological innovation that is fostered directly by the Corn Laws increases the population while at the same time improving the living conditions of the working class by lowering the costs of goods. In all of these ways the

nation grows economically and per capita income rises. See Paglin, *Malthus and Lauderdale*, p. 91.

51. J. R. McCulloch, a prominent disciple of Ricardo, countered this characterization of the towns as dens of iniquity. Instead, he argued, urban life provides greater cultural opportunities for the masses by exposing them to the high cultural pursuits which only cities can generate. For a discussion of McCulloch's views, see Coats, "The Classical Economist and the Labourer." Ricardo seems to have shared similar views; see *Works*, ed. Sraffa and Dobb, Vol. IX, pp. 192–193.

52. "I can hardly contemplate a more bloody revolution than I should expect would take place, if Universal suffrage and annual parliaments were effected by the intimidation of such meetings as have been latterly taking place. These people have evidently been taught to believe that such a reform would completely relieve all their distresses; and when they found themselves, as they most certainly would, entirely disappointed, massacre would in my opinion go on till it was stopt by a military despotism" (Malthus to Ricardo, October 14, 1819, *Works*, ed. Sraffa and Dobb, Vol. VIII, pp. 107–108).

"I am certainly not more inclined than I was before, to Radicalism, after witnessing the proceedings of Hunt, Watson and Co., if by Radicalism is meant Universal Suffrage. I fear, however, that I should not think the moderate reform which you are willing to accede to, a sufficient security for good government. Your scheme of reform, if I recollect right, is as much too moderate, as the universal suffrage plan is too violent,—something between these would give me satisfaction. Do you think that any great number of the people can really be deluded with the idea that any change in the representation would completely relieve them from their distresses? There may be a few wicked persons who would be glad of a revolution, with no other view but to appropriate to themselves the property of others, but this object must be confined to a very limited number, and I cannot think so meanly of the undertakings of those who are well disposed, as to suppose that they sincerely believe a reform in Parliament would give them work, or relieve the country from the payment of the load of taxes with which we are now burthened, —neither do I observe in the speeches which are addressed to the mob any such extravagant expectations held out to them" (Ricardo to Malthus, November 9, 1819, *Works*, ed. Sraffa and Dobb, Vol. VIII, pp. 129–230).

53. Halévy, *Growth of Philosophic Radicalism*, p. 238.

54. Malthus's *Essay on Population* went through six editions. For a discussion of the alterations from one edition to the next, see Bonar, *Malthus and His Work*, Book I; and the editor's introduction in Thomas Malthus, *An Essay on Population and a Summary View of the Principles of Population*, ed. Anthony Flew (Harmondsworth; Penguin Books, 1970).

55. T. R. Malthus, *Principles of Political Economy Considered with a View to Their Practical Application*, 2nd ed. (1836; rpt. New York: Augustus M. Kelley, 1951), p. 334.

56. Ibid., p. 209.

57. The principal positive check to population seems to be famine, since this is the consequence of population's outstripping its means of subsistence. Other positive checks are sufficient to forestall this particular check. For example, dis-

ease, plagues, harsh weather, and famine are all forms of misery that result directly from nature. Vice, on the other hand, consists of those social circumstances such as "unwholesome occupations, severe labor . . . extreme poverty, bad nursing of children, great towns, wars" (Malthus, *An Essay on Population*, Vol. II, p. 14).

58. The preventive check, however, does not merely refer to self-control. In Malthus's opinion, these checks must be labeled as vice: "Promiscuous intercourse, unnatural passions, violations of the marriage bed, and improper arts to conceal the consequences of irregular connections, are preventive checks that clearly come under the head of vice" (Malthus, *An Essay on Population*, Vol. I, p. 14). Contraception, for Malthus, also fell under the rubric of vice.

59. Ibid., Vol. II, p. 214.

60. Ibid., pp. 186–187.

61. Ricardo to Trower, 24 June 1818, *Works*, ed. Sraffa and Dobb, Vol. VII, p. 270.

3. Daniel Raymond on Wealth without a Working Class

1. Edward Gibbon Wakefield, *England and America: A Comparison of the Social and Political State of Both Nations* in *The Collected Works of Edward Gibbon Wakefield*, ed. M. F. Lloyd Prichard (Glasgow: Collins, 1968), pp. 470–499.

2. Ibid., p. 489.

3. Evsey Domar, "The Causes of Slavery or Serfdom: A Hypothesis," *Journal of Economic History* 30 (1970): 18–32; Stanley Engerman, "Some Considerations Relating to Property Rights in Man," *Journal of Economic History* 33 (1973): 43–65; and Edmund S. Morgan, *American Slavery, American Freedom: The Ordeal of Colonial Virginia* (New York: Norton, 1975), especially chapters 6–7 and pp. 11–12.

4. Gavin Wright, *The Political Economy of the Cotton South: Households, Markets, and Wealth in the Nineteenth Century* (New York: Norton, 1978), pp. 44–49; Robert Lawrence Sherry, "Petty Bourgeois Agriculture in the Nineteenth Century United States" (Ph.D. diss., Yale University, 1979), pp. 1–15; and Diane Lindstrom, *Economic Development in the Philadelphia Region, 1810–1860* (New York: Columbia University Press, 1978), pp. 8–18. For an opposing view, see Paul W. Gates, "Problem of Agricultural History, 1790–1840," *Agricultural History* 46 (1972): 33–58; and Clarence H. Danhof, *Change in Agriculture: The Northern United States 1820–1870* (Cambridge: Harvard University Press, 1969), p. 280.

To be more accurate, Wakefield believed that yeoman farming in the United States could be made compatible with capitalism by means of a protective tariff. Following a line of reasoning similar to Henry Carey's, Wakefield suggested that a tariff would integrate the farm into a capitalist market (Wakefield, *The Collected Works*, pp. 491–497).

5. Gates, "Problem of Agricultural History," pp. 58, 80–85; and Sherry, "Petty Bourgeois Agriculture," pp. 119–120, 156–159. The classic work on household manufacture remains Rolla Tryon, *Household Manufacture in the United States, 1640–1860* (Chicago: University of Chicago Press, 1917). See Sherry, "Petty Bourgeois Agriculture," pp. 123–125 for an assessment of Tryon's work.

6. Sherry, "Petty Bourgeois Agriculture," pp. 117–120, 136–142; Robert Brooke Zevin, "The Growth of Cotton Textile Production after 1815," in *The Re-*

interpretation of American Economic History, ed. Robert Fogel and Stanley Engerman (New York: Harper and Row, 1971), pp. 122–147; Lindstrom, *Economic Development*, pp. 8–18. This position runs counter to the export-led model of economic growth associated with the work of Douglas North, *The Economic Growth of the United States, 1790–1860* (New York: Norton, 1966). Lindstrom offers a summary and a critique of the export-led model in *Economic Development*, pp. 3–8.

7. Paul A. David, "The Mechanization of Reaping in the Antebellum Midwest," in *Technical Choice, Innovation and Economic Growth: Essays on American and British Experience in the Nineteenth Century* (London: Cambridge University Press, 1975); Thomas C. Cochran, "Did the Civil War Retard Industrialization?" in *The Economic Impact of the American Civil War*, ed. Andreano; and Stuart Bruchey, *Growth of the Modern American Economy* (New York: Dodd, Mead and Co., 1975), pp. 53–54, 78.

8. Practically, this division was overcome by importing European labor and introducing machinery, and ideologically it was resolved by the protectionist claim (especially in Henry Carey's work) that technology could overcome any labor constraint. The theoretical reconciliation of a protective tariff and westward expansion likewise occurred in politics when the Republican Party adopted a program that promised strong protection and a homestead act.

9. See, for example, Allen Dawley, *Class and Community* (Cambridge, Mass.: Harvard University Press, 1979), and John F. Kasson, *Civilizing the Machine: Technology and Republican Values, 1776–1900* (Harmondsworth: Penguin Books, 1976), chapters 1 and 2.

10. Bernard Bailyn, *The Ideological Origins of the American Revolution* (Cambridge, Mass.: Harvard University Press, 1972); Gordon Wood, *The Creation of the American Republic 1776–1787* (New York: Norton, 1972); Gerald Stourzh, *Alexander Hamilton and the Idea of Republican Government* (Stanford: Stanford University Press, 1970); Pauline Maier, *From Resistance to Revolution: Colonial Radicals and the Development of American Opposition to Britain, 1765–1776* (New York: Vintage, 1974); Lance Banning, "Republican Ideology and the Triumph of the Constitution, 1789 to 1793," *William and Mary Quarterly* 31 (1974): 167–188; and Pocock, *The Machiavellian Moment*, Part 3.

11. Pocock, *The Machiavellian Moment*, pp. 524–525, compares Court and federalist ideas as follows:

> The American republic proposed from its inception to offer a fresh solution to this ancient problem; the terms of this solution were in some respects dramatically new, but in others a restatement of old. We have further grown used to the existence in British thought of an alternative or "Court" ideology, which emphasized that men were guided by interest and passion, that factions and parties were necessary rather than illegitimate, and that government must be carried on by a sovereign power, ultimately unchecked but capable of subdivision into self-balancing powers, which ruled men partly by conversion of those passions into perception of a common interest. It should be clear by now that important elements of this ideology reappear in the Federalist theory at just the points where the latter moves away from virtue and toward interest.

12. Winch, *Adam Smith's Politics*, pp. 178–180. Winch argues that Smith's logic was transported to the colonies via Hume.

13. Jefferson's opinion of Ricardo's work can be found in Ricardo, *Works*, ed. Sraffa and Dobb, Vol. X, p. 372. Jefferson translated Destutt de Tracy's *Treatise in Political Economy* (1818) and advocated it in the hope that it would become a standard work. See Michael O'Connor, *Origins of Academic Economics in the United States* (New York: Columbia University Press, 1944). De Tracy's work accepted the inevitability of inequality and the formation of a propertyless class. However, unlike the English school, he argued that its wage rate did not have to tend toward subsistence. Good government and an appropriate policy could alleviate the condition of the laboring class, offsetting decay and class struggle. Furthermore, he adopted a hard-currency position in an effort to minimize capitalist accumulation and prolong the period in which labor owned property.

14. Pocock, *The Machiavellian Moment*, pp. 538–539.

15. Ernest Lee Tuveson, *Redeemer Nation: The Idea of America's Millenial Role* (Chicago: University of Chicago Press, 1968); Sacvan Bercovitch, *The American Jeremiad* (Madison: University of Wisconsin Press, 1978); Paul C. Nagel, *This Sacred Trust: American Nationality 1798–1898* (New York: Oxford University Press, 1971); Pocock, *The Machiavellian Moment*, pp. 511–513; and David Brion Davis, *The Problem of Slavery in the Age of Revolution, 1770–1823* (Ithaca: Cornell University Press, 1975), chapter 7.

16. The classic works on the tariff debate are Ugo Rabbeno, *The American Commercial Policy: Three Historical Essays*, 2nd ed. (London: Macmillan, 1895); Edward Stanwood, *American Tariff Controversies in the Nineteenth Century*, 2 vols. (1908; rpt. New York: Russell and Russell, 1979); and F. W. Taussig, *The Tariff History of the United States*, 8th ed. (New York: G. P. Putnam's Sons, 1931). Numerous recent studies have emerged, attempting to quantify the effects of the tariff on industrial development and income distribution. For example, see Jonathan Pincus, *Pressure Groups and Politics in Antebellum Tariffs* (New York: Columbia University Press, 1977); Bennett D. Baack and Edward J. Ray, "Tariff Policy and Income Distribution: The Case of the United States, 1830–1860," *Explorations in Economic History* 11 (1973–1974): 103–117; Clayne Pope, *The Impact of the Antebellum Tariff on Income Distribution* (New York: Arno Press, 1975); Paul A. David, "Learning By Doing and Tariff Protection: A Reconsideration of the Case of the Antebellum United States Cotton Textile Industry," in *Technical Choice, Innovation and Economic Growth*; Robert Fogel and Stanley L. Engerman, "A Model for the Explanation of Industrial Expansion during the Nineteenth Century: With Application to the American Iron Industry," *Journal of Political Economy* 77 (1969): 306–328; Richard Edwards, "Economic Sophistication in Nineteenth Century Tariff Debates," *Journal of Economic History* 30 (Dec. 1970): 802–838.

17. North, *Economic Growth*, chapters 4–5, pp. 61–65.

18. Malcolm Rogers Eiselen, *The Rise of Pennsylvania Protectionism* (1932; rpt. New York: Garland, 1974), pp. 37–42. See also William Freehling, *Prelude to Civil War: The Nullification Controversy in South Carolina, 1816–1836* (New York: Harper and Row, 1968).

19. Michael Holt, *The Political Crisis of the 1850s* (New York: John Wiley, 1978), chapter 2.

20. James Shenton, *Robert John Walker: A Politician from Jackson to Lincoln* (New York: Columbia University Press, 1961), pp. 81–86.

21. Eiselen, *The Rise of Pennsylvania Protectionism*, pp. 25, 48–49; Michael Hudson, *Economics and Technology in 19th Century American Thought: The Neglected American Economists* (New York: Garland, 1975), pp. 88–92; and Earl L. Bradsher, *Mathew Carey: Editor, Agitator and Publisher* (1912; rpt. New York: AMS Press, 1966). For an example of Carey's writings, see *Addresses of the Philadelphia Society for the Promotion of National Industry*, 5th ed. (1820; rpt. New York: Garland, 1974); and *Essays on Political Economy: or, The Most Certain Means of Promoting the Wealth, Power, Resources and Happiness of States, Applied Particularly to the United States* (1822; rpt. New York: Augustus M. Kelley, 1968).

22. O'Connor, *Origins of Academic Economics*, p. 31.

23. A collection of Condy Raguet's journalism can be found in *The Principles of Free Trade, Illustrated in a Series of Short and Familiar Essays: Originally Published in the Banner of the Constitution* (Philadelphia: Carey, Lea and Blanchard, 1835).

24. Henry Lee, *Report of a Committee of Citizens of Boston and Vicinity, Opposed to a Further Increase of Duties on Importations*, ed. Michael Hudson (1827; rpt. New York: Garland, 1974).

25. See Carl William Kaiser, Jr., *History of the Academic Protectionist–Free Trade Controversy in America before 1860* (Ph.D. diss., University of Pennsylvania, 1939).

26. O'Connor includes Lawrence, McVickar, Vethake, and Newman in the category of clerical writers. His representative figure is Francis Wayland. See *Origins of Academic Economics*, chapter 5.

27. See Alexander Everett, *Journal of the Proceedings of the Friends of Domestic Industry: In General Convention Met at the City of New York, October 26, 1831*, ed. Michael Hudson (New York: Garland, 1974); and Willard Phillips, *Manual of Political Economy with Particular Reference to the Institutions, Resources and Conditions of the United States* (Boston: Hilliard, Gray, Little and Wilkins, 1828). These economists did not reject the central concepts of classical political economy. Everett employed a Ricardian logic to show that the terms of trade were unfavorable to the United States, thereby justifying protection, while Phillips attached protectionist definitions to his classical system. Thus, unlike the American school, the New England protectionists did not develop a distinctive and utopian economics. Consequently, the working class remained a problematic category in their system. Phillips stated the problem in this way:

> Of all the wide territory to which, in a rude state of society, he had an equal right in common with others, nothing remains to him but his freedom of the highways, and he cannot step beyond their limits, without trespassing upon a monopoly that is guarded by the law. But if he is not a slave; if he has the free right to use of his faculties and corporal strength, he is, to all practical purposes, more wealthy than a savage who has the undisturbed right of hunting and fishing within the widest limits. (Phillips, *Manual of Political Economy*, p. 10.)

28. This dichotomy between Northern and Southern economists shows the protracted and complex transformation of republican ideology from a rhetoric of

virtue to one of interest. In his disagreement with Gordon Wood that American federalist thought marked the end of the classical republican tradition, J. G. A. Pocock wrote:

> [I]t can now be further argued that the vocabulary of virtue and corruption persisted in American thought, not merely as a survival slowly dying after its tap-root was cut, but with a reality and relevance to elements in American experience that kept it alive and in tension with the consequences that followed its partial abandonment in so crucial a field as constitutional theory and rhetoric. If Americans had been compelled to abandon a theory of constitutional humanism which related personality to government directly and according to its diversities, they had not thereby given up the pursuit of a form of political society in which the individual might be free and know himself in his relation to society. The insistent claim that the American is the natural man and America founded on the principles of nature is enough to demonstrate that, and the pursuit of nature and its disappointments can readily be expressed in the rhetoric of virtue and corruption. (Pocock, *The Machiavellian Moment*, pp. 526–527.)

29. See Cecilia Kenyon, "Men of Little Faith: The Anti-Federalists on the Nature of Representative Government," *William and Mary Quarterly* 12 (1955): 3–43.

30. The only biography of Raymond is Charles Patrick Neil, *Daniel Raymond: An Early Chapter in the History of Economic Theory in the United States* (1897; rpt. New York: Garland, 1974). No independent study exists of Raymond's writings; the most complete examination of his work can be found in Ernest Teilhac, *Pioneers of American Economic Thought in the Nineteenth Century* (New York: Macmillan, 1936).

31. See Alfred A. Cave, *An American Conservative in the Age of Jackson: The Political and Social Thought of Calvin Colton* (Fort Worth: Texas Christian University Press, 1969).

32. Although Colton's *Public Economy for the United States* (New York: A. S. Barnes, 1848) is not intellectually the equal of Raymond's *Elements*, Colton's treatise nonetheless rivals the *Elements* in its opposition to the classical tradition:

> This new and reformed state of society, commonly and not inaptly called republicanism, rejects with indignation and scorn the idea of those relations which constitute the basis of the system of Smith, Ricardo, Say, McCulloch, and others of that school. . . .
>
> What we have to say, then in elucidation of the American System, . . . and in contradistinction from the system of the economists above cited, is, that the former is opposed to the latter: opposed in the original elements of the social state; opposed in the organization of those elements; opposed in the main objects of such organizations; and opposed in its grand results, moral, political, and commercial. As it cannot be denied, that the commercial results are the ultimate objects which most concern all parties, as well as that they are the great aims of public economy, so neither can it be denied— that they are influenced and controlled by social organization; and it is this controlling power which renders it necessary to erect an American system of public economy on the American basis. (Colton, *Public Economy*, p. 168.)

Colton's opposition to the classical school is based on his identification of the natural social order and republican government with independent labor, placing him again in agreement with Raymond:

> There is no reason to be deplored in this malpractice [the separation of labor from the means of production], a moral cause, we fear, which aimed forever to exclude labor from its rights. It reversed the order of nature, and transferred the cause to the place of the effect. It is not capital, in the common, or in what the economists have made the technical sense of the term, that was designed to employ labor, and this condescension to enslave it; but it is labor which in nature occupies the first place, and which was designed to be the employer of its own creations. That which is commonly called capital, can do nothing, is worth nothing without labor. Labor is not only its parent, but its efficient and vivifying power. (Ibid., p. 46.)

Thus, like Raymond, Colton believes that a republic depends on a virtuous, moral population. However, unlike the classical theory which associates virtue with a static personality and the subordination of individual interest to the common good, the American school identifies "virtue" with interest and a dynamic personality. The state ensures that interest and growth do not destroy the conditions that guarantee a moral republican citizenry, namely, the preservation of independent labor.

33. Neil, *Daniel Raymond*; and Joseph Dorfman, *The Economic Mind in American Civilization 1606–1865*, Vol. II (New York: Viking Press, 1946), p. 573.

34. Thomas R. Dew, *Lectures on the Restrictive System Delivered to the Senior Political Class of William and Mary College* (1829; rpt. New York: Augustus M. Kelley, 1969).

35. William G. Giles, *Political Miscellanies* (Richmond: n.p., 1829), sections 32–39.

36. *The Southern Patriot*, February 7, 1821, as cited in Dorfman, *The Economic Mind*, p. 573.

37. Kaiser, *Protectionist–Free Trade Controversy*, pp. 41–42; Dorfman, *The Economic Mind*, p. 566; O'Connor, *Origins of Academic Economics*, pp. 39–40; and Neil, *Daniel Raymond*, chapter 4.

38. Dorfman, *The Economic Mind*, p. 779, considers John Rae's *Statement of Some New Principles on the Subject of Political Economy* (Boston: Hillard, Gray and Co., 1834) "the ablest treatise on the protectionist side." While certainly far superior to Colton's work, Rae's text, in my opinion, does not attain the intellectual stature of Raymond's *Elements*. It is true that Rae's treatise does not contain the same contradictory structure as Raymond's, but this apparent strength indicates its inferior quality. Rae's work discusses economics solely in terms of "national wealth," ignoring for the most part the actual economic processes of the market. Raymond's work combines these two dimensions, creating the text's contradictory structure. In combining these two levels of analysis Raymond presents a more thorough examination of the economy than Rae does.

39. Smith, *The Wealth of Nations*, pp. 320–321.

40. By equating profits with a capitalist's personal revenues, Smith creates a difficulty in his theory of accumulation. Economic growth can only take place when the capitalist increases productive expenditures. In Smith's analysis the funds designed for growth come out of the capitalist's revenues. The capitalists

refrain from consuming the necessaries and conveniences of life in hope that by investing these savings in expanded reproduction they will be able to increase future revenues—i.e., profits. By investing their savings in expanded production, the capitalists employ additional productive laborers. For this reason Smith conceives of capitalist saving and investment as nothing more than a transfer of revenues from the capitalist class to the working class. But here the problem arises: How can personal abstinence produce the additional means of production required for expanded reproduction? The articles of consumption accumulated by the capitalists through self-denial may afford additional necessaries and conveniences of life needed to sustain an expanded work force, but they cannot be converted into tools and machines required to actually engage the labor force in the production process. In fact, these commodities are lacking altogether within Smith's component theory of value. All that is accounted for in that theory are the means of consumption—i.e., the worker's wage, the capitalist's profits, and the landlord's rents. This is not to say that Smith ignores the means of production as an element within his analysis.

As Hollander points out in discussing this problem in *The Economics of Adam Smith*, Smith does take up the question of the means of production or capital goods in several places. For example, in his formulation of a nation's gross and net revenue, Smith includes fixed capital as a cost that must be deducted from gross revenue. Under the rubric "fixed capital" he includes useful machinery, profitable buildings, improvements in land, and acquired and useful abilities in the labor force. Fixed capital, however, cannot correspond to a revenue. If it were to be included as a part of profits, then, a portion of the capitalist's income could no longer be considered as personal income. Moreover, given the competitive struggle among capitalists, that portion of profits going to expand fixed capital would increase more rapidly than the consumptive expenditures of both capitalists and productive workers. Personal consumption would negate Smith's basic assumption that human needs directly structure production.

41. Daniel Raymond, *The Elements of Political Economy in Two Parts*, 2nd ed. (1823; rpt. New York: Augustus M. Kelley, 1964), Vol. II, p. 399; hereafter cited as *EPE*.

42. Dorfman, *The Economic Mind*, chapter 14, offers a summary of the labor economists' writings. Also see Edward Pessen, *The Most Uncommon Jacksonians: The Radical Leaders of the Early Labor Movement* (Albany: State University of New York Press, 1970), especially chapter 11; and William B. Scott, *In Pursuit of Happiness: American Conceptions of Property from the Seventeenth to the Twentieth Century* (Bloomington: Indiana University Press, 1977), Part 2.

Of course, Raymond has little in common with Brisbane or Owen, but there are striking similarities between Raymond's language and that of Skidmore and Pickering, since both authors attempted to ensure labor's right to property in a world of commodity production for profits. In his *The Rights of Man to Property* (1829, rpt. New York: Burt Franklin, 1966), Skidmore proposed a system of confiscation and redistribution to ensure an equitable distribution of property. John Pickering argued in *The Working Man's Political Economy* (1847: rpt. New York: Arno, 1971) that a homestead act would resolve the problem of a propertyless class.

43. *EPE*, Vol. I, p. 30.
44. Ibid., p. 36.
45. Ibid., p. 40.
46. Ibid., pp. 106–107.
47. Ibid., p. 35.
48. Ibid., p. 48.

49. Teilhac, *Pioneers*, p. 20, argues that Raymond's concept of national wealth implies state planning. Thus, he characterizes Raymond's thought as socialist, or more precisely, national socialist. This characterization is quite misleading, since it implies similarities between Raymond's ideas and the economic and political currents in the years between the two world wars. Even if one wishes to characterize Raymond's thought and that of national socialism as "petty bourgeois," the determinants of that class during each of these periods are radically different.

50. *EPE*, Vol. I, p. 57.
51. Ibid., pp. 124–125.
52. Ibid., p. 192.
53. Ibid., p. 202.
54. Ibid., Vol. II, pp. 11–12.
55. Ibid., pp. 69–72.
56. Ibid., Vol. I, p. 292.
57. Ibid., pp. 293–294.
58. Ibid., pp. 257–258.
59. Ibid., Vol. II, chapter 7.
60. Ibid., Vol. I, pp. 198–199.
61. Ibid., p. 91.
62. Ibid., pp. 86–88.
63. Ibid., pp. 197–199.
64. Ibid., p. 198.
65. Ibid., pp. 108–109.
66. Ibid., p. 117.
67. Ibid., pp. 118–119.
68. Ibid., p. 126.

69. In arguing that protracted crises are the result of capitalist parsimony, Raymond relies in part on Malthus's theory of underconsumption. However, Raymond only draws on that part of Malthus's theory that describes the source of underconsumption as capitalist parsimony. Raymond rejects both Malthus's adherence to Smith's notion that growth is dependent on savings and Malthus's solution to the problem of underconsumption, which he locates in the landlord's expenditures.

70. *EPE*, Vol. I, p. 219.
71. Ibid., Vol. II, chapters 4–12.
72. Ibid., p. 7.
73. Ibid., pp. 7–8.
74. Ibid., p. 9.
75. Ibid., p. 8.

76. Raymond's theory begs comparison to Locke's. In general, these writers follow traditional Christian natural law, which (1) seeks in nature a normative

means to evaluate positive law, (2) discovers this standard in natural laws through reason as well as through revelation, (3) views these laws as consistent with the human drive for self-preservation and the rational need to find salvation, and (4) uses natural law to establish the legitimacy of political power.

In particular, Raymond and Locke agree, with minor differences, on the motivation, means, and ends of the social compact. Where the two differ is on the degree of economic inequality in the original state. For Locke, a large propertyless class is consistent with increased productivity whereas Raymond comes to the opposite conclusion.

This difference leads to contrary institutional structures. Locke, like Raymond, does not view the right to property as absolute and justifies the propertyless class's political exclusion on the grounds that only this will induce the propertied class to enter a social contract. The propertyless can rationally accept this provision since their situation will improve in a propertied owners' state when compared to the state of nature. For Raymond, the differences between the two classes is not so great that the propertied need fear the propertyless.

Furthermore, there is some disagreement as to the moral presuppositions of the state and consequently to its range of action. Locke's theory is a purely instrumentalist one. Certainly, Raymond's theory falls in this category, since the economy is the region for moral improvement. There is an important qualification, however. Raymond insists that the state has the responsibility to preserve natural limits to economic inequality and so must intervene in the economy in ways that may be contrary to particular ends.

77. *EPE*, Vol. II, pp. 203–204.

78. Daniel Raymond, *The Elements of Constitutional Law* (Cincinnati: n.p., 1845), p. 27.

79. Constitutional law, too, finds its justification through "the exercise of right reason." Since it is a progressive science, Raymond believes that advances can be made, but these always have to be shown consistent with "truth" (Ibid., pp. xiv–xv).

80. See Chapter 4.

81. *EPE*, Vol. II, p. 207.

82. Ibid., pp. 170–171.

83. Ibid., pp. 210–213.

84. Ibid., p. 213.

85. Ibid.

86. The connection between the tariff and the employment of marginal or underutilized labor can be found in Alexander Hamilton, "Report on Manufactures," in *The Reports of Alexander Hamilton*, ed. Jacob E. Coore (New York: Harper, 1964). The labor that Hamilton refers to is that of women, children, and seasonal workers.

87. The limited effect of the protective tariff on the market may be stated in yet another way. The protective tariff will expand productive labor within knowable limits but not effective labor (*EPE*, Vol. II, p. 213).

88. Ibid., pp. 229–230.

89. Ibid., pp. 230–231.

90. Ibid., p. 242.

91. Ibid., p. 245.

92. Ibid., p. 244.

93. Ibid., p. 219.

94. Ibid., pp. 251–252.

95. Ibid., p. 9.

96. Ibid., chapter 6.

97. Ibid., pp. 120–124.

98. Raymond's recommendation that the state create an effectual demand to compensate for the disease of accumulation is another example of his regulatory spirit. He does not believe that the public debt which arises from such expenditures necessarily creates a "monied aristocracy." His optimism seems startling, given his diatribes against England's creditor class. Yet Raymond reasons that while a national debt may transfer wealth from one sector of the population to another, a national debt will not inflict any great hardships on the nation as long as an equal division of property exists. Under those conditions, claims on the national debt will be evenly distributed within the population (Ibid., pp. 310–331).

99. In an article written for the *American Whig Review* in 1848, Raymond denounced the Democratic administration for reducing the price of land. The administration hoped that a reduction in the price of land would increase sales and federal revenues, thereby reducing the need for a tariff. See Daniel Raymond, "The President's Message and the Report of the Secretary of the Treasury," *American Whig Review* 7 (1848): 384–396.

4. Daniel Raymond on Protecting the Republic from Slave Capital

1. *EPE*, Vol. I, p. 64, and Vol. II, p. 39.

2. Ibid., Vol. I, pp. 18–20.

3. Ibid., p. 22. Raymond's political philosophy seems to continue the Puritan tradition, which combined elements of St. Augustine with social contract theory. For a discussion of Puritan political thought, see Perry Miller, *The New England Mind: The Seventeenth Century* (1939; rpt. Boston: Beacon Press, 1970), pp. 418–422.

4. *EPE*, Vol. I, pp. 27–28.

5. Ibid., p. 222. For a general treatment of Puritan thinking on the relationship between the state and civil society and on the religious significance of technology, see Miller, *The New England Mind*, pp. 161–180, 422–431. T. H. Breen, *The Character of the Good Ruler* (New York: Norton, 1970), and Richard L. Bushman, *From Puritan to Yankee* (New York: Norton, 1970), trace the continuing secularization of Puritan political thought and practice.

6. *EPE*, Vol. II, p. 54.

7. Ibid., p. 33.

8. Ibid., p. 57.

9. Ibid., pp. 45–52.

10. Ibid., chapter 5.

11. Ibid., p. 81.

12. Ibid., p. 58.

13. Ibid., pp. 69–70.

14. Ibid., pp. 59–60.

15. Ibid., p. 36.

16. For Raymond, the general problem facing the statesman, regardless of period, is "first to what extent shall [pauperism] exist—Second, in what form shall it exist" (Ibid., p. 54).

17. Ibid., Vol. I, pp. 16–17.

18. Ibid., p. 17.

19. Ibid., Vol. II, pp. 395, 400.

20. Ibid., p. 358.

21. Ibid., pp. 361–362.

22. Ibid., p. 362.

23. Ibid., p. 363.

24. Ibid., p. 368.

25. Ibid., pp. 364–368.

26. Ibid., p. 420.

27. Ibid., pp. 365–366.

28. Ibid., p. 366.

29. Ibid., p. 373.

30. Ibid., p. 420.

31. Ibid., p. 371.

32. Raymond also discusses increased repression against the slave population and diffusion of it through expansion into the western territories as a possible means by which to eliminate the harmful effects of slavery. He believes that both of these strategies are hopeless.

33. *EPE*, Vol. II, p. 370.

34. Ibid., p. 374.

35. Ibid., p. 374.

36. Ibid., p. 375.

37. Ibid., p. 379.

38. Ibid., p. 390.

39. This point remains true even if we consider Ricardo's adaptation of Malthus's theory. Unlike Malthus, Ricardo does not believe in the natural inequality of individuals; nor does he oppose, in principle, universal suffrage. Nonetheless, he accepts Malthus's theory of population and his proposal to repeal the poor laws. For an examination of the effect of the poor laws in dividing England along class lines, see Perkin, *Modern English Society*, pp. 183–196.

40. *EPE*, Vol. II, p. 82.

41. Raymond believes that the planters can still be saved from the corrupting influence of slavery. Manumission offers them that possibility.

42. *EPE*, Vol. II, p. 368.

43. Ibid., p. 230.

44. Ibid., p. 358.

45. Ibid., pp. 379–380.

46. Charles S. Sydnor, *The Development of Southern Nationalism, 1819–1848* (1948; rpt. Baton Rogue: Louisiana State University Press, 1968), p. 12.

47. Robert Russel, *Economic Aspects of Southern Sectionalism, 1840–1861* (New York: Russell and Russell, 1924), pp. 261–265.

5. Thomas Roderick Dew on Accommodating the Republic to History

1. Major Wilson, *Space, Time and Freedom: The Quest for Nationality and the Irrepressible Conflict, 1815–1865* (Westport: Greenwood, 1974), dissents from the commonly held position that the American System declined as an important factor in American politics after the presidency of John Quincy Adams. See also William Freehling, "Spoilsmen and Interest in the Thought of John C. Calhoun," *Journal of American History* 52 (1965–1966): 239–241; and Richard B. Latner, "The Nullification Crisis and Republican Subversion," *Journal of Southern History* 43 (1977): 28–30. The opposing view may be found in George Dangerfield, *The Awakening of American Nationalism, 1815–1828* (New York: Harper, 1965), pp. 298–300; and Welter, *The Mind of America*, pp. 122–126.

2. Marvin Meyers, *The Jacksonian Persuasion: Politics and Belief* (Stanford: Stanford University Press, 1957); and John William Ward, *Andrew Jackson—Symbol for an Age* (1955; rpt. London: Oxford University Press, 1976), are the best accounts of Jacksonian rhetoric.

3. Edward Pessen offers a summary of recent research on the second-party system in his *Jacksonian America: Society, Personality, and Politics* (Homewood: Dorsey Press, 1969), pp. 154–179. Richard P. McCormick, *The Second American Party System: Party Formation in the Jacksonian Era* (Chapel Hill: University of North Carolina Press, 1966), remains the major study on the subject. Samuel Flagg Bemis, *John Quincy Adams and the Union* (New York: Knopf, 1965), pp. 11–32, 126–152; and Robert Remini, *Martin Van Buren and the Making of the Democratic Party* (New York: Columbia University Press, 1959) as well as *The Election of Andrew Jackson* (New York: Harper & Row, 1963) are also useful in understanding the rise of the second-party system. See also James Roger Sharp, *The Jacksonians versus the Banks: Politics in the States after the Panic of 1837* (New York: Columbia University Press, 1970) pp. 5–23.

4. Both David Potter, *The Impending Crisis, 1848–1861* ed. Don E. Fehrenbacher (New York: Harper, 1976) pp. 7–17, and Dangerfield, *Awakening*, pp. 299–300, view Jacksonian democracy as a nationalist movement even though it opposed the nationalism of the American System. Hans Kohn, *American Nationalism: An Interpretative Essay* (New York: Macmillan, 1957), and Paul C. Nagel, *One Nation Indivisible: The Union in American Thought, 1776–1861* (New York: Oxford University Press, 1964), develop the notion of a unique American nationalism and the divergent currents within it. Wilson explores some of the conflicting concepts of American nationalism in the antebellum period as noted by Kohn and Nagel. For an understanding of the antebellum conception of America's mission in the historical process, see David Nobel, *Historians Against History: The Frontier Thesis and the National Covenant in American Historical Writing Since 1830* (Minneapolis: University of Minnesota Press, 1965), pp. 3–17; Fred Somkin, *Unquiet Eagle: Memory and Desire in the Idea of American Freedom* (Ithaca: Cornell University Press, 1967), chapter 2; and Welter, *The Mind of America*, pp. 3–76.

5. Potter, *The Impending Crisis*, pp. 405–447. For an analysis of the sectional strains caused by the annexation of Texas, see Frederick Merk with Lois Bannister Merk, *Fruits of Propaganda in the Tyler Administration* (Cambridge: Harvard Uni-

versity Press, 1971); and *Slavery and the Annexation of Texas* (New York: Knopf, 1972).

6. Dorfman, *The Economic Mind*, Vol. II, pp. 637–712; Richard Hofstadter, "William Leggett, Spokesman of Jacksonian Democracy," *Political Science Quarterly* 58 (1943): 581–594; Pessen, *The Most Uncommon Jacksonians*, Part 3; and Scott, *In Pursuit of Happiness*, pp. 55–60.

7. While free-trade doctrine conformed to the needs of the Jacksonian coalition in general, classical political economy had a more vigorous following among the Planters. Even though the Plain Republicans advocated liberal economic values, this wing of the alliance remained tied to fixed moral values and, consequently, was unprepared for the upheavals of capitalist economic development, which their policies ironically promoted. See Meyers, *The Jacksonian Persuasion*, pp. 10–12; Wilson, *Space, Time and Freedom*, p. 8; Welter, *The Mind of America*, pp. 90–95; and Sharp, *The Jacksonians Versus the Banks*, pp. 320–325.

In the Northeast, classical political economy became associated with the "clerical school," which was centered in the elite universities with a myriad of ties to merchants, bankers, and other socioeconomic elites. For this reason, free-trade doctrine in the Northeast became a weapon against Jacksonian democracy and its attack on the banks. As sectors of the South became disillusioned with Jacksonian policies, renegade Jacksonians could find sympathizers in the "clerical school." See O'Connor, *Origins of Academic Economics*, pp. 279–286; and Hudson, *Economics and Technology*, pp. 26–33.

8. Dangerfield characterizes the piecemeal approach of Jacksonian politics as "an absurd distortion of the nominalist position" (*Awakening*, p. 300). For a political explanation of Jackson's negative economic policies as well as an account of their positive impact, see Bruchey, *Roots of American Economic Growth*, pp. 124–127. Morton Horwitz describes how antebellum law served political ends while remaining above party politics; see *The Transformation of American Law, Seventeen Eighty to Eighteen Sixty* (Cambridge, Mass.: Harvard University Press, 1979).

9. The democratic movements of the period raised the issue of majority versus minority rights. At the center of this debate was the antidemocratic forces' fear of wanton attacks on property by a poor or propertyless majority. For an overview of the controversy surrounding democratic white manhood suffrage, see Chilton Williamson, *American Suffrage from Property to Democracy 1760–1860* (Princeton: Princeton University Press, 1968); Merrill D. Peterson, ed., *Democracy, Liberty, and Property: The State Constitutional Conventions of the 1820s* (Indianapolis: Bobbs-Merrill, 1966); Melvin Fletcher Green, "Democracy in the Old South," in *Democracy in the Old South and Other Essays*, ed. J. Isaac Copeland (Kingsport: Vanderbilt University Press, 1969); and Charles S. Sydnor, *The Development of Southern Sectionalism, 1819–1848* (Baton Rouge: Louisiana State University Press, 1968), pp. 273–293.

10. Conservative Southerners used the term "agrarianism" to describe democratic movements. The term itself came from the popular movements in ancient Rome which forcibly expropriated property—hence, the connection in many Southern minds between democracy and attacks on private property (Welter, *The Mind of America*, pp. 107–108). The term was frequently used by John C. Cal-

houn; see August O. Spain, *The Political Theory of John C. Calhoun* (New York: Octagon Books, 1968), p. 91.

11. Wilson, *Space, Time and Freedom*, pp. 73–91; Freehling, *Prelude to Civil War*; and Latner, "The Nullification Crisis and Republican Subversion," pp. 19–38.

12. Historians have debated whether Calhoun's class analysis can be taken seriously or whether it should be understood as a tactic in his general strategy to protect Southern interests. Those historians who have argued for a sectional interpretation of Calhoun's writings have, for the most part, dominated the literature. See Sydnor, *Development of Southern Nationalism*, pp. 211–212; Frederic Bancroft, *Calhoun and the South Carolina Nullification Movement* (Baltimore: Johns Hopkins Press, 1928) pp. 172–173; Charles M. Wiltse, *John C. Calhoun: Nullifier, 1829–1839* (Indianapolis: Bobbs-Merrill, 1949), pp. 87–88, 160; Jesse Carpenter, *The South as Conscious Minority, 1789–1861: A Study in Political Thought* (New York: New York University Press, 1930), pp. 77–82; and Freehling, "Spoilsmen." Of these, Freehling's is the most provocative, since he challenges Calhoun's logic. According to Freehling, Calhoun at times argues that politics is above economic interest and at other times that economics determines politics. For this reason Freehling discounts Calhoun's theoretical integrity and explains his concept of a concurrent majority in purely sectional terms.

My essay suggests a resolution to the dichotomy that Freehling uncovers in Calhoun's thought. In examining Dew's work, I argue that the problem of governmental abuse is determined by both political and economic factors. The analysis of Dew also holds for Calhoun's *A Disquisition on Government*. Thus, it can be suggested that Freehling's isolation of an inconsistency in Calhoun's theory is in fact a consequence of Freehling's reading, which demands that governmental tyranny be either a result of political spoilsmanship or economic interest.

The opposing view, which takes Calhoun at his word regarding class, is perhaps best represented by Richard Current, "John C. Calhoun, Philosopher of Reaction," *Antioch Review* 1 (1943), pp. 223–234. However, whereas Freehling recognizes both an economic and a political dimension to Calhoun's logic, Current only sees the economic one. Also see Dangerfield, *Awakening*, pp. 285–287; and Spain, *Political Theory of John C. Calhoun*, pp. 251–275.

13. James C. McGregor, *The Disruption of Virginia* (New York: Macmillan, 1922), pp. 16–26; Peterson, ed., *Democracy, Liberty, and Property*, pp. 276–277; and Freehling, *Prelude*, pp. 22–23, discuss the planter-yeoman conflict. Genovese, *Political Economy of Slavery*, pp. 226–235, discusses the planters' fear of a propertyless class.

14. The most recent economic study on the yeoman farmer is found in Wright, *The Political Economy of the Cotton South*, pp. 24–32. The classic work remains Frank L. Owsley, *Plain Folk of the Old South* (Baton Rouge: Louisiana State University Press, 1949).

Recent historiography has argued that yeomen farmers for the most part did not develop as a major political opponent to the planters, at least as long as personal ties between the two social classes were maintained. See Eugene Genovese, "Yeomen Farmers in a Slaveholders' Democracy," *Agricultural History* 49 (1975): 331–341; and Carl Degler, *The Other South: Southern Dissenters in the Nineteenth*

Century (New York: Harper, 1974), p. 94. While this is certainly true, conflict still persisted throughout the period and into the Confederacy. The planter/yeoman strife in Virginia and South Carolina in the pre-1848 period is touched on in this essay. The Southwest did not escape this conflict; see, for example, Roger W. Shugg, *Origins of Class Struggle in Louisiana* (Baton Rouge: Louisiana State University Press, 1939). During the Confederacy the antagonism persisted. See Charles H. Wesley, *The Collapse of the Confederacy* (1937; rpt. New York: Russell and Russell, 1968), pp. x–xi, 82–83; Ella Lonn, *Desertion During the Civil War* (Chapel Hill: University of North Carolina Press, 1945) pp. 3–5; and Georgia Lee Tatum, *Disloyalty in the Confederacy* (Chapel Hill: University of North Carolina Press, 1934), pp. 3–24.

15. Wright, *The Political Economy of the Cotton South*, pp. 40–41, describes the nature of this problem and the growing economic gap between planters and yeomen during the antebellum years.

16. Opposition to the banks could be included in this list. As in the other issues, Jacksonian opposition to the banks had its own internal contradictions. However, these contradictions were not as deeply intertwined with sectional antagonisms (Sharp, *The Jacksonians versus the Banks*, pp. 328–329); see Chapter 6 of this book.

17. Dangerfield, *Awakening*, p. 283.

18. George M. Stephenson, *The Political History of the Public Lands from 1840–1860* (1917; rpt. New York: Russell and Russell, 1967), pp. 27–29; Helene Sara Zahler, *Eastern Workingmen and National Labor Policy, 1829–1862* (1941; rpt. New York: Greenwood Press, 1969), pp. 125–126; Frederick Merk, *History of the Westward Movement* (New York: Knopf, 1978), pp. 234–235; and Scott, *In Pursuit of Happiness*, pp. 60–64.

19. Not all Westerners accepted distribution, since it was argued that Congress would rather only wait until the price of land rose. Nonetheless, a distribution-preemption act was passed in 1841, pleasing Westerners and tariff advocates (primarily Northeasterners) while irritating Southerners. The act passed only because the South was able to attach a clause on the bill significantly lowering tariffs. Thus, land distribution was linked to the tariff question (Stephenson, *The Political History of Public Lands*, pp. 28–29).

20. The connection is illustrated in the Webster-Hayne debate of 1830. Senator Foot of Connecticut initiated the debate in the Senate when he proposed a resolution inquiring into the advantages of a temporary restriction on the purchase of western lands. Senator Benton of Missouri opposed the resolution and opened the opportunity for a closer South-West alliance. Acting on behalf of Vice-President Calhoun, Senator Robert Hayne defended Benton's position in an effort to consolidate the alliance. However, when Senator Webster of Massachusetts responded, the debate shifted from land policy to constitutional questions of minority rights and nullification. See Merk, *History of the Westward Movement*, pp. 231–233; and Freehling, *Prelude*, pp. 183–186.

The connection between majority rule and minority rights was also made with regard to land policy. Southerners condemned the radical schemas of Evans and Skidmore and organizations such as National Reform and the Industrial Congresses since they represented forces hostile to private property. Zahler, *Eastern Workingmen*, pp. 74–75.

21. Southern expansionism has long been a theme in American historiography. For an analysis which links political and sectional concerns, see Merk, *Slavery*. The Southwest's support for the homestead is documented by Gerald Wolff, "The Slavocracy and the Homestead Problem of 1854," *Agricultural History* 40 (1966): 101–112. A treatment of the South's difficulty in maintaining a South-West alliance can be found in Charles M. Wiltse, *John C. Calhoun: Sectionalist, 1842–1850* (Indianapolis: Bobbs-Merrill, 1951), pp. 233–245; Allan Nevins, *Ordeal of the Union: Fruits of Manifest Destiny, 1847–1852* (New York: Scribner's, 1947), pp. 26–33; and Arthur Bestor, "The American Civil War as a Constitutional Crisis," *American Historical Review* 69 (1964): 327–352.

22. Thomas R. Dew, "An Address," *Southern Literary Messenger* 2 (December 1836): 765.

23. Stephen Scott Mansfield has written a useful biography of Dew entitled "Thomas Roderick Dew: Defender of the Southern Faith" (Ph.D. diss., University of Virginia, 1968). Mansfield is also the author of "Thomas Roderick Dew at William and Mary: 'A Main Prop of that Venerable Institution,'" *Virginia Magazine of History and Biography* 75 (1965): 29–42. Other treatments of Dew include Dorfman, *The Economic Mind*, pp. 895–908; Lowell H. Harrison, "Thomas Roderick Dew: Philosopher of the Old South," *Virginia Magazine of History and Biography* 57 (1949): 390–404; William Somner Jenkins, *Pro-Slavery Thought in the Old South* (Chapel Hill: University of North Carolina Press, 1935); Kenneth Stampp, "An Analysis of Dew's *Review of the Debate in the Virginia Legislature*," *Journal of Negro History* 27 (1942): 380–388; and Theodore Whitfield, *Slavery Agitation in Virginia, 1829–1832* (Baltimore: Johns Hopkins Press, 1930), pp. 135–142.

24. Mansfield, "Defender of the Southern Faith," pp. 113–114. For a treatment of Virginia politics during these years, see Henry H. Simms, *The Rise of the Whigs in Virginia, 1824–1840* (Richmond: William Byrd Press, 1929), pp. 215–246; and McCormick, *The Second American Party System*, pp. 178–198.

25. A discussion of tariffs may be found in Chapter 3.

26. See Tribe, "Economic Property and the Theorization of Ground Rent."

27. Two important recent works have examined the influence of the Scottish enlightenment on American Southern thought: Wills, *Inventing America*; and Henry May, *The Enlightenment in America* (London: Oxford University Press, 1976).

28. Dew quoted frequently from John Mill's work.

29. O'Connor believes Thomas Cooper to be the real founder of the Southern economic position (O'Connor, *Origins of Academic Economics*, pp. 48–56). Cooper's influence has certainly been recognized by other historians, such as Dorfman, *The Economic Mind*, pp. 527–538, 844–848; Freehling, *Prelude*, pp. 98–99; and Dumas Malone, *The Public Life of Thomas Cooper, 1783–1839* (New Haven: Yale University Press, 1926), pp. 281–336. Whether Hudson's evaluation is correct or not is a matter for future research; however, Cooper's writings on the tariff and on political economy in general fall below Dew's.

Dew's basic theoretical problems can also be found in Thomas Cooper's work on political economy, *Lectures on the Elements of Political Economy* (1830; rpt. New York: Augustus M. Kelley, 1971). Like Dew, Cooper believes the basic antagonism in the advanced state to be that between worker and capitalist: "If the capitalist therefore finds it worth his while to manufacture the article, it is because he obtains his profit at the expense of the health and the comfort of the worn out starving operative" (p. 349).

Cooper attempts to solve this problem. In examining the alternative solutions Cooper rejects those offered by what he considers the "mechanic's political economy." In this grouping Cooper includes the English labor-Ricardian Thomas Hodgskin and the American radical Thomas Skidmore. These writers see labor rather than capital as the dynamic in the economic process—a conceptual error, Cooper believes, which will lead to an attack on private property. Universal white manhood suffrage makes such possible attacks all the more real for Cooper. To counter the mechanics' program and the utopian proposals, Cooper offers a reform program he believes will alleviate the economic conflict of the advanced stage. These reforms fall into three categories: (1) to limit the economic power of the church and aristocracy, (2) to limit the powers of government, and (3) to alleviate the material suffering of the working class by improving its moral being.

In Cooper's opinion, of all the commercial nations in the world, the United States approximates most closely the natural order and requires least in the way of reform. Yet even if the United States adopted all the relevant reforms suggested by Cooper, it would not be able to eliminate the economic class struggle.

30. Ricardo, *Principles*, pp. 147–161.

31. The following summary is taken from Dew, *Lectures on the Restrictive System*, pp. 28–37; hereafter cited as *LR*.

32. Aghiri Emmanuel, *Unequal Exchange: A Study of the Imperialism of Trade* (New York: Monthly Review Press, 1972), contains a useful critique of Ricardo's theory of comparative advantage.

33. *LR*, p. 39.

34. *LR*, p. 41.

35. *LR*, pp. 45–46.

36. Lucio Colletti, *From Rousseau to Lenin: Studies in Ideology and Society* (New York: Monthly Review Press, 1974), pp. 149–155.

37. *LR*, p. 10.

38. *LR*, p. 8.

39. In *A Digest of the Laws, Customs, Manners and Institutions of the Ancient and Modern Nations* (New York: D. Appleton and Co., 1852), Dew analyzes world history to describe the process whereby the individual has become the dominant category amond civilized nations. Two societies stand out as noteworthy, the ancient world of Greece and the feudal order of the European Middle Ages. The former period illustrates Dew's contention that the individual is the principal foundation on which modern civilization rests. Dew treats in detail the enormous achievements of ancient Greece, denoting their relevance to problems in his period. Despite his great admiration for the ancient world, however, Dew finally considers it flawed. The individual is subordinated to the state rather than the state to

the individual, as in the modern world. This fact differentiates the two periods and is the reason, according to Dew, for ancient Greece's restricted development.

In contrast, Dew finds little to admire in the feudal order, dominated by a capricious noble ruling class. He devotes his attention to this period because it offers the immediate link between the elements of the commercial world and the historic process. As Dew views it, the rise of the cities and the emergence of commerce provide the historic material out of which the free individual commodity producer has been formed.

Although the conditions for modern life have been established by the decline of the feudal economy, the true break into the modern world is in the revolutionary process initiated by the American and French revolutions. While Dew places these revolutions on the same historic plane, he is critical of the French model. Dew praises the French Revolution for its attempt to institute the principles of the advanced order in a nation that has been dominated by aristocratic and clerical ruling classes. However, he finds excesses in that process which demand condemnation. Unlike the American experiment in republican government, the French Revolution has not produced constitutional checks capable of peacefully resolving political strife and preserving the legitimate end of government. Consequently, Dew characterizes modern French political history by its continual dictatorial rule by mobs or armies. In this respect, France has been unable to resolve the historic dilemma of establishing a legitimate (i.e., a republican) government despite its enormous achievements in ending "feudality and priestcraft." The French Revolution had erred by making individual freedom absolute rather than conditional.

From this it is evident that Dew maintains a bourgeois conception of natural rights despite his rejection of their applicability to all people. Unlike the ancient conception, nature in Dew's theory does not fix ends to be emulated but rather endows humanity with a will that freely pursues subjective developmental ends.

40. *LR*, p. 9.

41. A history of republican theory may be found in Pocock, *The Machiavellian Moment*.

42. Ibid., pp. 513–526; and Wood, *The Creation of the American Republic*, pp. 593–618.

43. For a discussion of the functionalist reinterpretation of classical political theory by liberal political science, see Jürgen Habermas, *Theory and Practice* (Boston: Beacon Press, 1973), pp. 41–81. Also see M. I. Finley, *Democracy Ancient and Modern* (New Brunswick: Rutgers University Press, 1973), chapter 1.

44. Dew, in fact, frequently quotes from James Mill's works. The incompatibility between the classical notion of virtue and the modern concept of government as a well-constructed machine is discussed by Habermas, *Theory and Practice*, chapter 1; Pocock, *The Machiavellian Moment*, pp. 324, 404–405, 524–525.

45. For the eighteenth-century formulation see Dugald Stewart, *Lectures on Political Economy* (1855; rpt. New York: Augustus M. Kelley, 1968), Vol. II, pp. 402–456; for the nineteenth century, see James Mill, *The Article on Government, reprinted from the Supplement to the Encyclopedia Britannica* (London: J. Innes, n.d.).

46. *LR*, pp. 12–13.

47. Ibid., pp. 8–10.

48. Stewart, *Lectures*, pp. 438–440, argued that the British aristocracy was a political entity in which only one member of a noble family received any special privilege. Thus, the nobility functioned in civil society as a nonprivileged group, making its interests common with those of the people.

49. *LR*, p. 178.

50. Dew was trained in an antidemocratic tradition. See John A. Smith, *Lectures on Government* (Philadelphia: Thomas Dobson and Son, 1817).

51. *LR*, pp. 178–179.

52. Ibid., p. 181.

53. Wood, *The Creation of the American Republic*, pp. 471–518.

54. A federal system solves the problem of establishing a republic in a large territory. According to Dew, it also prevents the bitter feuds that occur when numerous independent republics are located in a given area. Dew developed his ideas on the federal system at length in "An Address on the Influence of the Federative System of Government Upon Literature and the Development of Character," *Southern Literary Messenger* 2 (March 1836): 261–282.

55. Dew's tone in the *Lectures* is restrained when he discusses secession. By 1836 his attitude has changed. In "An Address on the Federative System," Dew boldly asserts that the South must break its ties with the Union if Southern grievances are not redressed.

56. *LR*, p. 179.

6. Thomas Roderick Dew on Black Slavery as the Republic's Check on the Working Class

1. William Freehling argues that the connection between majoritarian rule and abolitionism has been made by South Carolina nullifiers and contributes to their opposition to the tariff. See p. 257.

2. The Nat Turner rebellion is still embroiled in controversy as a result of William Styron's novel *The Confessions of Nat Turner* (New York: Random House, 1967). John B. Duff and Peter M. Mitchell, eds., *The Nat Turner Rebellion: The Historical Event and Modern Controversy* (New York: Harper and Row, 1971), offer a useful introduction to the continuing debate on the subject. For an account of the rebellion, see Stephen B. Oates, *The Fires of Jubilee: Nat Turner's Fierce Rebellion* (New York: Harper and Row, 1975). Eugene Genovese has written a stimulating article on slave rebellions in the Western Hemisphere entitled "Slavery—The World's Burden," in *Perspective and Irony in American Slavery*, ed. Harry P. Owens (Jackson: University Press of Mississippi, 1976).

3. As quoted in Joseph Clarke Robert, *The Road from Monticello: A Study of the Virginia Slavery Debate of 1832*, Historical Papers of the Trinity College Historical Society, no. 24 (Durham: Duke University Press, 1941). Robert's work provides a useful account of the debate and the historical circumstances surrounding it. Also see Whitfield, *Slavery Agitation in Virginia*; Sydnor, *The Development of Southern Sectionalism*, pp. 227–228; and Degler, *The Other South*, pp. 16–17.

4. Robert, *The Road from Monticello*, pp. 9–11; Robert McColley, *Slavery and Jeffersonian Virginia* (Urbana: University of Illinois Press, 1964), pp. 114–140; and Mansfield, "Defender of the Southern Faith," chapter 3.

5. Robert, *The Road from Monticello*, p. 24.

6. Lewis C. Gray, *History of Agriculture in the Southern United States to 1860* (New York: Peter Smith, 1941), Vol. II, pp. 914–915; Sharp, *The Jacksonians versus the Banks*, p. 245; and Robert, *The Road from Monticello*, p. 9.

7. Robert, *The Road from Monticello*, p. 11.

8. Gray, *History of Agriculture*, p. 916; Sydnor, *The Development of Southern Sectionalism*, pp. 83–84; Carter Goodrich, "The Virginia System of Mixed Enterprise: A Study of State Planning of Internal Improvements," *Political Science Quarterly* 64 (1949): 355–387.

9. Robert, *The Road from Monticello*, p. 8; and Sharp, *The Jacksonians versus the Banks*, pp. 246–247.

10. Robert, *The Road from Monticello*, p. 9; and Sharp, *The Jacksonians versus the Banks*, p. 248.

11. Sharp, *The Jacksonians versus the Banks*, p. 248.

12. Robert, *The Road from Monticello*, p. 211.

13. Sharp, *The Jacksonians versus the Banks*, pp. 247–248, 255–259; Gray, *History of Agriculture*, pp. 919–920; and Avery O. Craven, *Edmund Ruffin, Southerner: A Study in Secession* (1932; rpt. Baton Rouge: Louisiana State University Press, 1972), pp. 47–72. For an interesting discussion of the contradictory character of the agricultural reform movement, see Genovese, *Political Economy of Slavery*, pp. 124–154.

14. C. W. Hill, Jr., *The Political Theory of John Taylor of Caroline* (Cranbury: Associated University Presses, 1977).

15. Sharp, *The Jacksonians Versus the Banks*, pp. 259, 266–267; Gray, *History of Agriculture*, p. 920. Sharp notes that the farm areas which were more developed tended to favor soft money, while those which were less developed tended to distrust banks and in some cases advocated hard money. Furthermore, Sharp found that those eastern districts which were economically diversified depended less on slave labor than other areas and were more likely to be Whig. Given this relationship between Whiggery and capitalist development, it is not surprising that Whigs were disproportionately represented among antislavery forces (Degler, *The Other South*, p. 95). However, as Dew's career illustrates, Whiggery and proslavery were not antonyms.

16. Both commercial and independent farmers are commodity producers to whom land, the means of production, and labor are all commodities. However, the purposes of their market activities differ. The difference can be seen by comparing the two forms of commodity circulation. The first form begins with a commodity, say, corn, and through exchange ends with another commodity, e.g., iron. Here the circuit is commodity-money-commodity (c-m-c). The second form begins with money and ends with money; in order for this circuit to make sense, the final sum of money must be larger than the initial quantity. This circuit can be represented as follows: m-c-m' where ' expresses an augmentation of the original value.

In the first circuit the aim of production is the satisfaction of actual needs associated with particular commodities. In contrast, the second form is primarily concerned with the general augmentation of wealth. For this reason farming becomes a means to an end—the expansion of value—rather than end in itself.

While this distinction can be made, it is nonetheless ambiguous given the conditions of antebellum agriculture. A family farm may engage in market activities by selling those products the family does not need, i.e., by selling its economic surplus. The family's relationship to the market may change as it attempts to increase its wealth by specializing in the production of particular staples for the market. When such units structure the market, the market in turn affects the unit as the need for money increases to facilitate exchange and to pay off debts. The growing dependency on the market may be exacerbated by commercial crises which plunge the family farm deep into debt or may even force bankruptcy.

When such specialization has advanced, soft money or bank credit no longer functions in a fashion amiable to simple commodity production, since bank credit effectively "dematerializes" money. As bank credit replaces gold and circulates as bank notes, then a source of credit exists that is not directly linked to production. These bank notes may in fact facilitate economic development so long as no crisis creates a demand for hard money (gold) to meet payments. Of course, an extension of credit may itself promote a crisis of overproduction. Thus, bank credit, on the one hand, encourages economic growth and, on the other hand, contributes to crises. Both of these effects extend market relationships. The first proliferates the money nexus through debt, and the second centralizes wealth through the appropriation of indebted independent producer's property. (For a detailed discussion of the distinction between commercial and bank credit, see Suzanne DeBrunhoff, *Marx on Money* [New York: Urizen Books, 1976]). Thus, soft money promotes the transformation of simple commodity production into capitalist production, a tendency inherent in simple commodity production.

The Jacksonian polemics against the banks, then, may be seen as an attempt to preserve the noncapitalist character of commodity production. Of course, not all Jacksonians opposed banks in principle, only a central bank. For these Jacksonians a decentralized bank would help proliferate credit and encourage democratic economic growth. Thus, the division between pro-and anti-Jacksonian forces cannot simply be considered in terms of procapitalist and anticapitalist policies. Dew, for example, opposed a central bank on political grounds but defended banking in general, unlike many of his Southern compatriots. For this reason Bray Hammond can argue, in *Banks and Politics in America: From the Revolution to the Civil War* (Princeton: Princeton University Press, 1957), pp. 82–83, that the Jacksonians were nothing more than businessmen in disguise. And Sharp must agree, although he concedes that it is one of history's greatest ironies that Jacksonian policy encouraged capitalist development.

17. Robert, *The Road from Monticello*, pp. 29–36.

18. As quoted in ibid., p. 63.

19. Ibid., pp. 39–40.

20. Ibid., p. 66.

21. Ibid., p. 68.

22. Peterson, ed., *Democracy, Liberty and Property* p. 284; and McCormick, *The Second American Party System*, pp. 179–180.

23. As quoted in Peterson, ed., *Democracy, Liberty and Property*, pp. 307–308.

24. McGregor, *The Disruption of Virginia*, pp. 49–65.

25. Mansfield, "Defender of the Southern Faith," pp. 18–21.

26. Thomas Roderick Dew, *Review of the Debate in the Virginia Legislature of 1831 and 1832* (1832; rpt. Westport: Greenwood Press, 1970), p. 5; hereafter cited as *RD*.

27. Ibid., p. 5.

28. For Dew, serfdom characterizes the agricultural stage of development in which the aristocracy has a monopoly on land. The dependency of the serfs on their lords is reenforced by the unstable governments of the period.

29. Gavin Wright argues that the basic economic unit of the antebellum period was the family farm. In comparing Northern and Southern farms, Wright evaluates the effectiveness with which each stimulated technical—i.e., capitalist—development. See Wright, *The Political Economy of the Cotton South*, pp. 43–44. For an insightful discussion of the limits of Southern plantation production, see Richard Garrett, "Primitive Accumulation in the Antebellum South" (Ph.D. diss., New School for Social Research, 1978).

30. Two points need to be made regarding the above characterization of the antebellum South. First, the conceptualization starts from the historical. Since it was the world market that actually constructed and then perpetuated slavery, the South is treated in relationship to the development of the world capitalist market. In the stage of development under investigation, capitalism has a tendency to preserve precapitalist relationships in order to acquire necessary raw materials. This stage, therefore, differs from the period of finance capital, in which there is a tendency to invest directly in the production process of lesser developed nations or regions, thereby eroding the previous forms of production. For a discussion of the stages of capitalist development in relation to a theory of international trade, see Patrick Clawson, "The Internationalization of Capital in the Middle East," (Ph.D. diss., New School for Social Research 1979), pp. 38–61. On the question of American slavery's origins, see Marx, *Capital*, Vol. I, pp. 765–772; Domar, "The Causes of Slavery or Serfdom; Morgan, *American Slavery*, chapters 6–7, 11–12; Wright, *The Political Economy of the Cotton South*, p. 11.

Consequently, there is no need to refer to or construct some general notion of a "slave mode of production." Southern slavery is understood in relationship to capitalist development; the particular effects of slavery on that development can be understood within a theoretical and historical account of capitalist development. For an attempt to construct a general theory of slavery deduced from the "abstract" elements of production in general, see Barry Hindress and Paul Q. Hirst, *Pre-Capitalist Modes of Production* (London: Routledge and Kegan Paul, 1975). Robert Padgug provides a useful summary of Marxist studies on ancient and modern slavery in "Problems in the Theory of Slavery," *Science and Society* 40 (1976): 3–27. For an assessment of Marxist studies of Southern slavery by a leading non-Marxist expert in the field, see Stanley Engerman, "Marxist Economic Studies of the Slave South," *Marxist Perspectives* 1 (1978): 148–168.

Second, although the South was divided into numerous geographic sections and produced a variety of agricultural goods, cotton unified the region. As the major export crop, cotton determined both the direction of economic growth and the value of slave labor. Wright, *The Political Economy of the Cotton South*, argues this point cogently. Gray, *History of Agriculture*, remains the most comprehensive work on Southern agriculture. There are numerous state-based studies of slavery which treat the effects of geography and local conditions on plantation life. For example, see Ralph Flanders, *Plantation Slavery in Georgia* (Chapel Hill: University of North Carolina Press, 1933); Orville Taylor, *Negro Slavery in Arkansas* (Durham: Duke University Press, 1958); and Chase Mooney, *Slavery in Tennessee* (Bloomington: Indiana University Press, 1957).

31. The capitalist circuit contains three phases: the circuit of productive capital, that of commodity capital, and that of money capital.

$$M_1 \overset{\overset{\text{II}}{\text{L}}}{\underset{\text{Mp}}{-\!-}} C_1 \ldots P_1 \ldots C_1' \underset{\text{III}}{-\!-} M_1' \overset{\text{I}}{-\!-} M_2 \overset{\overset{}{\text{L}}}{\underset{\text{Mp}}{-\!-}} C_2 \ldots P_2 \ldots C_2' -\!- M_2'$$

M: money
C: commodities
L: labor power
Mp: means of production
P: production

I: circuit of commodity capital
II: circuit of money capital
III: circuit of productive capital

Cotton entered a capitalist circulation process as commodity capital, even though it was not produced under purely capitalist conditions. Productive capital remained on a precapitalist basis since wage labor was not employed. See Marx, *Capital*, Vol. II; Christian Palloix, "The Internationalization of Capital and the Circuit of Social Capital," in *International Firms and Modern Imperialism*, ed. Hugo Radice (Harmondsworth: Penguin, 1975); and Clawson, "Internationalization of Capital," pp. 38–51.

32. The profitability of slavery has long been a thorny subject in United States historiography. Despite the controversy, recent studies indicate both that slavery was profitable and that slave owners employed concepts of profitability. For an introduction to this tedious subject, see Hugh Aitken, ed., *Did Slavery Pay? Readings in the Economics of Black Slavery in the United States* (Boston: Houghton Mifflin, 1971). Also see Wright, *The Political Economy of the Cotton South*, pp. 139–144.

33. While disagreement exists regarding the capitalist character of the slave South, a consensus has emerged regarding the "rational" character of the labor process. See, for example, Keith Aufhauser, "Slavery and Scientific Management," *Journal of Economic History* 33 (1973): 811–824; and Eugene Genovese, *Roll Jordan Roll: The World the Slaves Made* (New York: Pantheon, 1974), especially Book II, Part 2.

For a discussion of plantation management, see Jacob Metzer, "Rational Management, Modern Business Practices and Economies of Scale in the Antebellum Southern Plantation," *Explorations in Economic History* 12 (1975): 123–150. Wright, *The Political Economy of the Cotton South*, p. 81, agrees that plantations were run efficiently, but he challenges Metzer's claim that there was a relationship between management and economics of scale.

34. Wright, *The Political Economy of the Cotton South*, p. 50, compares the development of technology in Northern and Southern agriculture. The South lagged far behind the North in both the ratio of improved acreage and farm work-

ers and the ratio of value of farm implements and machinery to farm workers. The South also had far fewer patents in mechanical inventions than the North, indicating the absence of any economic compulsion to substitute machine for labor (pp. 107–108).

35. Robert E. Gallman, "Self-sufficiency in the Cotton Economy of the Antebellum South," *Agricultural History* 44 (1970): 19–23; Diane Lindstrom, "Southern Dependence upon Interregional Grain Supplies: A Review of the Trade Flows, 1840–1860," *Agricultural History* 44 (1970): 101–114; and Louis M. Hacker, *The Course of American Economic Growth and Development* (New York: John Wiley and Sons, 1970), pp. 78–79.

36. Owsley, *Plain Folk of the Old South*; Harold Woodman, *King Cotton and His Retainers: Financing and Marketing the Cotton Crop of the South, 1800–1925* (Lexington: University of Kentucky Press, 1968), chapter 15; and Wright, *The Political Economy of the Cotton South*, pp. 24–29.

37. Eugene Genovese, *The Political Economy of Slavery: Studies in the Economy and Political Society of the Slave South* (New York: Random House, 1967), pp. 167–171.

38. George D. Green, *Finance and Economic Development in the Old South: Louisiana Banking, 1804–1861* (Stanford: Stanford University Press, 1972), p. 10.

39. Woodman, *King Cotton*, pp. 115–118; Green, *Finance and Economic Development*, p. 9; and Genovese, *The Political Economy of Slavery*, p. 21.

40. From the planter's side, the commercial and money circuit may be viewed as merchant's and usurer's capital because of the precapitalist character of the production process (Clawson, "Internationalization of Capital," p. 46). However, because the Southern plantation was integrated into a capitalist circuit and because the planters had to expand value, it can be argued that capital had incorporated the master-slave relationship in its domain. The peculiarity of this economic process defines the preindustrial capitalist character of this master-slave relationship.

41. On Southern nationalism, see Avery O. Craven, *The Growth of Southern Nationalism, 1848–1861* (Baton Rouge: Louisiana State University Press, 1968); and Potter, *The Impending Crisis*, pp. 1–17. Russel, *Economic Aspects of Southern Sectionalism*; and Weymouth Jordan, *Rebels in the Making: Planters' Conventions and Southern Propaganda*, Confederate Centennial Studies, no. 7 (Tuscaloosa: Confederate Publishing Co., 1958), explore the connection between Southern nationalism and Southern economic independence. For a discussion of classical political economy's analysis of slavery in light of current research, see Howard Temperly, "Capitalism, Slavery and Ideology," *Past and Present*, no. 75 (1977), pp. 94–118.

42. *RD*, p. 26.

43. Ibid., pp. 11–12.

44. Ibid., pp. 12–13.

45. Ibid., p. 13.

46. Ibid., "Advantages Which Have Resulted to the World from the Institution of Slavery," pp. 28–35. Dew's concept of race does not depend on the alleged biological differences between blacks and whites. While not reducible to the notion of class, race nonetheless derives its basic features and meaning for Dew from the

wage labor/capital relationship in classical political economy. Indeed, Malthus assigns behavioral characteristics to the English working class that separate them from the capitalists as if the two were discrete "biological races."

In this way, Dew's thought on the matter resembles numerous scholarly analyses of American slavery which explain the institution in terms of labor requirements for capitalist expansion. See Eric Williams, *Capitalism and Slavery* (Chapel Hill: University of North Carolina Press, 1944), chapters 1 and 3; and J. H. Plumb, "Slavery, Race and the Poor," in *In the Light of History* (Boston: Houghton Mifflin, 1973).

The opposing view primarily attributes the rise of slavery, and its defense by Southern intellectuals, to cultural and psychological propensities among whites. The best study from this perspective is Winthrop D. Jordan, *White over Black* (Harmondsworth: Penguin Books, 1969). Channing, *Crisis of Fear*, has drawn out the implications of Jordan's notions, as well as those found in Allan Nevins's monumental study of the Civil War (*Ordeal of the Union*), in explaining South Carolina's reasons for secession. According to Channing, irrational racial fear fundamentally influenced South Carolina to break its ties with the Union in order to determine the relationship of white and black without the interference of the federal government. In arguing his case, Channing overlooks the interconnection between race and class and the "fear" of the laboring population prevalent among property owners in the period. Without this connection Channing cannot fully link the concepts of class, race, minority rights, economic growth, and secession, and thus he reduces South Carolina's drive toward independence to a psychological problem. Furthermore, while Channing presents an impressive array of material to bolster his argument, the argument itself rests on a theory of psychology which is never developed.

47. During the antebellum period the question of "race" received considerable "scientific" attention. Since Dew did not write a treatise on the subject, his precise thinking on the subject is unknown. For an introduction to the antebellum literature on race, see William Stanton, *The Leopard's Spots: Scientific Attitudes Toward Race in America, 1815–1859* (Chicago: University of Chicago Press, 1960); and George Fredrickson, *The Black Image in the White Mind: The Debate on Afro-American Character and Destiny, 1817–1914* (New York: Harper and Row, 1971).

48. George Tucker, a prominent professor at the University of Virginia, employed similar arguments to claim that abolition was an economic inevitability in *The Laws of Wages, Profits and Rent, Investigated* (Philadelphia: E. L. Carey and A. Hart, 1837). For this reason Tucker could support the American Colonization Society.

49. Thomas R. Dew, "The Improvements of the James and Kanawha Rivers: Mischievous Effects of the Immigration to the West," *Farmer's Register* 3 (1835): 138–140.

50. *RD*, pp. 66–68.

51. Ibid., pp. 112–113.

52. Thomas R. Dew, "An Address on the Influence of the Federative System of Government upon Literature and the Development of Character," *Southern Literary Messenger* 2 (1836): 277.

7. Jacob N. Cardozo on Making Slavery Work

1. The proslavery argument has been the subject of numerous scholarly inquiries. The basic work on the subject remains Jenkins, *Pro-Slavery Thought in the Old South*. Other important works are W. B. Hesseltine, "Some New Aspects of the Pro-Slavery Argument," *Journal of Negro History* 21 (1936): 1–14; U. B. Phillips, *The Course of the South to Secession* (1939; rpt. New York: Hill and Wang, 1964), chapter 5; Carsel, "The Slaveholder's Indictment of Northern Wage Slavery"; Morrow, "The Proslavery Argument Revisited"; Charles G. Sellers, Jr., "The Travail of Slavery," in *The Southerners as Americans*, ed. Charles G. Sellers (Chapel Hill: University of North Carolina Press, 1960); Genovese, "The Logical Outcome of the Slaveholders' Philosophy: An Exposition, Interpretation and Critique of the Social Thought of George Fitzhugh of Port Royal, Virginia," in *The World the Slaveholders Made*; David Donald, "The Proslavery Argument Revisited," *Journal of Southern History* 37 (1971): 3–18; and Robert Shalhope, "Race, Class, Slavery and the Antebellum Southern Mind," *Journal of Southern History* 37 (1971): 557–574.

2. Genovese, *The World the Slaveholders Made*.

3. Freehling, *Prelude*, pp. 108–117. Freehling's work is the authoritative study on the subject and has greatly influenced the narrative of this essay. Other useful works on the subject include Chauncey Boucher, *The Nullification Controversy in South Carolina* (Chicago: University of Chicago Press, 1916); Bancroft, *Calhoun and the South Carolina Nullification Movement*; Wiltse, *John C. Calhoun: Nullifier*; Sydnor, *The Development of Southern Sectionalism*, chapters 8 and 9; Wilson, *Space, Time and Freedom*, chapter 4; and Latner, "The Nullification Crisis and Republican Subversion."

4. Freehling, *Prelude*, chapter 1.

5. Ibid.

6. Ibid., pp. 89–91; Sydnor, pp. 42–49; McCormick, *The Second American Party System*, p. 7, n. 1.

7. Freehling, *Prelude*, pp. 89–97, Sydnor, chapter 6.

8. Freehling, *Prelude*, pp. 97–126; Sydnor, p. 178; Malone, *The Public Life of Thomas Cooper*, p. 295.

9. Freehling, *Prelude*, pp. 127–132; Malone, *The Public Life of Thomas Cooper*, pp. 294–299.

10. Freehling, *Prelude*, pp. 131–133.

11. Ibid., pp. 237–241; Wilson, *Space, Time and Freedom*, p. 77.

12. The best work on Cardozo's writings is Melvin M. Leiman, *Jacob N. Cardozo: Economic Thought in the Antebellum South* (New York: Columbia University Press, 1966). See also Dorfman, *The Economic Mind*, Vol. II, pp. 551–566, 852–862; and Abram C. Flora, Jr., "Economic Thought in South Carolina, 1820–1860" (Ph.D. diss., University of North Carolina, 1957).

13. Beginning in articles in the *Southern Patriot* in 1818, Cardozo vigorously opposed the protective tariff. After the enactment of the Tariff of Abominations he wrote a series of articles which were later published in 1830 in a pamphlet entitled *The Tariff: Its True Character and Effects Practically Illustrated* (in *Notes on Political Economy*, ed. Joseph Dorfman (Clifton: Augustus M. Kelley, 1972).

14. Ibid., pp. 211–214.

15. There were three stages in the Southern antebellum debate on manufacturing. The first two periods, 1790–1815 and 1828–1840, were determined by economic fluctuations in the Southern agrarian sector. The third period was also influenced by economic conditions; however, sectional considerations became the main impetus for the renewed interest in economic diversification. Abolitionism, the decline of Southern political power, the sectional conflicts arising from expansion, and the rise of new political parties pushed Southerners to dream of economic independence. See Robert Starobin, *Industrial Slavery in the Old South* (London: Oxford University Press, 1970), pp. 190–193, 204–206; Russel, *Economic Aspects of Southern Sectionalism*, pp. 9–55; Chauncey Boucher, "The Ante-Bellum Attitudes of South Carolina Towards Manufacturing and Agriculture," *Washington University Studies*, vol. 2, no. 2 (April 1916), pp. 243–263; and Ronald T. Takaki, *A Pro-Slavery Crusade: The Agitation to Reopen the African Slave Trade* (New York: Free Press, 1971), chapter 7.

16. Starobin, *Industrial Slavery*, pp. 206–214; and William Gregg, *Essays on Domestic Industry: or an Inquiry into the Expediency of Establishing Cotton Manufactures in South Carolina* (Charleston: Burges and James, 1845).

17. Cardozo, *Notes on Political Economy*, ed. Dorfman, pp. 11, 37–38; hereafter cited as *NPE*.

18. Ibid., pp. iii–iv.

19. For a discussion of Ricardo's theory of rent, see ibid., p. 39.

20. Ibid., p. 39.

21. Ibid., pp. 39–40.

22. Ibid., p. 40.

23. Ibid.

24. Ibid.

25. Ibid.

26. Cardozo agrees with Smith that one is rich or poor according to the amount of labor one can command. Ricardo objects to this statement if labor is to be taken as a standard measure of value. According to Ricardo, labor is subject to the same fluctuations in its value as any other commodity and therefore cannot function as a standard measure of value. Commenting on Malthus's selection of labor as a standard measure, Ricardo concurs with Malthus's statement that "the accumulation of capital, and its efficiency in the increase of wealth and population, depends almost entirely upon its power of setting labour to work; or, in other words, upon its power of commanding labour" (*Notes On Malthus*, in *Works*, ed. Sraffa and Dobb, Vol. II, p. 90). Although Ricardo accepts this statement, he asserts that it has no relevance for selecting labor as the standard measure of value. Cardozo employs Smith's proposition to indicate a relationship between economic growth and labor. Cardozo does not develop labor as the standard measure of value; in fact, he does not address this problem.

27. Cardozo does not argue that machinery creates a surplus laboring population by substituting fixed capital for circulating capital. According to Cardozo, fixed capital is not derived from circulating capital, since the latter is falling in price. As more fixed capital is employed to reduce the money wages of labor, a proportional demand for labor arises. Because the process of substitution is grad-

ual, Cardozo believes there cannot even be a temporary formation of a surplus laboring population. See *NPE*, chapter 3.

28. *NPE*, pp. 40–41.

29. According to Cardozo, Ricardo has not been able to perceive the natural law regulating population because of the effects of mercantilist policies in England. These artificial policies were designed to promote an excess laboring population in order to provide a cheap and docile labor force. The residue of these policies has created the appearance that population moves independently of accumulation. For an account of the influence of Malthusian population theory on Southern pro-slavery thought, see Joseph J. Spengler, "Population Theory in the Ante-Bellum South," *Journal of Southern History* 2 (1936): 360–389.

30. *Southern Patriot*, Feb. 26 and Feb. 28, 1842, March 2, March 3, and March 10, 1842.

31. Cardozo, "Rents," in *NPE*, pp. 215–216.

32. As quoted in Leiman, *Jacob N. Cardozo*, p. 219.

33. As quoted in Ibid., p. 217.

34. *Southern Patriot*, Feb. 9, 1838.

35. *Southern Patriot*, July 30 and July 31, 1835.

36. As quoted in Leiman, *Jacob N. Cardozo*, p. 215.

37. For a discussion of the transition from craft manufacture to industrial capitalist production, see Marx, *Capital*, Vol. I; Dobb, *Studies*, pp. 255–281; Stephen Marglin, "What Do Bosses Do? The Origins and Functions of Hierarchy in Capitalist Production," *Review of Radical Political Economy* 6 (1974): 60–112; Melvin Kransberg and Joseph Gies, *By the Sweat of Thy Brow: Work in the Western World* (New York: G. P. Putnam's Sons, 1975), chapters 10 and 11; and Ross Thomson, "The Origin of Modern Industry in the United States" (Ph.D. diss., Yale University, 1976).

38. The hiring-out system was not significant in a statistical sense but rather in a qualitative sense—that it offered a solution to the problem of capitalist accumulation based on slave labor. According to Starobin, *Industrial Slavery*, pp. 19–20, four-fifths of the slaves used in manufacturing were owned by the manufacturers. He unfortunately does not inform the reader how he arrived at these figures. Despite these numbers, Starobin still attributes much importance to the hiring-out system. He asserts that the system developed more rapidly as the South became more industrialized. Furthermore, he argues that the hiring-out system converted a rigid institution into a flexible one. He highlights its flexibility when he compares slave labor's responsiveness to market fluctuations with wage labor's (pp. 178, 182). His position is summarized when he states that the hiring system "permitted employers to obtain labor without making heavy investments in Negroes" (p. 135).

Claudia Dale Goldin, *Urban Slavery in the American South, 1820–1860* (Chicago: University of Chicago Press, 1976), is more precise in describing the extent of the hiring-out system. The 1850 census, according to Goldin, does not provide information concerning the ownership of slaves used in Southern cities. To overcome this problem, Goldin devises a category of slave "useship" to determine the percentage of persons using various numbers of slaves. Goldin finds nearly one-quarter of all slaves employed in Charleston in 1850 were in work situations that demanded ten or more slaves. While few slaves were employed in industrial settings such as textile mills, the concentration of slaves in such work activities as the railroads, the ports, the shipping trades, and other commercial pursuits demonstrates the applicability of slaves in large numbers in nonagricultural production. The 1860 census manuscript provides information on the hiring of slaves, but that information varies from state to state. Despite the deficiency in the data, the census manuscript reveals, according to Goldin, that the hiring out of slaves was quite common, especially in the more industrial Virginia cities of Richmond, Norfolk, Portsmouth, Lynchburg, and Fredericksburg. Richmond, for example, had eighteen hiring agents who matched slaves for hire with potential employers (pp. 35–36).

For additional information on slave hiring and the development of manufacturing in the South, see Clement Eaton, "Slave-Hiring in the Upper South: A Step Toward Freedom," *Mississippi Valley History Review* 46 (1960): 663–678; Richard Wade, *Slavery in the Cities* (New York: Oxford University Press, 1964); Fred Bateman, James Foust, and Thomas Weiss, "Profitability in Southern Manufacturing: Estimates from 1860," *Explorations in Economic History* 12 (1975): 211–232; and Fred Bateman and Thomas Weiss, "Comparative Development in Antebellum Manufacturing," *Journal of Economic History* 35 (1975): 182–208.

39. *Southern Patriot*, Feb. 26, 1842.
40. Goldin, *Urban Slavery*, p. 124.

INDEX

Marshall, John, 105
Marx, Karl, xxiii–xxiv, xxvii, xxviii;
    on Smith, 12
Memminger, C. G., 125
Mercantilism. *See* Smith, Adam
Mill, James, 19, 20, 21, 24
Missouri Compromise of 1820, 41,
    86, 122
Monarchy, English, 3, 5, 16–17, 39
Monopoly: economic effects of, 14, 15,
    29, 60–61; on land, 9, 14, 15–16,
    29; Malthus on, 28, 29; Raymond
    on, 60–61, 64; Smith on, 13, 14,
    15–16, 60–61

National debt, 3, 4, 5, 47, 163n98
Nat Turner rebellion, 85, 87, 104, 105,
    106, 124
Natural foundations of society, xxvii,
    7, 12, 13–15, 16, 21, 40–41, 73, 90,
    118–119, 157–158n29
Natural law, xxv, 7, 8, 47, 48, 58–59,
    60, 68, 69, 70, 73
Natural limits to growth, 22, 26, 28,
    30, 34–35, 121–122, 126–128, 130,
    153–154n57. *See also* Agriculture,
    diminishing returns in
Natural origins of wealth, 10, 25, 29, 55
Negro Seaman controversy, 86, 122
New Model Army, 41
Niles Register, 42
Nullification, 82, 84, 86, 121–125;
    crisis, 42, 123

Ohio resolution for emancipation,
    86, 122
Owen, Robert, 30, 34, 131

Parliament, English, 3, 4, 39, 53
Pauper labor. *See* Labor, pauper-
    ization of
Peel, Sir Robert, 19
Peterloo Massacre, 20
Philadelphia Free Trade Convention,
    87
Phillips, William, 43, 46, 157n27
Pickering, John, xxix, 67
Plain Republicans, alliance of, with
    southern planters, 82–83, 85–86,
    104, 166n7

Plantation system: in capitalist circuit,
    176n31, 177n40; economic effects
    of, 38, 110, 115–116, 135–136,
    175n30; in world market, 110, 115,
    135, 175n30
Planters, southern, 78–79, 89,
    106–107, 135; alliance of, with
    Plain Republicans, 82–83, 85–86,
    104, 166n7; isolation of, 19; political
    views of, 83–86, 104, 108, 122–
    124, 166n14; relation of, to yeomen,
    83, 85, 107; on tariff, 20
Pocock, J. G. A., xxvii, 155n11,
    158n28
Political economy, classical, xxix, 44,
    68, 85, 90, 96, 109, 118, 130–131,
    157n27, 166n7; as a discipline,
    xxvii–xxviii, 14
Poor laws, 71, 77, 164n39
Precapitalist economic aspects: of En-
    gland, xxvi, xxvii, 12–13, 18, 20,
    22, 88; of the North, xxvi, 38, 48,
    65, 80–81, 92, 141n19; of the
    South, xxvi, xxviii, 38, 90, 91–92,
    119, 141n19, 175n30
Price: natural, 29, 52, 150–
    151n39; necessary, 28–29, 31, 52,
    150–151n39, 152n49; saving, 52,
    57, 69
Primogeniture, 9, 14, 15, 20, 31, 47, 53
Production, means of: capitalist's rela-
    tion to, 9, 10, 11–12, 50, 57, 93,
    141n19; labor's relation to, 8, 9, 10,
    12, 44, 47, 50, 57, 91, 93, 141n19;
    landlord's relation to, 9, 10
Profit: Cardozo on, 128–131; Dew on,
    92–94; falling rate of, 15, 25–26,
    28, 29, 31, 93, 94, 111, 116, 126;
    Malthus on, 28, 29, 30, 31, 32;
    Ricardo on, 24–26; Smith on, 11,
    15, 46–47
Property: Cardozo on, 132; challenges
    to, 4, 20, 22, 23, 27, 33, 36, 63, 79,
    84, 117–118, 132; and citizenship,
    4, 33, 36, 123; as defense of slavery,
    79, 84, 117; Dew on, 117–118; Mal-
    thus on, 33; Raymond on, 51, 52,
    59, 63, 79, 162n76; Ricardo on, 25,
    27, 36; rights to, 13, 52, 59, 79,
    162n76; Smith on, 13

Van Buren, Martin, 82, 87
Virginia, 85, 87, 91–92, 104–109,
117, 124; constitutional convention
of, 108; economic geography of,
105–107; House of Delegates of,
104; politics of, 104–108; racial
population of, 106; slavery in,
104–108

Wages: Cardozo on, 128–130, 131;
Dew on, 92–94, 95; Malthus on,
28, 128; Raymond on, 52, 56;
Ricardo on, 24–26; Smith on,
10–11
Wakefield, Edward Gibbon, 37–38,
154n4
Walker, Robert, 42
Walker Tariff, 42
War of 1812, 123
Washington, George, 105
Wealth: Malthus on, 33; Raymond on,
49–51, 55, 56, 58, 73, 79; Ricardo
on, 23–24, 26; Smith on, 10–11,
12, 13, 46; sources of, 10–11, 12,
13, 23, 33, 46, 51, 55, 149n30; as use
value, 12. *See also* Land, as a source
of wealth; Natural origins of wealth
Wealth of Nations, xxx, 7, 12, 13, 14,
15, 18, 22, 65

West, Edward, 21
Whigs: American, 44–45, 65, 82, 106,
173n15; English, 3, 4, 5, 16, 21, 23,
39
William and Mary College, 87
Working class, xxiii, xxx, 7, 20–21,
44, 89, 91; Cardozo on, 126, 128,
131–133, 135; Dew on, 102, 111–
112, 118–119; Malthus on, 23,
33–35, 101, 153n52; political demands of, 21, 33, 102, 132–133; as
problem for political theorists, 7,
10, 23, 33, 89, 101–102, 132–133;
Raymond on, 56, 65, 66, 70–72 (*see
also* Labor, independent); Ricardo
on, 23, 25–26, 27–28, 33, 35–36,
101, 148–149n22, 153n52; Smith
on, 10–11, 13–14, 15, 33, 101. *See
also* Labor; Propertyless class; Revolution, working-class; Slavery, effect
of, on working class
Wright, Gavin, xxvi

Yeoman farmers, 53, 83, 85, 86, 90,
107, 108, 110, 111, 122, 167n14; alliance of, with industrialists, xxv,
xxvi, 38; and bank credit, 173–
174n16; relation of, to southern
planters, 83, 85, 107